Frederick James Furnivall

Early English Poems and Lives of Saints

Frederick James Furnivall

Early English Poems and Lives of Saints

ISBN/EAN: 9783337005641

Printed in Europe, USA, Canada, Australia, Japan

Cover: Foto ©Thomas Meinert / pixelio.de

More available books at **www.hansebooks.com**

EARLY ENGLISH POEMS

AND

LIVES OF SAINTS,

(WITH THOSE OF THE WICKED BIRDS PILATE AND JUDAS.)

COPIED AND EDITED FROM MANUSCRIPTS IN THE LIBRARY
OF THE BRITISH MUSEUM

BY

FREDERICK J. FURNIVALL, M.A. CAMBR.,

ONE OF THE HONORARY SECRETARIES OF THE PHILOLOGICAL SOCIETY;
EDITOR OF LONELICH'S AND DE BORRON'S 'SEYNT GRAAL'; ROBERD
OF BRUNNE'S 'HANDLYNG SYNNE', AND WILLIAM OF WADINGTON'S
'MANUEL DES PECHIEZ'.

PUBLISHED FOR THE PHILOLOGICAL SOCIETY

BY

A. ASHER & CO., BERLIN.

1862.

PREFACE.

THE chief grievance of an Honorary Secretary is, that certain Members of his Society *will not* send him for press the Papers they have read at the Society's Meetings. Beg for them as he will,—by letter, word of mouth, through mutual friends, by special visits,—out of some Members no Papers can be got. What then is left for the unhappy Official, but to write Papers himself, or copy MSS. to fill the volume that his refractory friends have left vacant? The former branch of the alternative was out of my reach, so I grasped the latter, and the reader must not blame me if he thinks my basket of fruit a bad sub-stitute for the second course of strong meat that he expected and ought to have had.

Sir Frederick Madden, the keeper of the Manuscripts at the British Museum, kindly directed me to the earliest unprinted English MSS. under his charge. Of these Roberd of Brunne's *Handlyng Synne* was the most important, but it was too long for our Society, and I have therefore edited it for the Roxburghe Club. Next came the short Poems that stand first in the present volume, all before 1300; and then the Lives of the Saints (Harleian MS. No. 2277, about 1305-10 A. D.) of which I took a few whose titles or contents caught my fancy, including those of the two accursed ones, Pilate and Judas Iscariot. These not making a sufficient number of pages in our close print, I added, 1. a few songs from the incomplete and later duplicate of the noble Vernon MS. in the Bodleian Library,—having time to collate one only with the earlier copy—; 2. the fragment on the Corrupt state of the Nunneries (p. 138-148) from a Cotton MS. temp. Hen. VI; 3. three Poems on Old Age, Earth, and the Faults of the Monks and People of Kildare (which I had, after copying, set aside as

having been printed in the *Reliquiæ Antiquæ*), and lastly the
twice-printed 'Land of Cokaygne', the airiest and cleverest piece
of satire in the whole range of Early English, if not of English,
poetry. A short abstract of the Poems the reader will find in
'the Contents', and he will see that however uninteresting the
titles of 'Sarmun', 'Moral Ode', 'Lives of Saints' may appear,
information and amusement are yet to be drawn from the pieces
themselves. He can get a lesson in the Geography and Ecclesi-
astical divisions of England (p. 48-9), hear about going to school
at Oxford (p. 41), and studying there art, Arsmetrike—'a lore
þat of figours al is, and of drauȝtes as me draweþ in poudre and
in numbre iwis'—and Divinity (p. 77); of the heriot beast being
paid on a tenant's death (p. 83); of preachers for the Crusades
(p. 79); of the pomp, bell-ringing, and show of horses and squires
at Bishops' progresses to consecrate new Churches (p. 44, l. 43-6),
and many an other scene of English life. He will find too the
Old-Englishman's special sin of Envy[1] denounced (p. 20), his
Greed, and Pride[2], and other faults; will hear Sunday-trading
condemned (p. 16), and see the rough mason running from his
work to catch and kiss the country-girls coming to market with
their eggs (p. 45), which of course get broken in the struggle.
If the reader should doubt whether the Saint—mightier than
'all the king's horses and all the king's men'—'can set Humpty-
Dumpties together again', he will at least not object to the
poet's reflection, that if egg-mongers now could so get their
broken eggs made whole, 'they might hop over ditches where
they would, and both wrestle and fight' (p. 45, l. 69, 70). The
treatment of the 'puir deil' in those days too was hard,—to
be talked to pleasantly by a blacksmith-saint till he had heated
his tongs redhot, and then to be treacherously caught and 'tuengde
and schok' by the nose till the trustful being yelled and hopped

[1]   And Englys men namely
         Are þurghe kynde of herte hy.
         A forbyseyn ys toldé þys,
         Seyde on Frenshe men and on Euglys.
         Frenshe men synne yn lechery
         And Englys men yn enuye.
                 Roberd of Brunne's *Handlyng Synne*, p. 131, l. 4150-5.
[2] cp. A noþur Mon proudeþ. as doþ a poo. p. 129, l. 18.

and brayed, and had to fly home through the lift, shouting in all men's ears 'Out! What hath the baldpate done! What hath the baldpate done!'—was manifestly unfair. The punishment of lustful young women also was judicious (p. 73); the Virgin had odd cases brought before her for decision (p. 59); and Judas murders his father—'smot hym with a ston bihynde in the pate'—marries his mother, hangs himself, his womb bursts amid atwo, 'his gvttes' fall to ground, and through the hole goes out his 'liþer gost'. But it is not for the oddities of subject or phrase that one values these poems; it is for their language that the student, and for their earnestness that the man, holds them of worth. The words first used in most of them were registered by our lost friend Herbert Coleridge, in his *Glossarial Index to the Printed English Literature of the Thirteenth Century*, and most of the new words in the remainder of them will be found at the end of the present Selection. For the deeper feeling in some of the Poems, I need only refer to the simple and touching confession of shortcomings and sins in the 'Moral Ode', to the trust and joy of the Songs of 'Merci' and '*Deo gracias*' (p. 118-130), the self-abasement shown in the 'Sarmun' (p. 1-7), the tender love of the 'Christ on the Cross' (p. 20-1), and the triumphant faith of the Martyrs who gave up their lives for God (p. 101-6).

Of Rhyme, the text contains one noteworthy specimen, 'the Rhyme-beginning Fragment' (p. 21-2), of which the man most capable to speak in England—whose hand we have, alas, so long missed from our pages—writes as follows:

Edinburgh, Aug. 30, 1860.

My dear Furnivall,

I am on my rambles, and your letter of the 20th has been following me.

The rhyme which has attracted your attention belongs to the kind, which is called "inverse rhyme". You will find something about it in the *History of English Rhythms*—in the chapter on rhyme.

I do not however remember to have seen so ancient or so elaborate a specimen as the one you have sent me. It is very curious, and to me interesting.—With all best wishes I am

Yours truly

E. Guest.

The proofs of the text I have read with the MSS., and endeavoured to make them accurate copies of the originals, though with expansions of the ordinary contractions for *er*, *ri* &c., and insertions of commas occasionally. Some final *es* in italics, to help out the rhythm, I inserted in the first few pages, as noticed in the note to p. 1, but soon gave this up; and the later final *es* represent the flourishes of the scribe at the end of certain of his words ending in *i*. In the lines whose rhythm cannot be in any way made good without the insertion of a final *e* at the end of a word, there the reader may insert it (as erroneously omitted by the scribe), but not otherwise. The doctrine of the critic of Dr. Pauli's edition of Gower's *Confessio Amantis* as to the final *e* in Early English[1], is not strictly borne out by any MS., or any undoctored edition of one, that I have ever read; and far more experienced readers and better judges than I, have condemned the attempt to impose on a language constantly changing in words, inflexions, and spelling, written often by half-lettered men, a rigid rule applicable only to the well settled speech and literature of a cultivated nation.

3 Old Square, Lincoln's Inn,
    Dec. 17, 1861.   •

---

[1] In the grammatical system of the 14th century, the final *e* invariably marked the objective case singular .. In adjectives, both the objective in the singular, and all the cases in the plural, are marked by the final *e* .. In verbs the final *e* marked invariably the infinitive mood, and the plurals of all the tenses, when the final *-en* was discontinued .. The final *e* also marked the adverbial form of words, and distinguished the adverb from the preposition. *Gentleman's Magazine*, Third Series, vol. 2, p. 647-9, June, 1857.

CONTENTS.

---

[1] After the text was printed I found that Mr. Wright had this poem in his
notes to the 2nd volume of the Chester Plays, for the Shakspere Society.

be-ginne at is heued. and loke to is to. (13)
þou ne findest in is bodi. bot anguis and wo.

punishment; it shall end' (68). Little know they its heat and
bitter blasts (69-70). Who would give ending pleasure for
endless pain (71-2)? The bread of sin is sweet, and so is
wild deer's flesh; but *he* buys it too dear who gives his neck
for it (73). A full belly talks lightly of hunger (74), but if
a man had tried a little hell-fire, he'd think otherwise of it 27
(75-6); no earthly wealth could get him endless joy (78). *Of
the Judgment.* There may we dread (80), for all that was
hidden here shall be uncovered (81), every man's life shall be
known (82). The penitent shall not be ashamed, but others
shall be lost (83-4). The Doom shall soon be over (85), and
hard men and makers of evil laws shall be punished (86).
Doers of good shall go to heaven (89), and of evil to hell (90)
where they shall dwell without end (91): no relief will there
be (92), for not again will Christ break hell (93), and none 28
else can do it (94). Our Lord bought us with his blood (95),
and we'll not give a bit of our bread for His love (96).
Death came in through the old devil's spite (98), and for our
first father's guilt have we fallen into misery (99-100), else
we might have lived in bliss for ever (101). Great was thus
the sin for which all died (102); and if, for that, such ven-
geance was taken, what shall *we* do who sin so oft (104)?
Full long shall we be in hell, if Adam was there so many
hundred years for one bare sin (105-6). *God's mercy* is not
less than his might (107), and the devil himself might have
it if he would seek it (108). But Hell's King is merciless 29
(109); he who most does his will gets worst reward—a bath
of boiling pitch (110). God keep us from it (111)! and I will
warn you as wise men and the Book say (113-14). *Of the
Pains of Hell.* There is hunger and thirst for evil misers
(116); change from chill to heat, and heat to chill (117); with
no relief (119). The unsteadfast walk ever, seeking rest and
finding none,—wearily up and down as water driven with the
wind (120-2); and quarrellers shall bathe in ever-boiling pitch
(124). Fire is there that ever burns, unquenchable by sea, or 30
Avon stream, or Stour (125-6), and in it shall be those who
were full of foul tricks (127), who loved robbery, whoredom,
and drunkenness (128), were liars (129), lovers of others' wives
and deserters of their own (130), hoarders of goods (131), and
stingy men (132), those greedy of silver and gold (133), doers
of untrueness (134) and the evil Spirit's teachings (135). Ad-
ders, snakes, efts, and toads, shall tear and fret the evil
speakers and envious (138). Never sun shines there, nor
moon, nor star (139), but only foul smoke and darkness (140).
There lay loathly fiends (141) and frightful wights (142), dread

Satanas and old Beelzebub (143). No heart can think, or
tongue tell, how great is the pain of hell (144); but the greatest
is, that the damned know it is endless (146). Heathen men are
there (147); and wicked Christians (148), whom neither money,
prayers, nor alms, shall help (149-50). Let each shield him-
self while he can, and warn his friend, as I have done (151);
and leave what God has forbidden, and do what He has com-
manded (153). Love God and your fellow-Christian (154), all
hangs on these two words (155). But it is hard to stand, and   32
easy to fall, unless Christ gives us strength (157-8); if we
worked for God as we do for goods and gain, we should have
more of heaven than earls or kings do (159-61). There, is
no thirst or hunger, death or age (162); but of it we think
too seldom, and of this world too oft (163-4), though here we
are a little while, and long elsewhere (165). Let us beware,
or the world will drown us (166). Most of us drink of one
devil's cup (167); but let us guard against sin with fasting,
alms, and prayers (169), leaving the broad street (170), and
going the narrow way—green and fair it is, though few tread
it (171). It is God's command (174), for which men leave   33
their own will (175); and will bring us with the fair few men
to heaven's king (176), with Whom is mirth and angels' song
(177), and neither ill nor wane (179). Some have less joy,
and some more, according to their deeds here (180). God
alone is their food, their life, their bliss (181), their clothing,
and their joy (182-3); their sun and nightless day (184). In
heaven is weal and rest (186), bliss without sorrow, and life
without death (187): neither sorrow nor sore (188). God alone
is the bliss of angels and men (189), but all shall not see
His light alike, only as they loved Him here (190-2). Christ   34
shall be enough for all his darlings (194), and of the sight of
Him is no satiety (195). God is so lovely in His godship that
no man can tell what mirth have those who are in His bliss
(196-7). To it may He bring us (198), and Christ grant us
here to lead such life that we may thither come. Amen.

LIVES OF SAINTS.

While he was in his mother's womb, her taper on Candlemas
day was miraculously lighted, and other folk lit their lights at   35
hers, typifying the light he should give to England (l. 1-20).
He was born A.D. 925, the first year of King Athelstan (21),
and brought up at Glastonbury (26). When grown up, he

**

St. Bastian was martyred (51). But Edmund quietly called on
God, and so Hyngar had his head cut off (56), and hidden in a
secret place in the wood of Eglesdon (61-6). There a wild   89
wolf finds it, and though his nature 'were betere to swolowe
hit', he licks and kisses it like his own whelp (70). After-
wards Christian men look for it, and when they come near,
the head calls out "Here; here; here" (79). They take it
up and carry it off with the body—the wolf yelling piteously
(86)—to St. Edmundsbury (89), where it was put in a noble
shrine (91), and the torn flesh became whole again (94), and
the head joined on to the body, but a thin red line, shining
like gold (98), was where the head had been cut off. And a
fair pilgrimage it is, to go there and honour that holy body
(100).

When she was eighteen, Maxentius commanded all his officials
to come to Alexandria to sacrifice to their gods (10). St.
Katherine sees their 'giddyhood' in worshipping idols, goes to
the Emperor (16), and asks him why he is so proud of his
Temple of lime and stone, and regards not the high Temple
of heaven, whose sun and moon and stars never weary (26):
on that he should think, forsake his idols, and honour God
(30). The Emperor bids her wait, and then questions her (39,   91
51). She says she is King Cost's daughter (47), that idols
are no help (50), and that the Emperor's soul will go to hell
(62). He sends for great clerks (68); fifty come (71), and the   92
maid is sent for (83). An angel comforts her (85), and she
taunts the Emperor with having so many Masters to dispute
against her only (92). One tells her that the soul cannot live
after death (100-3), and God cannot give her the life he had
himself lost; but she says that God was made of two things,   93
godhead and manhood (109), and arose from death to life (112).
Did not Plato the great 'philosophe' say that God was to be
scourged and drawn: and Balaam that a Star should arise of
Jacob's race (123)? By this the masters are confuted, and say they
will be baptised (136). The Emperor orders them to be burnt
(139), but the maiden comforts them (142); and after they are
burnt, they lie all whole, whiter and fairer in hue than ever
(150), no hair or clothes the worse. The Emperor offers Ka-
therine to be next to his Queen, and have her image, over-
gilt, set up to be honoured like a god's (161), if she will turn;
but she says she is God's spouse, and nothing shall take her
heart from Him (166). She is stript naked and scourged (168),
cast into prison and starved twelve days (173); but a white
dove brings her meat from heaven. Then the Empress, with

was to be a nun professed (304), and because thy father would
not consent, thy heart was sore oppressed. Now I have showed
thee what, for the most part, is the nuns' rule: for the most
part, not all, for some are devout and toward, and others lewd
and froward" (317). Then I thanked her, and resolved that
'nun wold I neuere be none' (329). 'But here peradventure   147
some man would say that I forsook a perfect way for a fan-
tasy or a dream' (338). No: dream was it none, nor fantasy,
but a gracious warning. See in Genesye, Chapytylle xxxiv,
how Dinah was defouled and thousands slain, because she
went out idly to see things (349). And you Nuns, your barb,
wimple, vail, and devout clothing, make men think you are
holy in living: then, be within as you are without, my ladies
dear. The garland of ivy green at a tavern door is a false
sign unless there be good wine within (358-61). Then, do
you leave your vices, and lewd customs, or you are the children   148
of false hypocrisy (372). Take good heed to this exhortation,
and behold the good conversation of the holy virgins here-
before, St. Clare, St. Edith, and many more, who fled from
sin on earth, and now are quit of all sorrow and woe (388).

¹ Printed before in Reliquiæ Antiquæ, vol. 2. Nos. XXXIV and XXXV
should be read. Of the writer of XXXIV, stanza 12 well says:
þe clerk þat þis baston wrowзte,
wel he woke, and slepe riзte nowзte;
and stanza 15:
þe best clark of al þis toun
craftfullich makid þis bastun.
Roberd of Brunne uses *baston* for a kind of rhyme, putting *baston* and
cowee together, and as *cowee* is a stanza in which the *tails* (or third line
tagged on to each of two rhyming couplets) rhyme (—see Guest II, 286,
and specimens in *The Sarmun*, p. 1, the Fragment on the Seven Sins,
p. 17 &c.), so *baston* may be the stanza in which the *tail* consists of a
rhyming couplet put on to another rhymed and unrhymed one, as in
the text. R. Brunne's passage about the 'ryme' of his *Chronicle* is,
If it were made in ryme couwee,
Or in strangere, or enterlace,

Whosè wl. com þat lond to.
Ful grete ponance he mot do.
Seuè ȝere in swine-is dritte.
180 He mot wade, wol ȝe·i-witte.
Al anon up to þe chynne.
So he schal þe lond i-winne.

þat rede Inglis it ero Inowe
þat couthe not haf coppled a kowe,
þat outhere in couwee, or in baston,
Som suld haf been fordon,
        (extract in *Handlyng Synne*, p. xxxii, l. 85-90, in Guest's
        English Rhythms, vol. 2, p. 282, and in Hearne's
        Langtoft, vol. 1.)
Of the *enterlace*, alternate, or any kind of interlaced rhyme, examples
are, the Signs before the Judgment, p. 7-12; the Fall and Passion,
p. 12-15, &c.

CORRIGENDA.

p. 6, st. 49, l. 3, for *heuesiþ is*, Mr. Wedgwood suggests *seue siþis*, seven times.

p. 16, l. 38, for *bemineþ* we should no doubt read *benimeþ*.

p. 22, VII, st. 5, for *hable* read *habbe*.

p. 34, IX, l. 10, for *here*, ? read *bere*.

p. 39, l. 180, *ne* should doubtless be *me*.

p. 50, l. 108, *þat* should doubtless be *þan*.

p. 107, l. 5, Gilbert's Life was not printed by the Percy Society.

p. 135, l. 75, ? for *likyng* read *lieyng*.

p. 146, l. 297, for *he-helde* read *be-helde*.

'bean frere' is somewhere printed for 'beau frere'.

EARLY ENGLISH POEMS.

I. A SARMUN.

[Against Pride, and Covetousness (16), and on the grave, the pains of hell and the joys of heaven.] (Harl. MS. 913, p. 16.)

1. þe grace of godde and[1] holi chirche
þro uertu of þe trinite:
 if ous grace soch workes to wirche;
þat helplich to ure sowles be.

2a. þes wordes þat ich speke nou last
in`latin. hit is iwritte in boke:
wel mow we drede and be agast;
þe dede beþ so lolich to loke.

2b. þer for he sciith . a : man hab munde
þat of þis lif þer commiþ ende:
of erþe and axen is ure kunde
and in to duste we schulliþ wende

3. So sciþ seint bernard in his boke
and techiþ vs ofte and lome:
to be hend if we wold loke
wel file hit is þat of us come

4. Man loke þin ein and þi nosse
þi mouþ. þin cris al aboute
fram þi girdil to þi hosse
hit is wel vile þat commiþ vte

5. Man of þi schuldres and of þi side
þou mi te hunti luse and flee
of such a park i ne hold no pride
þe dere nis nau te þat þou mighte sle

---

[1] In the MS. every *and* is written *a'* or is marked by a sign of contraction; and there are no hyphens, and no numbers before the lines. The final *es* in italics are inserted by the editor.

6.   If þou ert prute man of þi fleisse
    oþir of þi velle þat is wiþ-oute
    þi fleisse nis naȝte bot worme-is meisse
    of such a þing whi ert þou prute .

7.   Wormis of þi fleisse schul spring
    þi felle wiþ-oute nis bot a sakke
    ipudrid ful wiþ drit and ding
    þat stinkiþ lolich and is blakke

8.   Sire whar of is þe gentil man
    of eni oþer þan of þis:
    him silf mei se . if gode he can
    for he sal find þat so hit is

9.   Þat hit be soþ and noȝt les
    þou loke þi neȝbor whare and how
    þou loke in his biriles
    he was prute as ert þou

10.   Whate prude sastou se þar
    bot stench and wormis i-crop in dritte
    of such a siȝt we aȝt be ware
    and in vre hert hit hab i-writte

11.   Silk no sendale nis þer none
    no bise no no meniuer
    þer nis no þing a-boute þe bone
    to ȝeme þat was ihuddid here

12.   Þe wiked wede þat was abute
    þe wormis þat hit habbiþ al for-soȝt
    Alas whar of is man so prute
    whan al is pride sal turne to noȝte

13.   If man is prute of world-is welle
    ihc hold a fole þat he be
    hit commiþ . hit goþ . hit nis bot dwelle
    bot dritte gile and wanite

14.   Lo þat catel nis bot gile
    trewlich ȝe mov isee
    he nel be felaw bot awhile
    þou salt him leue oþer he sal þe

15.   Hit is mi rede while þou him hast
    þou spen it wel þat helplich be

for god. but þou nelt at þe last
oþer men sulle aftir þe .

16. Nouþe oþer mister men þer beþ
proȝ coueitise hi beþ iblend
þat wer leuer wend to þere deþ
þen spene þe gode þat god ham send

17. Þoȝ man hit hab hit nis noȝt his
hit nis ilend him bot alone
fort to libbe is lif i-wisse
and help þe nedful þat naþ non

18. Nou mani wrecche be-commiþ þralle
hi nul noȝt spene bot ȝime in store
be-com hi beþ þe deuil-is þralle
niȝt and dai hi libbeþ in sore .

19. for niȝt and dai is al har poȝte
how hi hit mow hab and winne
fast to hold and spene riȝt noȝte
and lediþ euer har lif in pinne

20. Þe wrecchis wringit þe mok so fast
up ham silf hi nul noȝt spened
ȝit hi sul dei at þe last
and to þe deuil hi sul wend.

21. Siþ such a wringer goþ to helle
for litil gode þat nis noȝt his
whate mai ich bi þe riche man telle
þat lediþ al is lif in blisse

22. Hit is as eþe forto bring
a camel in to þe neld-is ei
as a rich man to bring
in to þe blisse þat is an hei

23. Þeiȝ man be rich of lond and lede
and holdiþ festis ofte and lome
hit nis no doute he sal be dede
to ȝelde recning at þe dome

24. ȝe: sulle we ȝiue a-cuntis
of al þat we habbiþ ibe here
ȝe: of a verþing soþ i-wisse
of al þi time fram ȝer to ȝere

25. And bot þou hit hab ispend ariʒte
þe gode þat god þe haþ ilend
of ihsu [1] criste þou lesist þe siʒt
to helle pine þou worþe isend

26. Of helle pine we aʒt be ware
and euer more hit hab in poʒt
ac non nel be oþer i-ware
for ham silf be in i-broʒt

27. Þeiʒ freris prech of heuen and helle
of ioi and pine to mani man
al þat him þenchit bot dwelle: [a tale
as men tellip of wlonchargan

28. Ak ʒite þat ilk dai sal be
þer nis non þat nold him hide
so sore we sul drede to se
þe wondis of ihsu crist-is side

29. His hondes is fete sul ren of blode
þou woldist fle þou ne miʒt noʒ þan
þe sper þe nailes and þe rode
sal crie tak wrech of sinful man

30. Þe erþe þe watir þan sal sprede
route and driue al for-wode
nov ihsu crist we sul þe wrekke
of sinful man þat sadde þi blode

31. Boþe fire and wind lude sal crie
louerd nov let vs go to
for ich wl blow þe fire sal berne
vp sinful man þat haþ misdo

32. heuen and erþe sal crie and grede
and helle sal berne þou salt ise
o: sinful man wo worþ þi rede
whan al þis wrech sal be for þe

33. hit is so grisful forto loke
and forto hir þe bittir dome
angles sul quake so●seiþ þe boke
and þat þou hirist of [2] and lome

[1] The MS. has always *ihc* or *ihu* with a mark of contraction.
[2] ? for *ofte*.

34. Sei sinful man whi neltou leue
    þat al þing sal com to hepe
    wel aȝt þi hert proȝ ute cleue
    þin eiine blodi teris wepe
35. Hit is to late whan þou ert þare
    to crie ihsu þin ore
    while þou ert here be wel iware
    vn-do þin hert and liue is lore
36. Vn-do þin hert þat is iloke
    wiþ couetise and prvde þer an
    and þench þos wordis her ispoke
    for-ȝite ham noȝt ac þench apan
37. and bot þou nelt þench her apan
    fort vnderfonge gode lore
    i-wis for soþ as þou ert man
    þou salt hit rew bitter and sore
38. Man-is lif nis bot a schade
    nov he is and nov he nis.
    loke hou he mei be glade
    þoȝ al þis world miȝt be his
39. Wold he þench þe vnseli man
    in to þis world whate he broȝte
    a stinkind felle i-lappid þer an
    wel litil bettir þan riȝt noȝt
40. What is þe gode þat he sal hab
    oute of þis world whan he sal go
    a wikid wede whi sold i gab
    for he ne broȝt wiþ him no mo
41. Riȝt as he com he sal wend
    in wo and pine and pouerte
    takiþ gode hede men to ȝur end
    for as i sigge so hit sal be
42. I note whar of is man so prute
    of erþe axin fel and bone
    for be þe soule enis oute
    a uilir caraing nis þer non
43. mani man þenchit on is poȝt
    he nel noȝt leue his eir al bare

his eir sal fail and ber riȝt noȝte
and wast þe gode wel wide whare

44. Ich warne þe for i-sold hit sal
al þat þou wan here wiþ pine
a broþin eir sal wast it al
and be al oþeris þat was þine

45. Nouþ siþ þat þe world nis noȝt
and catel nis bot vanite
haue god in ur þoȝt
and of þe catel be we fre

46. Anouriþ god and holi chirch
and helpiþ þai þat habiþ nede
so god-is wil we sul wirch
þe ioi of heuen hab to mede

47. What is þe ioi þat man sal hab
if his lif he speniþ wel
soþ to sigge and noȝt to gab
þer nis no tunge þat hit mai tel

48. if i sal tel al þat i can
in holi boke as we can rede
hit is a ioi þat fallit to man
of hel pine he ne dar drede

49. þe man þat mai to heuen com
þe swete solas forto se
heuesiþ is briȝtir þan þe sun
in heuen sal man-is soule be

50. his bodi sal þer be al so
so fair and strang ȝe mou wel leue
iuil is euer fur him fro
þer nis no þing þat him sal greue

51. to met no drink þer nis no nede
no for no hungir he no sal kar
þe siȝte of god him sal fede
hit is wel miri to woni þar

52. þer beþ woningis mani and fale
gode and betir tak god hede
þe last word bint þe tale
wo best mai do: best is his mede

53. heuen is heiʒ boþe lange and wide
mani angles þer beþ an
boþe ioi and blis in euch side
þer in sal woni gode cristin man

54. þe lest ioi þat þer is in
a man sal know is owin frend
is wif is fader and al is kin
of al þis ioi þer nis non end

55. we sul se oure leuedi briʒte
so fulle of loue ioi and blisse
þat of hir neb sal spring þe liʒte
in to oure hert þat ioi iwisse

56. þe siʒte of þe trinite
þe mest ioi þat mai be-falle
boþe god and man in mageste
þe heiʒ king aboue vs alle

57. þe siʒt of him is ure vode
þe siʒt of him is ure virst
al ure iois beþ ful gode
þe siʒt of him is alir best

58. Be-seche we him mek of mode
þat soke þe milk of maid-is brest
þat boʒt us wiþ is dere blode
ʒiue us þe ioi þat euer sal lest .

59. Alle þat beþ icommin here
fort to hire þis sarmun
loke þat ʒe nab no were
for seue ʒer ʒe habbiþ to pardoun.

II. XV SIGNA ANTE IUDICIUM. (A fragment.)
(Harl. MS. 913, p. 20.)

1 þe grace of ihsu fulle of miʒte
proʒ prier of ure swete leuedi
mote a-mang vs nuþe aliʒte
and euer vs ʒem and saui.

5 Man and woman þou aȝtist tak gome
   þis world-is ending how hit ssal be
   þe wondres þat sal com be for þe dome
   þat ȝung and old hit sal ise

9 þe xv tokingis ichul ȝou telle
   as us techiþ ysaie
   þe holi gost him taȝt ful welle
   and he hit prechid for profecie

13 hit is iwrit in holi boke
   as clerkis hit mow se and rede
   þat no þing no man mai loke
   þat is so grisful forto drede

17 þer nis aliue so sinful man
   if he þer of wold tak kepe
   and he wold þench apan
   þat nold wel sore in herte wepe

21 Godmen takiþ nou gome
   of tokninges þat commiþ bi for
   þe children wiþ in þe moder wome
   wel sore sul dicce and drede þer for

25 wiþ in þe moder wom. hi sul grede
   vp ihsu criste euer to crie
   louerde crist þou red vs rede
   and of vs þou hab mercie

29 we wold louerd þat we ner
   in world icome forto bene
   and vnbeȝet of ure fader wer
   þat al þing nou sal suffri tene

33 Þe first tokning sal be þusse
   al for soþ we sul hit see
   and þat oþer sal be wors
   for soþ ȝe nou wel liue me

[The first tokyn]

37 þe sterris þat þou sest so brȝte
   in heuen aboue þat sit so fast
   for man-is sin sal ȝiue no liȝt
   ac sal adun to erþe be cast

41 as fair and briȝte as þou seest ham
   hi worþ be-com as blak as cole

and be of hiwe durke and wan
for man-is sin þat hi sul þole [1]
45 þer nis aliue so stidfast man
þat þer of ne sal agrise
him to hide he ne can
no whoder to fle in nonc wise
49 bot as bestis þat wer wode
a-ʒe oþir to crne. her and þare
for þi hi ne sul can no gode
see no lond hi ne sul spare
53 þan þe dede up sal arise
up har biriles forto sitte
of þilk dai hi sul agrise
and lok as bestis þat cun no witte
III. 57 þe þrid dai þan amorow
grisful hit sal be to loke
of moch weping and of sorow
as we fint in holi boke
61 þe sone þat nov schiniþ so briʒt
þilk dai þou salt i-se
wel grene and wan sal be is liʒt
and þat for dred so hit sal be
65 abute þe time of middai
he worþ as blak as þe cole
we mov sigge wailawai
moch is þe pine þat we sul þole
IV. 69 þe ferþ dai þat silf son
worþ as rede as hit wer fire
for ferd of dome þat he sold come
bi for ihsu þe heiʒ sire
V. 73 þe fifte tokning þat sal be-fal
þat allirkin maner beste
wel sore hi sul quake wiþ al
wil þat ilk dai sal lest
77 towar heuen be-hold sul hi
wiþ har mund and wiþ har poʒt

[1] In the MS. the stanzas that follow are written in two lines instead of four.

of ihsu crist merci to cri
þoȝ þat hi ne mou spek riȝt noȝt
81   alas louerd wat sul we tak
we þat abbiþ sin i-wroȝt
niȝt and dai we aȝt sore quake
whan we it sold þench in ure þoȝt
VI. 85 þe sixte dai ne lef ich noȝt
wan þes montis and þes hille
al for soþ hit wurþ ibroȝt
þes depe dalis for to fille
89 þer nis castel no ture none
þat euer was no be salle
imakid was of lime and ston
þat ne sal adun to-falle
93 no no tre in erþ so fast
mid al har rotis so fast ipiȝt
þat ne sal adun to-berst
þilk silue dai er hit be niȝt
VII. 97 þe sefþe dai hit sal grow aȝe
har crop adun har rote an hei
such wondris we sul i-se
for god-is wreþ þat sit an hei
101 þe iren sul blede. a wonder þing
þe þing þat bodi no flesse naþ non
for dred of þe heuen king
vnkundlich þing ded sal don
105 þan sal dei boþe poure and riche
ne sal þan þer wiþ stond no þing
al we sul ben ilich
boþe kniȝt and barun. erl. and. king
109 ne sal þer help castel no ture
palfrei chasur no no stede
no for al is moch honoure
þat he ne worþ wel sone dede
VIII. 113 þe eiȝt dai so is dotus
and þat ful wel þou salt se
ful of tene and angus
al þis dai so sal be

117 al þe see sal draw ifere
as a walle to stond up riȝt
and al þos watris þat beþ here
sal crie merci up god al miȝt

121 þe fissis þat beþ þer in iwroȝt
þe see so hard sal ham to-driue
þat hi wol wene in her þoȝt
þat god of heuen nis noȝt aliue

125 þan þe see sal draw aȝe
in to þe stid þer hit was
and euch uerisse watir þan sal he
be com to is owni plas

IX. 129 þe ix tokin sal be þus
þe wonderis þat worþ þilk dai
ouer al þat oþer sal deuers
wate hit is ich ȝow tel mai

133 þe holi man telliþ seint austin
þat þe skeis so sal spec þan
wan al þing so sal hab fine
in steuen as hit wer man

137 hi sul grede lude wiþ al
in uois of man up god to cri
as heuen and erþe sold to fal
god and man nouþ merci

141 louerd merci of miȝt
nouþ is al ur time ispend
for sinful man-is ein siȝt
ne let us neuer ben ischend

145 þer nis no seint in heuen abow
in al god-is ferred
þat þer of ne sal amoue
and of þilk tokin be aferd

149 þus vs telliþ seint Ieronime
and seint gregori al so
þat þan sal quake seraphin
and cherubin. þat beþ angles two

153 þer nis in heuen angil iwis
þat to oþer sal hab spech

so sore i-worþ adrad iwis
of ihsu crist-is gremful wreche
157 al þe fendis þat beþ in hel
wiþ grete din hi wol com þan
har mone þou salt hire ful wel
hou hi sul cri to god and man
161 O: man and womman þou take hede
hou þe fentis sul men har mone
wel aʒtist þe faire to lede
wile þou art in þis wreche wone
165 vp ihsu crist hi sulle cri
wiþ such a steuen of pine and wo
louerd ʒif vs ur herbegi
aʒe to helle. let us neuer go

XI. 169 þe .xi. dai fure windis sul rise
and þe reinbow þan sal fal
þat al þe fentis sal of agris
and be ifesid in to helle
173 for wolny nulni hi sul fle
and þat in to þe pine of helle
maugrei ham þer hi mot be
wiþ duble pine þer in to dwel

XII. 177 þe .xii. dai þe fure . elemens sul cri
al in one heiʒ steuene
merci ihsu fiʒ mari
as þou ert god and king of heuene.

(End of the fragment.)

III. THE FALL AND PASSION.
(Harl. MS. 913, back of p. 29.)

1 þe grace of god ful of miʒt . þat is king an euer was : [1]
mote amang us aliʒt . an ʒiue vs alle is swet grace .
3 me to spek an ʒou to lere . þat hit be worsip lord to þe :
me to teche an ʒou to bere . þat helplich to ure sowles be .

[1] For the a' (= and), an is printed here.

5 þat ic mote wiþ moch worþing . þroȝ is miȝt so hit ful fille :
   to ȝov schow is vp-rising . if hit be his swet wille .

7 al þat god suffrid of pine . hit nas noȝt for is owen gilt :
   ok hit was man for sin þine : þat wer for sin in helle ipilt .

9 þo lucifer steiȝ in pride . þat was angel in heuen so briȝte :
   vte of heuen he gan glide . an in to helle sone he liȝte .

11 an wiþ him mani an mo . þat no tunge ne miȝt telle :
   wiþ him fille adune al so : in to þe derk pit of helle .

13 Seue daies a seue niȝt . as ȝe seeþ þat falliþ snowe :
   vte of heuen hi aliȝt . an in to helle wer iþrow .

15 for þe prude of lucifer . þe teþe angle fille in to helle :
   au al þat to him boxum were . euer in pine hi mot dwelle .

17 har stides for to ful fille . þat wer i-falle for prude an hore :
   god makid adam to is wille . to fille har stides þat wer ilor .

19 Skil resun an eke miȝt . he ȝef adam in his mode :
   to be stidfast wiþ al riȝt . an leue þe harme an do gode .

21 god ȝaf him a gret maistre . of al þat was in watir an londe :
   of paradis al þe balye . whan him likid to is honde .

23 foules . bestis . an þe frute . saf o tre he him forbede :
   of paradis þe grete dute : an ȝit he sinied þroȝ iuil red .

25 to him þe dcuil had envie . þat he in his stid schold be broȝte :
   a serpent he com þroȝ felonie . an makid eue chonge hir poȝt

27 whi com he raþer to eue . þan he com to adam .
   ichul ȝou telle sires be leue . for wommau is lef euer to man .

29 womman mai turne man-is wille . whare ȝho wol pilt hir to :
   þat is þe resun an skille . þat þe deuyl com hir first to .

31 Ette he seid of þis appil . if þat þou wolt witti be :
   þe worþ as witti of miȝt an wille : as god him silf in trinite

33 hi nad bot þat appil i-ȝette . þat þe sin nas ido :
   glad was þe deuil wol ȝe i-wit . for þe sorow þat he sold to .

35 of paradis hi wer ute pilt . wiþ trauail har liuelode to winne :
   an vte flemid for har gilt . an neucr efte paradis to com inne .

37 In þe vale of eboir . his liuelod he most swink sore :
   wiþ sorow an care an dreri won . he liued .ix.c. ȝer an more .

39 aftir is lif þat he had here . nedis he most wend to helle :
   for þc trepas þat he did here . þere he most bide an dwelle .

41 God makid mankin more . ok to helle þe deuil ham broȝt :
   þat euir ham traiid þroȝ is lore . non fram him scapid noȝt .

43   god is prophetis to ham send . an seid hov hi sold be sauid:
      as bi Moyses þat am wend . a-ȝe þe propheci ȝit i-sinid.

45   god wist wel bi þilk say . þat bi no man þat was y-cor:
      whan bi prophetis no bi lai. þat communclich hine wer for-lor.

47   holi bok is fort fulfil . god is angle anon forþ send:
      as bi angle gabriel . þat to þe maid was iwend.

49   flees he took of maid mari . god an man-is kund to gadir:
      an þat was a gret maistri . þat þe doȝtir ber þe fader.

51   maid bere heuen king . þat is al ure creatoure:
      maid ber þe swet þing . þer for sso ne les noȝt hir flure.

53   God him ȝed an erþ here . xxxti winter an somdel mo:
      as holi writ vs gan lere . he suffrid boþe pine an wo.

55   man aȝens god so gilt . to heuen non sowle ne miȝte:
      fort god-is sone in rode was pilt . an wan vs heuen liȝt.

57   Iudas ne cuþe is lord noȝt hold. his owen disciple ȝit he was:
      for xxx peniis he him sold . ynom an ibund he was.

59   he was ibobid an i-smitte . an hi spette in is face:
      hi bede him rede if he cuþe witte . woch of ham al hit was.

61   he was ibund to a tre . an ibet wiþ scurges kene:
      þat al þe blode vt gan fle: ouer al is bodi hit was sene.

63   Siþ hi nom him as a þef . an lad him bi-for pilate:
      for he nas noȝt to ham lef. hi had to him grete hate.

65   pilat bed ham do har best . a-ȝe þe law be he nold:
      for no gilt bi him he nist . war for deþ suffri he ssold.

67   hi nailed him in hond an fete . as ȝe mow al i-se:
      for þe appil þat adam ete: deþ he þolid opon þe tre.

69   þe wikkid men nol leue noȝt . þat he wer fullich ded so:
      fort þer wiþ a sper hi ad him soȝt. an clef is swet hert atwo.

71   þer was in þe lond a kniȝt. þat het ȝosep of arimathie:
      þat louid ihsu wel ariȝt. an þoȝt is wel to honuri.

73   he wend to pilat swiþe snel . an be-soȝt him mercy:
      if hit wer is wil . þe bodi grant biri.

75   þo pilat had igrant is luue . glade y-noȝ ho was:
      he nem þat swet bodi adun . an biriid hir in a fair plas.

77   his moder stode him be side . an s$^{t.}$ jon ek al so:
      bitter teris vte gan glide . hir þoȝt hir hert wol a two.

79   hit nas no wonder þoȝ ȝo wep . for hir swet child alowe:
      wiþ nailes he was i-smit deþ . wiþ sper hi delet him in two.

81 al hir ioi was ago . þo ʒo him sei dei in rode:
for to ꝩep ʒe nad no mo . bot iiii bitter teris of blode.

83 who spekiþ of deil a-ʒe þat del . neuer such nas þer none:
as whan þat hi him be-held . as ʒho makid an seint Jon.

85 siþ hi seid at one moupe . þat he wolde destru temple an chirche:
an þat he was wel coupe . þat al falsnis schold wirche.

87 an vp pilat hi cried apan . eu[ri]chon at one vois:
þat he schold hold barabam . an do ihsu on þe crois.

89 In þis manere he was ipinsed . as his swet wil hit was:
an deþ for mankyn suffred . þe þrid dai vp he ros.

91 after þat he liʒt in to helle . þer al þe sowles wer i-wisse:
al his frendis he broʒt vt alle . in to ioi an heuen blis.

93 Whan in helle was seint ion . patriarkes an oþer mo:
hit isene þer scapid non . profetis þat god louid al so.

95 al in helle were i-fast . fort ihsu crist þroʒ is miʒte:
of þe pit vte he ham cast . an broʒt ham to heuen lyʒt.

97 þroʒ is deþ he ouer cam . as he is manhed siwed:
as profetis prechid in his name . so þat he deþ suffrid.

99 þo he rose fram deþ to liue . as telliþ daui þe king:
is godhed he gan to kiþe . holy boke telliþ is up-rising.

101 ihsu was sikir inoʒ . þat seid erlich . ic wol riʒt me:
an asnward wiþ vt woʒ . after þat deþ ouercom be.

103 þe .iii. dai he ros to liue . is lore riuedlich he send:
his deciplis he makid bliþe . þer after in þe world ham send.

105 of his lore forto preche . hoù hi lord ssold siu þe:
an þe sinful folk to tech . hou meri hit is to wiþ þe be.

107 an after he steiʒ to heuen aboue . þer ioi is þat euer lest:
an þer he sal al vs loue . in his swet blisful fest . amen.

IV. THE TEN COMMANDMENTS: against swearing, Sunday trading &c.
(Harl. MS. 913, p. 31 back.)

1 Nou ihsu for þi derworþ blode : þat þou schaddist for mankyn:
ʒif vs grace to wirch workis gode . to heuen þat we mot enter inn.
Man and womman ic red be ware . ʒure gret opis þat ʒe be leue:
and bot ʒe nul god nel ʒou spare . boþe lif and catel he wol ʒou reue.

5 hit nis no wonder for soþ i wisse: þat gret wrecbe ne fallip þer fore:
for we ne leuiþ of al is limmes. þat we ne habbiþ ham for-swore.
man is wors þan eni hunde. oþer he is to wild and wode:
þat we ssold edwite is worþi wound. þat he þolid for vre gode.
be a ware whose euer wol. al quelme and sorow þat euir is:
10 at þen end so find we sulle. þat for man-is sin it is
ic rede þat euch be ware i-wis. in as moch as þe is man:
whan ȝe sweriþ gret opis. in rode þou piltist him apan.
God commandid to ysay. þat he ssold wend and prech:
þat was in þe hil of syna. hou he ssold þe folke tech.
15 and to ssow ham god-is defens : boþe to ȝung and to olde.
of þe .x. commandemens. whos wold be sauid ham ssold hold.

I.   þe first comondemcnt is þis. o god we ssul honuri:
þe heiȝ king of heuen blis. his name wiþ wirssip to worþi.
loue þou him as he doþ þe. wiþ al þi miȝt an þi þoȝt:
20 we auȝt ful wel for hit was he. þat vs wrecchis so dere boȝt.
more harm is we doþ noȝt so. we louid þe ful dritte of grunde:
alas wrecchis whi do we so. hit mai noȝt hold vre lif a stunde:
ve beþ hi þe deuil be tauȝt. þat liuiþ oþ goddis mo þan one:
and makiþ goddis þroȝ wichcraft. þai ssul al to þe deuil gone.

II. 25 þe secunde so is þis. sundai wel þat ȝe holde:
to serue god þilk dai wis. boþe ȝung and eke olde.
and now þe sundai opunlich. men holt al har cheping:
wonder þat gode ne sent wreech. al an erþe vp mankyn.

III.   þe þrid is. fader moder to honuri . for euch man aȝt ful wel:
30 moch ten suffrid hi : her hi miȝt bring þe wrecche to wel.
hit fallip bi children þat beþ quede : as fariþ bi been in hiue:
whan fader ȝuief ham londe and leede: þe ȝung wol þe old ut driue:

IV.   þe verþ. loue þi neiȝbore. as þine owe bodi: non oþer þou him wil:
V. VI. þe fift wit þe fram licheri : þe sixt is no gode of man þou ne stel.
VII. 35 þe .vii. manslaȝt þou ne be : ne coueit noȝt neuer adel
VIII. IX. þoȝ þou be stuter þan is he : no is wif no is catel.
X.   fals witnes þou ne ber . for to destrei pouer no riche:
sore and bitter þe soule sal der . for hit bemineþ heuen-riche.
besech we him mild of mode . þat sok þe milk of maid-is brest:
40 þat boȝt vs wiþ is der blod . ȝiue vs euer in heuen rest . Amen.

[Lollai .l. litil child: whi wepistou so sore,—which has been printed
elsewhere—follows.]

V. FRAGMENT ON THE SEVEN SINS.
(Harl. MS. 913, f. 48 and 22.)

1. þe king of heuen mid us be
    þe fend of helle fram us tc
       to dai and euir more:
    to dai me ʒiue gode beginninge
    þe king of houen to worþing
       and speken of is lore.
2. and þat ʒe hit mote vnderstonde
    þe fend to mochil schamc and schonde
       þis predicacioune.
    and þat ʒe hit hold mote
    bodi and soulc to mochil bote
       and to saluaciounc.
3. Alle we beþ meiis and mowc
    and of one foule erþe i-sowe
       who so hit wold vnderstonde
    þis world-is wcl nis bot wowe
    þis wrecche lif nis bot a þrow
       al dai hit is gond.
4. Man . ne be þou neuer so riche
    be-hold whom þou art iliche
       whan þou ert al nakid
    be-þench þat þou salt i-worþe
    and for-roti to axin and erþc
       whar of þou ert makid
5. Clansi þe of þi misdede
    and lerne wcllc þi lif to ledc
       þe while þou art aliue.
    to nene frcnd þou nab triste
    bot to onc ihcsu criste
       to child no to wiue.
6. Mi leue frendis ic ʒou bi-seche
    ʒung . old . poure and reche
       herkcnþ to god-is speche:

in þe name of god. and S. marie
ȝoure sinful lif to amendie
   to-dai ic wol ȝow teche.

7. And þat he me let so wel to spek
to dai þe deuil-is staf to brek
   an wiþ him so to fiȝte.
perto. par charite ic ȝou crie
a pater noster. and auc marie
   in þe name of god al-miȝte.

8. Þat pees þat is in god-is huse
to dai be a-mangis vse
   proȝ is holi grace:
þat me giue lif. and gode ending
and to ȝou ȝiue gode lusting
   in þis silue place.

9. God him silf seiiþ in his gospel
mi leue frendis ic wol ȝou tel
   nimiþ to me gome:
o worde ic ȝou lie nelle
of heuen blis no pine of helle
   no of riche dome.

10. and of þe herrid sinnes seuene
whar for men lesiþ heuene
ic wol ȝou nemeni alle
and har namis ic wol ȝou teche
and hou hi wol men bi-peche
and make ham to falle.

I. 1 First at prude i wol be-gin. for hit is heuid of al sinne.
[Pride.]   ic hit wol ȝou do to wit. in holi boke hit is i writ.
3 Lucifer þat was so briȝte. þat fairist was of al wiȝte.
  wiþ oute god in heuen nas. non so fair als he was.
5 nas neuer non so fule ifund. as he in helle liþ abund.
  nad he no more gilte. whar for he was of heuen ipilte
7 a litil prude him was in-com. þer-for god him hauiþ be-nome.
  heuen blisse þat euer sal last. and in to helle he is cast.
9 þer he sal woni euer more. and is prude abigge wel sore.
  alas. man whi artu prute. whannin comniþ þi fair schrute.

11 mid whate þou art ischrid aboute. noȝte of þe man boute doute.
þine owen schond þou werist an . þat heliþ þi fleis and þi bone .
13 ic wol þat þou iwit wel . hit nis bote a hori felle.
þat is þine owen ·riȝt wede . beþenche þe man and hab drede.
15 man and womman vnderstond þis . be-tak euch beste his.
þat ert so fair mid bi gon . liuin. wollin. glouis. and schone.
17 þat þou art in hit so prute . ne sal þe leue neuer a cloute.
þer-for man ic þe for-bede . worldlich prude in hert and dede.
19 and lede þi lif bi godis rede . to loui god and hab drede.
þat þou be gode-is sone . and him to queme at þe dome.

II. 21 Coueitise is þat oþer . herkne nov leue broþer.

þer is mani man bi peiȝte . so þe fend him hauiþ iteiȝte .
23 þe man þat is coueituse . ne commiþ he neuer to god-is huse.
suche þer beþ al to fele . þat louiþ more þis world-is welle .
25 þan god þat haþ ham of erþe iwroȝte . and so swithe dere ham boȝte.
he nel is catel spen in wast . ac euer he hit witiþ fast.
27 he nold þat aliue nere . none so riche as he were.
and euer so he hauiþ more . þe faster he gaderiþ to store.
29 and euer he wol is lif so lede . in mochel sorow and in drede.
nel he neuer hab rest . is mochil mukke to witi fast.
31 þat ne mai in him slepe ¢um . lest is mukke be him be nome .
leuer him wer ȝiue of is blode . þan ani man of is gode.
33 nel he of oþir þing hede . but is fule bodi fede.
mid is siluir and is gold . noȝt is soule þat he schold.
35 a-þan is muk he sit a-brode . he þat þus doþ mid is gode.
he ne þenchith noȝt in is end . þat he sal of þis world wend.
37 and vnderstonde noȝt he nelle. what he is no whoder he schel.
his catel he weniþ witi wel . oc in his soule þenche he nelle.
39 with is siluir and is gold . he weniþ euer is lif hold.
whan he weniþ liuie wel . mid deþ adun fal he schel.
41 þe deuil benimiþ him is breþ . moch sorow þan he him deþ.
for is gode þe fend him deriiþ . and is soul to helle he feriiþ.
43 þe deuil is his executur . of is gold and is tresure.
þat he so moch trist to . loke nou hou he is ago.
45 þerfor man in alle wise . ic þe for-bede coueitise.
to world-is wel nab þou no triste. hit went awei so doþ þe miste.
47 her it is and her hit nis . al so fareþ þe world-is blis.
ne be he neuer so riche . whan he liþ a cold liche.

49 if he hauiþ an old clute. he mai be swiþe prute.
    whar mid i-helid he sal be. þat noman nakid him ise.
51 of what he gadred an is was. nis þis rewþ. alas. alas.
III. · þe þrid sin so is onde. þat mochil nuþe' is in lond.
53 and euir hi quemiþ þe fend of helle. in woch maner ic wol ʒou tel.
    leue breþerin herkniþ now. and ic wol ʒou tell how.
55 world-is wel falliþ vnliche. and noʒt euch man ilich.
    sum þer beþ þat cun noʒt libbe. sum þat hauiþ frendis sibbe.
57 and sum þer beþ þat swinkiþ sore. winne catel to hab more.
    ham silf fair to susteni. and euer more hi beþ nedi.
59 and sum þer beþ leue broþer. þat more haþ þan anoþer.
    and more loue of gode man. anoþer wol after þan.
    areri cuntake.

[ends abruptly.]

VI. CHRIST ON THE CROSS. (A fragment.)
(Harl. MS. 913, f. 28.)

Respice in faciem christi tui &c.   Augustinus.
pendens nudatum pectus. rubet sanguineum latus. regia
pallent ora. decora languent lumina. crura pendent marmorea.
rigat terre beatos pedes sanguinis unda. De istis auctoritatibus anglicum.

1   Be-hold to þi lord man. whare he hangiþ on rode.
    and weep if þou miʒt. teris al of blode.
    and loke to is heued. wiþ þornis al be-wonde.
    and to is felle so bi-spette. and to þe sper-is wnde.
5   bi-hold to is brest nakid. and is blodi side.
    stiniith is armis. þat sprad beþ so wide.
    his fair lere falowiþ. and dimmiþ is siʒte.
    þer-to is hendi bodi. on rode so is y-tiʒte.
    his lendin so hangiþ. as cold as marbre stone.
10 for luste of lechuri. nas þer neuer none.
    be-hold to is nailes. in hond and ek in fote.
    and how þe stremis erniþ. of is swet blode.
    be-ginne at is heued. and loke to is to.
    þou ne findest in is bodi. bot anguis and wo.

15 turne him uppe. turne him doune. þi swete lemman.
ouer al þou findist him. blodi oþer wan.

Dilexit nos et lauit nos a peccatis nostris in sanguine suo &c.

Leue for þe mi brest nakid. schiniþ glisminge.
mi side dep istunge. mi hondes sore bleding.

Quid misericordius ualet intelligi ipsi peccatori eternis tormentis
dampnato et vnde se redimat non habenti quam ut dicat deus ipse
peccatori . Dicit vero deus pater . Accipe unigenitum meum et da
pro te. et ille filius tolle me et redime te. Anglicum expone.

Man þou hast þe for-lor. and ful neiþ to helle ibor.
20 wend a-ȝe and com to me. and ic wol underfang þe.
for first ic makid þe of. noȝt. and siþ dere þe i-boȝt.
whan ic mi lif ȝef for þe. and i-hang was on tre. &c.

O homo; vide quid pro te patior sicut est dolor sicut dolor quo
crucior. ad te clamo qui pro te morior. uides penas quibus afficior.
uide clauos quibus confodior. si est tautus dolor exterior. interius
est planctus grauior.

Man bi-hold what ic for þe. þolid up þe rode tre
ne mai no kinnes wo be mare. þan min was þo ic heng þare.
25 hire me man to þe gredind. for loue of þe biter deiend.
loke mi pinis biter and strang. wan ic was nailed proȝ fot and hond.
for þe ic had hard stundes. dintes grete and sore wondes.
for þe biter drink ic dronk. and þou cunnest me no þonk.
wiþ-vte ic was ipinid sore. wiþ-in ic was mochil more.
30 for þou nelt þonk me. þe loue þat ich schowid þe &c.

[end.]

VII. A RHYME-BEGINNING FRAGMENT.

(Harl. MS. 913, f. 58.)

Loue hauiþ me broȝt in liþir poȝt.
poȝt ic ab to blinne:
blinne to þench hit is for noȝt;
Noȝt is loue of sinne.
Sinne me hauiþ in care ibroȝt.
broȝt in mochil vn-winne:

winne to weld ic had i-þoʒt;
þoʒt is þat ic am inne.
  In me is care. how i ssal fare.
  fare ic wol and funde.
  fare ic wiþ outen are
  ar i be broʒt to grunde.

VIII. A MORAL ODE.

(Egerton MS. 613, fol. 7-12; later copy, fol. 64-70.)

1. Ic[1] rem ælder þænne ic *wæs[2]. a winter[3] and a lore
   ic wælde more þanne ic dude. mi wit ah to ben more
2. Wel lange ic habbe child iben[4]. a worde & ec[5] a dede
   þech[6] ic beo a wintre cald. to ʒung ic[7] eom at[8] rede
3. Vnnvwt[9] lyf ic habbe ʒe-læd[10]. & ʒuet me þinh[11] ic lede
   þanne ic me bi-þanche[12]. wel sore ic me adrede
4. Mest al þæt ic habbe ydon. ys idelnesse and chilce
   wel late ic habbe me[13] bi-þoht. bute me god do milce
5. Fele ydele word ic hable i-queþen. syðen[14] ic speke cuþe
   & fele ʒuinge deden[15] i-do. þat[16] me of þinchet nuþe
6. Al to lome ic habbe a-gult. a werche[17] & ec a worde
   al to muchel ic habbe i-spend. to litel y-leid an horde
7. Mest al þat me likede ær. nu it me mys likeð[18]
   þe muchel folʒeþ his y-wil. him sulfne he bi-swikeð
8. Ic myhte[19] habbe bet i-don. hadde ic þer[20] y selþe
   nu ic wolde, ac ic ne mai. for elde ne for un-helþe
9. Elde[21] me is bi-stolen on. ær ic hit a-wuste
   ne myht ic isen be-fore me. for smeke ne for myste
10. Arʒe[22] we beoþ to done god. to vuele[23] al to þriste
    more eie stont[24] man of manne. þanne him det[25] of criste

---

* The *w* is the Anglo-Saxon þ, the & the 7. The hyphens and commas
are not in the MS. Some of the metrical points are inserted from the later MS.
 [1] Ich.   [2] þen ich.wes.   [3] awintre.   [4] ibeon. a weorde.   [5] ech.
 [6] þeh.   [7] tu ʒyng.   [8] a.   [9] Vn-nut.   [10] habb ilæd.   [11] þincþ.
 [12] þenche.   [13] me.   [14] iqueden. syððen.   [15] ʒunge dede.   [16] þe.
 [17] weorche.   [18] mis-lichet.   [19] Ich mihte.   [20] þo.   [21] Ylde.
 [22] ærwe.   [23] yfele.   [24] stent.   [25] do.

11. Þe wel ne deþ þe hwile he mei. wel oft hit hym scæl ruwen
    þenne hy mowen sculen & ripen. þer þe hi ær seowen

12. Don ec to gode wet ᵹe muᵹe. þa hwile ᵹe buð a life
    ne hopie no man to muchel. to childe ne to wyfe

13. Þe him selue for-ᵹut for wife. oþer ¹ for childe
    he sæl comen ² on vucle stede. bute hym god be ³ milde

14. Sende ec ⁴ sum god be-foren hym. þe hwyle ᵹe ben aliue ⁵
    for betere his on almesse before. þaune ben after vyue ⁶

15. Ne beo þe leure þan þi self ⁷. þi mei ne þi moᵹe ⁸
    ⁹for sot ys þat ys oþer mannes frond. betre þanne his oᵹe

16. Ne hopie wif to hyre were. ne were to his wife
    bue ¹⁰ for him selue æfrech ¹¹ man. þe whylc he bo alife

17. Wis is þe him sulf be-þenþ ¹². þa hwile þe he mot ¹³ libbe
    for sone willet him for-ᵹyten ¹⁴. þe fræmden & þo sibbe

18. Þe wel ne deþ þe wile he mai. ne scal he wanne ¹⁵ he wolde
    mani ¹⁶ mannes sor ᵹe swynch. habbet ofte alle vn holde ¹⁷

19. Ne solde no man don a ferst. ne sclakien ¹⁸ wel to done
    for mani man bi-hoted ¹⁹ wel. he ²⁰ it forᵹytet sone

20. Þe man þe wule siker ben. to habbe godes blisse
    do wel him silf þe wile he mai. þanne haued he it mid ²¹ ywisse

21. Þos ²² riche men wened ben sikere ²³. þurh walles ²⁴ & þurh diche
    he ded his eitte on ²⁵ sikere stede. þe hi send ²⁶ to heuene-riche

22. For þer ne þarf he ben of drad ²⁷. of fure ne of þeve ²⁸
    þer ne mai it hym bi-nimen ²⁹. þe loþe ne þe leue ³⁰

23. Þer ne þerf he habbe kare. of wiue ne of childe
    þider we sended suuel & bred ³¹. to litel ³² & to selde

24. Þider we solden drawen & don. wel oft & wel ᵹe-lome
    for þer ne scal me us nontbinimen ³³. mid wronge ne mid woᵹe ³⁴

25. Þider we scolde ᵹerne drawen & don ³⁵. wolde ᵹe me ileue
    for þer ne mai hit ou bi-nimen ³⁶. þe king ne þe scirreve ³⁷

---

¹ oðer. ² sceal cume. ³ beo. ⁴ æch. ⁵ hwile he mei to heuene.
⁶ seouene. ⁷ þene þe sulf. ⁸ mæi ne ði maᵹe. ⁹ sot is ðe is oðres.
¹⁰ beo. ¹¹ æurich. ¹² sulfne bi-þencð. ¹³ hwile he mote. ¹⁴ wulleð
hine for-ᵹite. ¹⁵ hwenne. ¹⁶ manies. ¹⁷ sare iswinch . habbeð oft
unholde. ¹⁸ slawen. ¹⁹ bi-hateð. ²⁰ þe. ²¹ ðen haueð he mid.
²² þes. ²³ weneð beo siker. ²⁴ walle. ²⁵ his a. ²⁶ þe sent. ²⁷ ðierf
beon of dred. ²⁸ þeoue. ²⁹ mei hi bi-nime. ³⁰ laðe ne ðe leoue.
³¹ sendet & sulf bereð. ³² lite. ³³ naht bi nime. ³⁴ mid wrancwise
dome. ³⁵ & don *omitted*. ³⁶ bi-nimen eow. ³⁷ ne se ireue.

26. Al þat beste þat ge we habbet[1]. þider we scolde sende
    for þer we it muwen[2] finden eft. & habben abuten[3] ende

27. Þe þe her det ani god. for to habben[4] goddes ore
    al he it scal finden þer. & hundred felde more

28. Þe þe ehte wile healden wel. þe wile he mai his welden
    ᵹiue his for godes luue. eft heo hit scullen a-finden[5]

29. Vre iswinch & ure tilþe. is efte iwuned to swinden
    ac þat we dot for godes luue. eft we it scullen afinden

30. Ne scal non vuel[6] ben vn-bout. ne non god vn-for-ᵹolde
    vuel we doð al to muchel. & god lasse þanne we scolde

31. Þe þe mest deð nu to gode. & þe þe lest to laðe
    ayþer to lutel & to muchel. scal þinchen eft hym baðe

32. Þer me scal vre werkes weᵹen. bi-foren þen heuene kinge
    & ᵹiuen us vre swinches lyen. after vre erninge

33. Eure ilc man mid þan þe he[7] haued. mai biggen heueriche
    þe þe more haued & þe þe lasse. boþe mai iliche

34. He alse mid his penie. þe þe[8] oþer mid his punde
    þat is þe wunder-likeste ᵹare[9]. þat ein man eure funde

35. And þe þe more ne mai don. bute[10] mid his gode þanke
    al se wel se þe haued. goldes feale manke[11]

36. And god[12] can more þanc. ðan þe him ᵹiued lesse
    al his werkes & his weics. is milce & ritᵹifnesse[13]

37. Lutel loc[14] is gode lef. þat comed of gode wille
    & eð-lete muchel ᵹyue. ðenne ðe heorte is ille

38. Heuene & erþe he ouer-sihð. his eᵹen bed so britte
    sunne. mone. dai. & fur. bud þustre to-ᵹenes his lithte

39. Nis him nout for-hole ni hud. so muchel bet[15] his mihte
    nis it no so derne idon. ne a swa þustre nihte

40. He wot wat deht[16] & þenchet. alle quike wihte
    nis no louerd swilc se is crist. na king swilc vre drihte

41. Heuene & herþe & al þat is. be loken in his honde
    he ded al þat his willes is. a watere & a londe

42. He makede fisses inne þe see. & fuᵹeles inne þe lofte
    he wit & walt[17] alle þing. & he scop alle scefte[18]

---

[1] þet betste þer we hedde.   [2] mihte.   [3] habbe bute.   [4] for habbe.
[5] þenne deð he his wel ihealden.   [6] nan uuel.   [7] he *omitted*.   [8] se ðe.
[9] wunder-lukeste ware.   [10] bute *omitted*.   [11] marke.   [12] And oft god.
[13] rihtwisnesse.   [14] lac.   [15] bið.   [16] deð.   [17] wealdeð.   [18] ealle ȝe sceafte.

43. He is ord abuten orde. & ende abuten ende
    he one is eure on elche stede. wende war þu wende
44. He is buuen vs & bi-neþen. bi-foren & bi-hinde
    þe þe godes wille ðe [1]. eiðer he mai him finde
45. Elche rune he i-hurd. & he wot alle dede
    he þurð-sihð elches mannes þanc. þat scal us to rede
46. Þo þe breked godes hese. & gultet so ilome
    wet sulle hi segge [2] oþer don. at þe muchele dome
47. Þo þe [3] luueden vnriht. & vuel lif ladde
    wat scullen hi seggen oþer don. þar engles bed of dredde
48. Hwat sculle we beren bi-foren us [4]. mid wan sculle we him
                             i-quemen [5]
    we þe neure god ne duden. þe heuenliche demen
49. Þer sculle ben deofles swo fele. þe wulled us for-wreien
    nabbet hi noþing for-ɤyte. of al þat hi ere seɤen [6]
50. Al þat we mis-duden her. hit wullet cuþe þere
    buten we habben it ibet. þe wile we her were
51. Al hi habbet an here i-write. þat we mis-duden here
    þei we it nulten ne i-seien [7]. hi weren vre i-fere
52. Hwet scullen horlinges do. þe swikele [8] þe for-sworene
    wi swo fele beod i-cleped. swa feuwe beod i-corene
53. Wi hwi were he bi-ɤite. to wan were hi i-borene
    þe sculle ben to deþe i-demd. & eure mo for-lorene
54. Elch man scal him sulne þar. bi-clepiean & ec demen [9]
    his aɤe werc & his iþanc. to witnesce he scal temen
55. Ne mai hym na man al swa. wel demen ne al sa rithte [10]
    for nan ni cnawed him swa wel. buten one dritte
56. Elc man wot him sulue best. his werc & his i-wille
    þe þe lest wot, seit ofte mest. & þe þe it wot [11] is stille
57. Nis no witnesse al so mochel. so mannes howe heorte
    hwa se segge þat he beo al [12]. him self wat best his smerte
58. Elc man scal him snelf demen. to deþe oþer to liue
    þe witnesse of his owe werc. to oþer ðis him scal driue

---

[1] deð.   [2] we seggen.   [3] þa ða.   [4] us *omitted.*   [5] we cweman.
[6] hi iseɤen.   [7] hi nuste ne ni seɤen.   [8] swikene.   [9] him ðer bi-clupien. & ech sceal him demen.   [10] ne swa rihte.   [11] ðe ðe hit wat eal.   [12] hal.

59. Eal þat cure ilc man hauod i-do. sutþe he com to manne
    swilc hit seie on boc[1] i-writen. he scal it þenche þanne[2]

60. Ac drihtc ne demed nanne man. after his bi-ginninge
    ac his[3] lib scal beo swilc. se bued his endinge

61. Ac ꝩif þe ende is euel, al it is uucl. & al god[4], ꝩif god is ende[5]
    god ꝩuue þat ure end beo god. & wite þet hc us lende[6]

62. Þe men þc nele do no god. nc neure god lif leden
    aer ded[7] & dom come to[8] his dure. he mai sore a-dredcn

63. Þat he nc muwe þenne bidde ore. for it itit ilome
    þi he is wis þe bit & be-ꝩit[9]. & bet be-fore dome

64. Þenne ded is ate[10] dure. wel late he biddet ore
    wel late he leted vucl weorc. þe hit ne mai do na marc

65. [11]Sunne let þe, & þu naht hire, þanne þus ne miht do no morc
    for-þi he is sot, þe swa abit, to habbe goddes hore

66. Þeh hweðer we it iluuet wel. for drihte sulf hit sede
    a wulche timc so eure þe man. of-þinchet his mis-dede

67. Oþer later oþer raþer. milce he scal i-meten
    ac þe þe nout naued[12] ibet. wel muchel he scal beten

68. Mani man seid wo recke of pine. þe scal habben ende
    ne biddc ic no bet beo a-lused[13]. a domesdai of bende

69. Lutel wat he hwat is pine. & lutel he it icwoweð[14]
    wilc hctc is þer soule wunet. hu biter wind þer blouwet

70. Hadde he ibeon þer anne dai. oþcr twa bare tide
    nolde he for al middan eard. þe þridde þer abide

71. Þat habbct ised þat comen þanne. þit wuste mid iwisse
    uuel is pine seoue ꝩer. for seoue nihtes blisse

72. And ure blisse þe ende hafh. for endeliese pine
    betre is wori water to drinke[15]. þcnne atter i-menge mid wine

73. Swunes brede is swuþe swetc. so is of wilde dere
    ac al to duerc he i-buꝩed[16]. þat ꝩiued þere-fore his swere

74. Ful wombe mai liht-liche speken. of hunger & of fasten
    swa mai of pine þe naht not. hu hi scullen ilesten[17]

75. Hadde he ifonded sume hwile[18]. he wolde al seggen oþcr
    eð-lete him werc. wif. & child. suster. & fader. & broþer

---

[1] si aboc   [2] iðenche ðennc.   [3] ac al his.   [4] & god.   [5] þcnne.   [6] lenne.
[7] dieð.   [8] æt.   [9] ðe beot & beat.   [10] deað is æt his.   [11] *st. 65 is omitted.*
abit = *abides, waits.*   [12] nafð naht.   [13] ilusd.   [14] icnaweð.   [15] weter idrunke.
[16] hi biȝð.   [17] hu pine sceal alesten.   [18] Hedde his a-fanded sume stunde.

76. [1]Al he wolde oþerluker don. & oþerluker þenche
ᵹanne he bi-þouhte on helle fur. þe nowiht ne mai aquenche

77. Eure he wolde inne wa her. & inne pine[2] wunien
wid þan þe mihte helle pine. bi-fluen & bi-scunien

78. Eð-lete him were al woruldes[3] wele. & al eordliche[4]
for to þe muchele murcð cume. þat is heuenriche[5]

79. I[6] wulle nu comen eft to þe dome. þat[7] ic eow er of sede
on þat dai, & at þe dome. us helpe crist & rede

80. Þþer we maᵹen beon eðe of drad[8]. & harde us adrede
þer elc sceal i-seo bi-foren him. his word & ec his dede

81. Eal scal ben þanne[9] cud. þat man luᵹen her & stelen
al scal ben þer vnwrien. þat men wruᵹen her & helen

82. We scullen alre manne lif. icnawe þer al so vre owe
þer sculle heueninges ben. þe heiᵹe & þe louᵹe

83. Ne scal þei noman scamien þer. ne þerf he him adrede
ᵹif him here of-pinched his gult. & beted his misdede

84. For heom ne scamet ne ne gramet. þe sculle beon iboruwene[10]
ac þe oþre habbet scame & grame. þat sculle beon forlorene[11]

85. Þe dom scal sone ben idon. ne last he nowit longe
ne scal him noman mene þer. of strengþe ne of wrange

86. Þo scullen habben hardne dom. þe here weren herde
þa þe euele heolden wreche men. & vuele laᵹes rerde[12]

87. Ac[13] after þan þe[14] he haued idon. he[14] scal þer beon idemed
bliþe mai he þanne buen. þe god haued[15] iquemed

88. Alle þo þat isprunge beð. of adam & of eue
ealle he sculle þuder come. for soþe we it ileued

89. Þo þe habbed wel idon. after heore mihte
to heuenriche[16] he scullen. ford mid vre drihte

90. Þo þe nabbeð god idon. & þer-inne beð ifunde
he scullen falle swiþe raþe. in to helle grunde

91. Þær[17]inne he scullen wuniẹ. buten ore & ende
ne brecð neuereuft crist helle dure. to lese hem[18] of bende

---

[1] Stanza 76 is omitted.   [2] wawẹ.   [3] eal woruld.   [4] eordliche blisse.
[5] cume. ðis murbðe mid iwisse.   [6] Ich.   [7] þe.   [8] dredde.   [9] ðen
ðenne.   [10] iboreᵹe.   [11] . & oðer fele sorᵹe.   [12] arerde.   [13] and.
[14] *omit* þe *and* he.   [15] hafð wel.   [16] scule faren.   [17] hi wuniẹ sculen
a & buten ende.   [18] for lese hi.

92. Nis no sellic þei heom beo wo. & hem beo ¹vneþe
    ²nele neureit crist þolie deð. for lesen heom of dieþe

93. Enes drihte helle brac. his frend he ut broutte
    him self he þolede dieð for hom. wel dorc he us bouhte

94. Nolde it mouwe don for mey³. ne suster for broþer
    nolde it sune don for fader. ne noman for oþer

95. Ure⁴ lauerd for his þreles. ipined was on rode
    ure bendes he unbond. & bouht us mid his blode

96. We ჳieued vneþe for his louue. a sticche of vre brede
    ne þenche we nout þat he scal deme. þo⁵ quike & to⁵ dede

97. Muchele luue he us cudde. wolde we it understonde
    þat vre eldrene mis-duden. we habbet vuele an honde

98. Dieð com in þis middenerd. þurh þe ealde deofles onde
    & synne & sorჳe & ჳe-swinch. a watere & ec⁵ alonde

99. Vres formes faderes gult. we abigget alle
    al his of-sprunge after hym. in herme is bi-falle

100. Þurst. & hunger. chule. & hete. eche & al unelþe⁶
    þurh dieð com in þis middenerd. & oþer vnisalþe⁷

101. Niere no⁵ man elles dieð. ne sic. ne non ⁸vn-ysele
    ac mihten libbe eure mo. a blisse & on hele

102. Lutel iþenchð mani man. hu muchel wes þe synne
    for ⁹þan þolied alle died. þe comen of here cunne

103. Here sunne & ec vre owen. sore us mai of þinche
    for in⁵ synne we libbet alle¹⁰. in sorewen & in swinche

104. Sudþe god nam swa muchele wreche. for ane misdede
    þe þat so muchel & swa⁵ oft mis doð. muჳen us sore¹¹ adrede

105. Adam & his of-spring. for one bare sunne
    was fele hundred wintre in helle. in pine & in vnwunne

106. And þo þe leded here lif | mid vnriht & mid⁵ wronge
    bute it godes milce do | sculle beo þer wel longe

107.   Godes wisdom is wel muchel. & al swa is his mihte
    & nis his milce nawiht lasse. ac bi ðes ilke wihte

108. More he one mai for-ჳiuen. þenne alfolc gulte cunne
    deofel suelf⁵ mihte habbe milce. ჳif he it ¹²bidde gunne

---

¹ un ieðe. ² sceal neure. ³ mei. ⁴ Vre ealre. ⁵ omits these.
⁶ unhelðe. ⁷ uniselðe. ⁸ un sele. ⁹ whan ealle þolied dieð. ¹⁰ alle
her. ¹¹ eaðe. ¹² bigunne.

109.   þe ðe godes milce sechð. iwis he mai is finde
  ac helle kinge is [1]oreles. wið þa þe he mai binde
110.   þe ðe deþ his wille mest. he haueþ wurst mede
  his beað scal beo wallinde pich. his bed berninde glede
111.   Wurs he deð his gode wiues[2]. þene his fulle feonde
  god sculde alle godes frend | a wihd scuche[3] freonde
112.   Neure on helle ic ne com | ne comen ic þer ne reche
  ðeh ich elches wurldes wele. þer inne mihte fecche
113.   þeh ic wulle seggen eow. þat wise men ut[4] sede
  and aboke [5]it is i-write. þer me mai it rede
114.   Ic it wulle segge heom | þe hem self it nusten
  & warnen heom wit heore hearme[6]. ɥif hi me wulled lusten
115.   Vnder-stondet nu to me. æidi[7] men & earme
  Ic wulle telle of helle pine. & warnie ow wið herme
116.   On helle is vnger & þerst. vuele tuo ifere
  þos pine þolied þo. þe were mete niþinges here
117.   þor is woninge[8] & wop. after eche strete
  hi fared fram hete to þe chele. fram chele to þe hete
118.   þanne hi beod in þe hete. þe chele[9] ðinchet blisse
  þenne hi comeð eft to chele. of hete hi habbed misse
119.   Aiþer hem deð wa inou. nabbet hi none lisse
  nuten hi weþer ded wurst. mid neure non[10] iwisse
120.   Hi walked eure & sechet reste. ac hi ne muɥen imeten[11]
  for þi hi nolden þo[12] wile | hi mithten here sunne beten[13]
121.   Hi seched reste þer non nis. ac[14] þi ne muwen ifinde[15]
  ac walked weri up & dun. al[14] se water deð mid winde
122.   þis beod þo þe weren her. on þonke vn-stedefaste
  & þo god bi-heten auht. & nolden it ilaste
123.   þo ðe god weorc bigunne. & ful enden hit nolden
  þe[16] weren her. & nuþe þer. & nusten wet he[17] wolden
124.   þere is pich þat eure wealð. þat sculle baþien inne
  þo þe ladde vuel lif. in feoh[18] end in iginne

---

[1] are lies.   [2] wines.   [3] swiche.   [4] us.   [5] hi hit write.   [6] unfreme.
[7] ɜedi.   [8] wanunge.   [9] chelecheð blisse.   [10] wheðer him deð wurs mid
nane.   [11] mugen imete.   [12] þi ði nolden.   [13] bete.   [14] ac *and* al
omitted.   [15] hi finde.   [16] nu.   [17] hi.   [18] feoht.

125. [1]Þer is fur þat eure barnð. ne mai hit nawiht quenche
     her-inne beod þe wes to lef. wrecche men to swenche
126. Þer is fur þat is vndredfelde | hatere þanne beo vre[2]
     ne mai it quenchen salt water. nauene strien[3] ne sture[4]
127. Þo þe were swikele men. & fulle of vuele wrenche
     þo þe ne mihte euel don. & lef was it to[5] þenche
128. Þo þe luueden reuing & stale. hordom. & drunke
     & þe[6] on þes deofles weorkes | bliþeliche swunke
129. Þo þe were so lease. þat me hi ne mihte ileuen
     med Ȝeorne domes men. & wrancwise reuen[7]
130. Þe oþre mannes wif wes lef. his awene cð-lete
     & þo þe sunegede muchel. on drunke & on[8] ete
131. Þe wrecchen bi-nemen hure ehte. & leiden huere on horde[9]
     þe lutel leten of godes bode[10]. & of godes worde
132. And of his owen nolde Ȝiuen. þer he sei þe nede
     ne nolde ihuren godes sonde. þer þe[11] sette his beode
133. Þo[12] þe weren[13] oþeres mannes þinc[14]. leure þanne ic scolde
     & weren al to gredi. of suelfer &[15] of golde
134. And þo[12] þe vntreunesse deden. Ȝam[16] hi ahte ben holde
     & leten þat hi scolde don. & duden þet hi wolde
135. Þo þe Ȝysceres[17] weren | of þis woruldes ehte
     & dude þat þe loþe gost. hem tihte & ec[18] tauhte
136. And alle þo[12] ðen eni wise. deoflen her iquemde
     þo beoð nu mid him | an helle for-don & for-dempde
137. Bute þo[12] þe ofþouhte sore. her here[19] mis-deden
     & gunnen here gultes beten. & betere lif leden
138. Þeor beð naddren & snaken. eueten & frude[20]
     þa tered & freteð þe uuele speken. þe nihtfulle[21] & þe prute
139. Neure sunne þer ne scinð. ne mone ne steorre
     þer is muchel godes hete. & muchel godes Ȝeorre
140. Eure þer is vuel smech. þusternesse & eie
     nis þer neure oþer liht. þanne þe swarte leie

---

[1] The later MS. transposes the stanzas 125 and 126, and begins 125
with: Þis is þe.   [2] hundred fealde hattre ðen vre.   [3] striem.   [4] i. e.
nor Avon stream nor Stour.   [5] wes to.   [6] a.   [7] ireue.   [8] a drunken
& en.   [9] Þe wrecche be-nam his ehte. & leide hes en horde.   [10] bibode.
[11] he.   [12] þa.   [13] wes.   [14] ðing.   [15] end.   [16] dude. þam ðe.   [17] witteres
and omits weren.   [18] to.   [19] of ðufte sare heore.   [20] frute.   [21] nið fulle.

141. Þer ligget laðliche fend. in stronge raketeie
    þat buð þe þe were mid gode. on heuene wel heie
142. Þer buð ateliche fend. & eisliche wihte
    þos sculle þa wrecchen i-son[1]. þe sunege þurð[2] sihte
143. Þer is þe loþe sathanas. & belsebuc þe[3] ealde
    Ieþe he[4] muwen ben of drard. þe hine sculled bi-helde[5]
144. Ne mai non heorte it þenche. ne no[6] tunge ne can telle
    hu muchele pine. &[7] hu vele. senden[8] inne helle
145. Of[9] þo pine þe þere bued[10]. nelle ic hou nout[11] leioᵹen
    nis it bute gamen & gleo. al þat man mai here dreoᵹen
146. Ac[12] ᵹet ne deð heom nout so wo. in þo loþe biende[13]
    bute þat hi witeð þat heore pine. ne scal neure habben ende
147. Þer buð þo heþenemen. þe were lawe lese
    þe heom nas nout of godes bode[14]. ne of godes hese
148. Vuele cristenemen. hi bud here i-vere
    þo þe heore cristen-dom. vuele heolden here
149. ᵹut hi bud a wurse stede. on þere helle grunde
    ne sculle hi neure comen vp[15]. for marke ne for punde
150. Ne mai heom noþer helpen þer. i-bede ne almesse
    for nis noþer inne helle. ore ne forᵹiuenesse
151. Sculde him elc[16] man þe wile he mai[17]. of þos helle pine
    and warnie æc[16] his frend þer wid. so ic habbe mine
152. Þo þe scilden heom ne cunnen. ic heom wulle teache
    ich kan beo ᵹif i[18] scal. lichame & soule liache[19]
153. Lete we þat god for-bet. alle mancunne[20]
    & do þe þat he us hat. & scilde we us wid sunne
154. Luuie we god mid vre heorte. & mid al vre mihte
    & vre emcristene alse[21] us suelf. swa us lerde drihte
155. Al þat me rat & singð[22]. be-fore godes borde
    al it hauged & bi-halt. bi þisse twam worde
156. Alle godes lawe he fulð. þe newe & þe[23] ealde
    he þe þos twa luue haued[24]. & wel hi wule healde

---

[1] i-fon. [2] suneᵹede ðurh. [3] belzebud se. [4] eaðe hi. [5] scule bi-
healde. [6] iðenche. ne. [7] na. [8] sunden. [9] Wið. [10] beoð. [11] eow
naht. [12] End. [13] ða laðe bende *and omits* bute *following.* [14] þe nes
naht of godes bi-bode. [15] vt. [16] ech. [17] muᵹe. [18] ich. [19] leche.
[20] manne cunne. [21] eal. [22] ræt & eal þat me singð. [23] ða.
[24] hafð.

157. Ac hi buð wunder erued helde. swa ofte we[1] gulted alle
    for it is strong to stonde longe. & liht it[1] is to falle

158. Ac drihte crist he ᵹiue us strencþe. stonde þat we mote
    & of alle vre gultes, unne us come[2] bote

159. We wilnied efter worldes[3] wele. þe longe ne mai ileste
    & leggeð al ure iswinch. on þinge un-stede-faste[4]

160. Swunche we for godes luue. half þat we doð for ehte
    ne were[5] we nout swa bi-cherd. ne swa vuele bi-cauhte[6]

161. ᵹif we serueden god. so we doð erninges
    more we haueden of[7] heuene. þanne eorles oþer[8] kinges

162. Ne muwen hi her[9] werien heom wid chele. wid þurst. ne wid
                               hunger
    ne wid elde[10], ne wid deð. þe eldre[10] ne þe ᵹeonger

163. Ac þer nis hunger ne þurst ne deþ. ne vnhelþe ne elde
    of þisse riche we þenchet oft. & of þere to selde

164. We scolden alle us bi-þenche. oft & wel ilome
    hwet we beð. & to þan[11] we sculle. & of wan we come

165. Hu lutel wile we beð her. hu longe elles ware
    hwat we muᵹen habben her. & whet elles hware[12]

166. ᵹif we were wise men. þis we scolden iþenche
    bute we wurþe us iwar. þes worlde us wule for-drenche

167. Mest alle men he ᵹiued drinke. of one deofles scenche
    he sceal him cunne sculde wel. ᵹif he him[13] nele screnche

168. Mid ealm[i]hties[14] godes luue. vte þe us bi-werien
    wid þes[15] wrecches worldes luue. þat he ne[16] mawe us derien

169. Mid fasten. & almesse. & ibede. werie we us wid sunne
    Mid þo wepnen þe god haued ᵹiuen | alle[17] mancunne

170. Læte we þe brode[18] stret. & þe[19] wei bene
    þe lat þe niᵹeðe del to helle of manne. & mo ic wene

171. Go we þene narewe[20] wei. & þene wei grene
    þer forð-fareð lutel folc. ac it is feir & scene

172. Þe brode[18] stret is vre iwil. ðe is us lod for to lete[21]
    þe ðe al folewed[22] his wil. fared bi þusse strete

---

[1] *omits* we *and* it.   [2] cume to.   [3] woruld.   [4] unstedefeste.   [5] beo.
[6] bi-kehte.   [7] hedden en.   [8] her &.   [9] *omits* her.   [10] ulde . uldre.
[11] beoð to whan.   [12] finde þere.   [13] hine.   [14] ealmihtiᵹes.   [15] ðises.
[16] *omit* ne.   [17] biᵹiten.   [18] brade.   [19] ðene.   [20] nærewne.   [21] to
forlæte.   [22] eal folᵹeð.

173. Hi muwen lihtliche gon. mid ðere nuðer[1] hulde
　　　ðurh ane godliese wude. in-to ane bare felde

174. Þe narewei is godes hes. þer-forð farð wel feuwe
　　　þat buð ða þe heom sculdeð ᵹeorne. wid elche un-ðeawe

175. Þos goð un-ieþe to-ᵹeanes[2] þe cliue. aᵹean þe heᵹe hulle
　　　þos leteð al here aᵹen wil. for godes hese to fulle

176. Go we alle þene wei. for he us wulle bringe
　　　mid·þo faire fewe[3] men. be-foren heuene kinge

177. Þer is alre meruþe[4] mest. mid englene songe
　　　þe þis[5] a þusent wintre þer. ne þincð him noht to longe

178. Þe þe lest haued. haueð[6] so muchel. þat he ne bit no more
　　　þe ðe blisse for ðos for-lat. it him mai rewe sore

179. Ne mai non vuel ne non wane[7]. beon inne godes riche
　　　ðeh þer beð wunienges[8] fele. elc oþer vn-iliche

180. Sume þer habbet lasse murhðe. & sume habbed more
　　　after þan þe hi[9] dude her. after þan þe hi swonke[10] sore

181. Ne scal þer ben bred ne win. ne oþer cunnes este
　　　god one[11] scal beo eche lif. & blisse. & eche reste

182. Ne scal þer beo fou[12] ne grei. ne cunig ne ermine
　　　ne ocquerne[13] ne martres cheole. ne beuer ne sabeliue

183. Ne scal þer beo sced[14] ne scrud. ne woruld wele none
　　　al þe murhðe þe me us bi-hat. al it scal beo god one

184. Ne mai non murhðe beo so muchel. so is godes sihte
　　　he is soð sunne & briht. & dai a-buten nihte

185. He is elches godes ful. nis him noþing ᵹit[15] vten
　　　no god nis him wane. þe wunied him abuten

186. Þer is wele abute grame[16]. & reste abuten swinche
　　　þe mai & nele þider come. sore it him scal ofþinche[17]

187. Þer is blisse abuten treᵹe. & lif abuten deaþe
　　　þe eure scullen wunien þer. bliþe muwen ben eþe

188. Þer is ᵹeoᵹeðe bute ulde. & hele abuten vn-helðe
　　　nis þer sorewe ne sor. ne neure nan vn-sealþe

189. Þer me scal drihte sulf i-seon. swa he is mid iwisse
　　　he one mai & scal al beo. engle & manne blisse

---

[1] under.　[2] gað unieðe ᵹeanes.　[3] te feawe feire.　[4] murhðe.　[5] is.
[6] haueð hafð.　[7] ne nawane.　[8] wununges.　[9] omits hi.　[10] swanc.
[11] aue.　[12] fah.　[13] aquierne.　[14] scier.　[15] na wið.　[16] gane.　[17] The
later MS. ends here.

190. And ðeh ne beod heore eȝe naht. alle iliche brihte
Oi nabbed hi nouht ilichc. alle of godes lihte

191. On þisse liuc hi neren nout. alle of one mihte
ne þer ne scullen hi habben god. alle bi one ȝihte

192. Þo scullen more of him seon. þe luuede him her more
& more icnawen & iwiten. his mihte & his ore

193. On him hi scullen finden al þat man mai to lesten
hali boc hi sculle iseon. al þat hi her nusten   .

194. Crist scal one beon inou. alle his durlinges
he one is muchele mare & betere. þanne alle opere þinges

195. Inoh he haued þe hine haueð. þe alle þing wealdeð
of him to sene nis no sed. wel hem is þe hine bi-healdeð

196. God is so mere & swa muchel. in his godcunnesse
þat al þat is. & al þat wes. is wurse þenne he & lesse

197. Ne mai it neure no man oþer segge mid iwisse
hu muchele murhðe habbet þo. þe beod inne godes blisse

198.   To þere blisse us bringe god. þe rixlet abuten ende
penue he vre soule vn-bint. of licames bende

199. Crist ȝyue us leden her swilc lif. & habben her swilc ende .
þat we moten þuder come. wanne we henne wende. Amen.

LIVES OF SAINTS.

IX. ST. DUNSTAN.
(Harl. MS. 2277, fol. 51.)

Seint Dunstan was of Engelond: icome of gode more
2 Miracle oure louerd dude for him: er he were ibore
For þo he was in his moder wombe: a candelmasse day
4 Þer folc was at churche ynouȝ: as to þe tyme lay
As hi stode mid here liȝt: as me doþ ȝut nou
6 Here liȝt aqueynte oueral: here non nuste hou
Her liȝt hit brende suyþe wel: and her liȝt hit was oute
8 Þat folc stod in gret wonder: and also in grete doute
And hi speke ech to oþer: in whiche manere hit were
10 Hou hit queynte so sodeynliche: þe liȝt þat hi here
¶ As hi stode and speke þerof: in gret wounder echon
12 Seint Dunstanes moder taper: afure worþ anon

þat heo huld on hire hond: heo nuste whannes hit com

14 þat folc stod and bihuld: and gret wonder þerof nom

Ne non nuste wannes hit com: bote þurf our louerdes grace

16 þerof hi tende here liȝt: alle in þe place

¶ What was þat oure louerd crist: þe liȝt fram heuene sende

18 And þat folc þat stod aboute: here taperes þerof tende

Bote of þat holi child: þat was in hire wombe þere

20 Al Engelonde scholde þe bet beo iliȝt: þat hit ibore were

þis child was ibore neoȝe hondred ȝer: and fyue and tuenti ariȝt

22 After þat oure suete louerd: in his moder was aliȝt

þe furste ȝer of þe crouning: of þe king Adelston

- 24 His moder het kenedride: his fader Herston

¶ þo þis child was an vrþe ibore: his freond uome þerto hede

26 Hi lete hit do to Glastnebury: to norischi and to fete

To teche him eke his bileue: pater noster and crede

28 þe child wax and wel iþeȝ: for hit moste nede

¶ Lute ȝeme he nom to þe wordle: to alle godnisse he drouȝ

30 Ech man þat hurde of him speke: hadde of him ioye ynouȝ

þo he was of manes wit: to his vncle he gan go

32 þe archebischop of Canterbury: seint Aldelm þat was þo

þat makede wiþ him ioye ynouȝ: and euere þe lengere þe more

34 þo he seȝ of his godnisse: and of his wyse lore

For deynte þat he hadde of him: he let him sone bringe

36 Bifore þe prince of Engelond: Adelstan þe kynge

þe kyng him makede ioye ynouȝ: and grantede al his boue

38 Of what þinge so he wolde bidde: if hit were to done

þo bad he him an abbei: þat he was forþ on ibroȝt

40 þi* þe toun of Glastnebure: þat he ne wornde him noȝt   [*?þi]

¶ þe king grantede his bone: and after him also

42 Edmund his broþer þat was king: in his poer ido

To Glastnebury wende sone: þis gode man seint Dunstan

44 þo beye þe kynges him ȝeue leue: Edmund and Adelstan

¶ Of þe hous of Glastnebure: a gret ordeynour he was

46 And makede moche of gode reule: þat neuer er among hem nas

Ac þat hous þat furst bigonne: four hondred ȝer bifore

48 And eke þreo and vyfti: er seint Dunstan were ibore

For þer was ordre of monekes: er seint patrik com

50 And er seint Austyn to Engelonde: brouȝte cristendom.

And seint patrick deide tuo hondred : and tuo and vyfti ȝer
52 After þat oure suete leuedi: oure louerd here ber
Ac none monckes þer nere furst: bote as in hudinge echon
54 And as men þat drowe to wyldernisse: for drede of godes fon.
¶ Seint Dunstan and seint Adelwold: as oure louerd hit bisay
56 I-ordeyned to preostes were: al in one day
þer after sone to Glastnebury: seint Dunstan anon wende
58 He was abbod þer ymaked: his lyf to amende
¶ And for he nolde bi his wille: no tyme idel beo
60 A priuei smyþþe bi his celle: he gan him biseo
For whan he moste of orcisouns: reste for werinisse
62 To worke he wolde his honden do : to fleo idelnisse
Scruie he wolde poure men: þe wyle he miȝte deore
64 Al þe dai for þe loue of god : he ne kipte of hem non hure
And whan he sat at his wore þer: his honden at his dede
66 And his his hurte mid ihesu crist: his mouþ his bedes bede
¶ So þat al at one tyme: he was at þreo stedes
68 His honden þer, his hurte at god: his mouþ to bidde his bedes
þerfore þe deuel hadde of him: gret enuye and onde
70 O tyme he cam to his smyþþe: alone him to fonde
Riȝt as þe sonne wende adoun: riȝt as he womman were
72 And spac wiþ him of his wore: wiþ laȝinge chere
And seide þat heo hadde wiþ him: gret wore to done
74 Treoflinge heo smot her and þer: in anoþer tale sone
¶ Þat holi man hadde gret wonder: þat heo was and þere
76 He sat longe and biþoȝte him: longe hou hit were
He biþoȝte him ho hit was: he droȝ forþ his tonge
78 And leide in þe hote fur: and spac faire longe
Forte þe tonge was al afure: and sippe stille ynouȝ
80 Þe deuel he hente bi þe nose: and wel faste drouȝ
He tuengde and schok hire bi þe nose: þat þe fur out blaste
82 Þe deuel wrickede her and þer: and he huld euere faste
He ȝal and hupte and drouȝ aȝe: and makede grislish bere
84 He nolde for al his biȝete: þat he hadde icome þere
Mid his tonge he snytte hire nose: and tuengde hire sore
86 For hit was wiþinne þe nyȝte: he nemiȝte iseo nomore
Þe schrewe was glad and bliþe ynouȝ: þo he was out of his honde
88 He fleȝ and gradde bi þe lifte: þat me hurde in-to al þe londe

Out what haþ þe calewe ido: what haþ þe calewe ido
90 In þe contrai me hurde wide: hou þe schrewe gradde so
As god þe schrewe hadde ibeo: atom ysnyt his nose
92 He ne hiȝede no more þiderward: to hele him of þe pose
¶ þe holi abbot seint Dunstan: hadde gret poer
94 Wiþ king Edmund þat was þo: and was al his consailler
After king Edmundes deþ: a good while was a gon
96 þat Edwyne his sone was ymaked king: and noȝt after anon
þis Edwyne hadde vuel red: and þerafter drouȝ
98 Wiþ seint Dunstan he was wroþ: siker wiþ gret wouȝ
¶ Of his abbey he dude him out: and dude him schame ynouȝ
100 þe more schame þat he him dude: þe more þe gode man louȝ
He drof him out of Engelond: and let him grede fleme
102 þis gode man wende forþ wel glad: ne nam he neuere ȝeme
To þe abbey of seint Amand: biȝunde see he drouȝ
104 And soiournede þer longe: and ladde god lyf ynouȝ
¶ After kyng Edwynes lyue: Edgar þat was his broþer
106 Was king ymaked: for he was nher þan enie oþer
Suyþe god man he bicom: and louede wel holi churche
108 And ech man þat him perto radde: after him he gan wirche
Me tolde him of seint Dunstan: þat his broþer drof of londe
110 Mid vnriȝt for his godnisse: and gan him vnderstonde
¶ After him he sende anon: þat he come aȝe sone
112 And bileue his consailler: of þat he hadde to done
Seint Dunstan com hom aȝen: and faire was vnderfonge
114 Ladde his Abbey al in pees: fram whan he was so longe
Wiþ þe king he was suyþe wel: and was al his consailler
116 Moche me spac of his godnisse: boþe fur and nher
Hit biful þat þe bischop: of wircetre was ded
118 þe king and þe archebischop Ode: þerof nome here red
¶ þo þe holi abbot seint Dunstan: bischop hi makede þere
120 To makie him heȝere in godes lawe: his wille þeȝ hit nere
Somme eschte þe archebischop: of Canterbury sire Ode
122 Wherfore hi him bischop makede: and his grace were so gode
For he schal, quaþ þis gode man: after me her beo
124 Archebischop of Canterbury: þat me schal iseo
¶ What saistou, þis oþer seide: þu spext folliche iwis
126 Nostou nomore þan þi fot: vppe god al hit is

  ¶ Leoue freond, quaþ þis godc man: ne þorc ȝe ne blamie noȝt
128 Wel ic wot what mie loucrd crist: in mie mouþ haþ ibrouȝt
    As ho saiþ of þulke þinge: þat he haþ in ine ised
130 Telle ic mai what schal bifalle: after þat ich am ded
    Bischop he was of Londone and Wircetre: and hulp boþe two
132 Of Londone and of Wircctre: and bischop was of boþe also
  ¶ Hit biful þat þe archebischop: of Canterbury was ded
134 Þe pope and þe kyng Edgar: þerof nome here red
    And makede þe gode seint Dunstan: archebischop þorc
136 Gode men þat him iknewe: wel glad þerof were
    Cristendom in Engelond: to god stat he drouȝ
138 And riȝtes of holi churche: he huld vp faste ynouȝ
    He fondede þurf al Engelond: þat ech persoun schulde cheose
140 To witien him fram lecherie: oþer his churche leose
  ¶ Seint Osewold was þulke tyme: bischop of wyrcestre
142 And seint Adelwold also: bischop of Roucestre
    Þis tuei bischopes and seint Dunstan: were al at one rede
144 And Edgar þe gode king: to do þis gode dede
  ¶ Þis preo bischops wende forþ: þurf al Engelonde
146 And eche liþer persoun caste out: þat þer nemiȝte non atstonde
    Here churchen and here oþer godc: clanliche hi bynome
148 And bisette hit in pore men: þurf þe popes grant of Rome
    Eiȝte and fourti Abbeyes: of Monckes and of nonne
150 Of þe tresour hi arerde in Engelond: of persones so iwonne
    So hit was wel bet biset: þan hit was er in schrewe
152 For whanne gode maistres beoþ: som god hi wolleþ schewe
  ¶ Gode were þis preo bischops: þat o tyme were þo
154 Þe betere is Engelond for hem: and worþ euere mo
  ¶ Oure louerd ȝaf an vrþe: seint Dunstan faire grace
156 Þat o tyme as he was: in a priueie place
    His fader and his moder ek: in þe ioye of heuene anheȝ
158 After þat hi dede were: aperteliche he seȝ
    Wel gret loue oure louerd him cudde: whan he schewede þere
160 So moche of his priueite: þe while he alyue were
    As he lay anoþer tyme: in his reste anyȝt
162 He seȝ þe ioye of heuene: and þe place þerinne wel briȝt
    Angles he hurde also singe: a murie song þer inne
164 Þat me singeþ ȝut in holi churche: whan me doþ þe masse singe

Kirieleyson. christeleyson: was þe murie note and song
166 þis holi man þat þis ihurde: ne poȝte hit him noȝt longe
¶ Wel auȝte he to heuene come: after his ende day
168 Whan he þe while he was alyue: so moche of heuene isay
Harpe he louede suyþe wel: þeron he couþe ynouȝ
170 A day he he sat in solaȝ: and a lay þeron drouȝ
¶ þe harpe he heng bi þe wowe: þo hit was tyme to ete
172 þo hit was ȝare þerto ibrouȝt: he sat adoun at his mete
Of heuene he gan þenche sone: of þe ioye þat was þere
174 Of þe ioyfulle blisse þat þer was: of halewen þat þer were
He sat as he were ynome: so moche þeron he þoȝte
176 His harpe he heng bi þe wowe: of wham he lute roȝte
¶ Bigan to cuþe his holi poȝt: ded treo þeȝ hit were
178 As oure louerdes wille was: as hi hurde alle þat þer were þere
Al bi him silue he gan to harpe: a murie steuene iwis
180 þat ne singeþ ȝut in holi churche: þat an englisch is þis
Alle halewene soule glade beoþ: þat in heuene beoþ ido
182 þat suyeþ oure louerdes way: and for him schadde also
Here blod for his suete loue: þerfore hi schulle wone
184 And kynges beo bouten ende: wiþ crist godes sone
þis anteyn þat murie is: þat folc ihurde alle
186 Hou þe harpe song al bi him silf: þer he hong bi þe walle
Fair grace oure louerd him schowede þere: whan þe dede treo
188 So schulde singe of þulke ioye: þat he scholde inne beo
Louerd ihered beo þi grace: and þi miȝte also
190 þat þu woldest her alyue for him: such miracle do
¶ þo þis holi man hadde ylyued: an vrþe menie a daie
192 And his endedai was neȝ icome: as he him silue isaie
A holi þursday he worþ sik: as hit ful in þe ȝere
194 He let ofsende his freond: þat specials to him were
His men þat him seruede eke: he let hem clipie also
196 And forȝaf hem al here trespas: þat hi him hadde misdo
And assoillede hem of here sinne: and in godes bendes lay
198 And so he lay al þulke tyme: and also þane friday
He let clipie þe saterday: þe freres bifore him alle
200 And bed alle godneday: and seide hem what scholde bifalle
And let him do alle his riȝtes: and oure louerdes flesch nom
¶ His soule wende out of þe wordle: and sone to heuene com

Neoȝe hondrcd ȝer and fourscore: in þe eiȝteteoþe ȝere
204 He deide after þat oure lcuedi: oure louerd an vrþc bere
Nou suete louerd seint Dunstan : þat oure archebischop were
206 Bring ous to þe ioye of heuene: as angles þi soule bere.

[Seint Aldelm the Confessour follows;
   then, Seint Austyn þat cristendom: brouȝte in-to Engelonde;
   then, Seint barnabe þ'apostle; & Seint Teofle,
for whom,
'A fair miracle oure leuedi dude: þat brouȝte him out of þulke wo
As heo menle oþere dude: ic mot ȝut telle mo'.
   On p. 61 back, is:
Ou marie þat is so moche: þi milce and þyn ore
so murie hit is to telle of þe: þat ȝut we mote more.

   The fifth miracle is that of]

X. AN OXFORD STUDENT.
(Miracles, Harl. MS. 2277, fol. 63.)

A kniȝt þer was in Engelond: by norþe her biside
A ȝung child he hadde bi his wyf: as god wolde hit scholde bitide
Þe moder adai while hit was ȝung: to churche hit broȝte
Þe child bihuld þe rodc in churche: and stod in grete þoȝte
5 Moder, he seide, what is þe man: þat ȝund anhongod is
¶ Sone, quaþ þe leuedi, hit is: oure louerd iwis
For ous he was so anhonge: and to deþe ibroȝt
To bringe ous to þc ioye of heuene: he haþ ous deorc iboȝt
Wel auȝte we þanne, quaþ þe child: seruie him wiþ wille
10 And what is þulke faire womman: þat stent bi him so stille
Hit is his moder, quaþ þe leuedi: þat oure suete leuedi is
Ou ma dame, quaþ þe child: wounder me þinȝþ hit iwis
¶ Stod heo bi him þo me him slouȝ: þe leuedi seide ȝe
Awey ma dame, quaþ þis child: miȝtestou so bi me
15 Hou miȝte heo iseo quelle hire child: þat hire hurte ne brac atuo
Moche del was on hire hurte: and sorinysche also
Þeȝ þis child were ȝung: of þis deol ofte siþe hit þoȝte
Selþe wher he euere were: out of his hurte he hit brouȝte

þis child was sippe ido to scole: hit lurnede wel ynouȝ
20 So þat he com to Oxenford: þo he to manne drouȝ
Selþe hit com out of his poȝt: what so he iseȝe
þe deol þat oure leuedi hadde: þo heo iseȝ here sone deye
¶ Hit biful sippe in a tyme: as hit doþ bi menie on
þat he dude a dedlich synne: so ne dude he neuere non
25 He nolde noȝt, as manie on wolleþ: ligge þeron longe
To a frere he wende to schrifte: his penance to afonge
Repentant he was ynouȝ: of þulke liþere dede
And bisouȝte him for þulke sinne: þat he for him bede
And þat he bede to oure leuedi for þulke sor: þat heo hadde on
hire þoȝt
30 þo he seȝ hire sone anhonge: and in stronge deþe ibroȝt
þat heo ȝyue me grace and wille: þe leuedi milce and freo
Sorie ynou in hurte: for mio sinne to beo
þat he bad eke him silf: boþe niȝt and day
34 For þe deol of hire sone: þo heo dim ded isay
¶ He hadde þe while he lyuede: þulke bone in mone
þat oure leuedi þo he was ded: him cudde and eke hire sone
Atte laste at Oxenford: at scole he gan deye
þe furste day he was iwist: as þe maystres iseye
Tuey clerkes þat were ouer him: þat suyþe wel his freond were
40 þat wiste his bodi niȝt and day: and were next þe bere
Ech man amorwe bote hi tueye: wende hom in his ende
Felawe, quaþ on, hit is tyme: þat we þe taperes tende
Abyd, quaþ þoþer, a stounde: þat þis maistres come
44 Hit nis noȝt riȝt þe tapres tende: bote hi were her some
¶ As þis tuey clerkes were alone: adoun hi lynede stille
So þat hi werþe a slepe: as hit was godes wille
As hi slepe, hem þoȝte boþe: þat hi angles meniee iseȝe
Here felawes soule þat þer lai ded: to heuene lede heȝe
¶ Oure leuede as to teche þe wey: hire silue ȝeode bifore
50 And openede þe dore of heuene: þat þe soule were in ibore
¶ þo heo tofore oure louerd com: adoun heo sat a kneo
Sone, heo saide, lo, her mie freond: þat wel haþ iserued me
Vnderfong him into þi ioye: oure louerd aȝe sede
Leoue moder ic auȝte wel: þeȝ þu neuere ne bede

55 For an vrþe he bad mie milce ofte: for þe deol þat þu iseȝe
   And þat sor in þin hurte: þo þu me seȝe deye
   Wel fawe ic him wole afonge: as riȝt is þat ich do
   And among myn halewen him onoury: and þu schalt also
¶ Þo sende oure leuedi fram heuene: to þe tapres liȝt anon
60 Þat aboute þe bodi stede: and tende hem echon
   Þe clerkes awoke anon: as hi slepe boþe per
   And fonde þe tapres alle itend: as hem poȝte in slepe er
¶ Þo come þe maistres as riȝt was: þe seruise for to do
   And þo hit was to ende ibrouȝt: and þe bodi ibured also
65 Þe clerkes to here priue maistre: tolde al þat hi seȝe
   Þat oure leuedi to oure louerd seide: in þe ioye of heuene heȝe
   And hou hi onourede him for þe munde: þat he hadde her in mode
   Of þe deol þat oure leuedi hadde: of hire sone in þe rode
   Hi ȝeode forþ to þe frere: þat his schriftfader was
70 Somme of þe maistres priueiliche: and tolde him of þat cas
¶ Þe frere seide þat hit was soþ: þat he hadde er in mode
   Þe deol þat oure leuedi hadde: þo hire sone deide on þe Rode
   Þe miracle was þo iholde soþ: of þis holi childe
   Wiþ eche þing al day we seoþ: oure leuedi suete and mylde

XI. THE JEWS AND THE CROSS.
(Harl. MS. 2277, fol. 64.)

1 Gywes hatieþ oure leuedi moche: and hire suete sone also
  Þat is isene in manie dede: þat þe schrewen habbeþ ido
3 Oure leuedi day in haruest: þat so holi is and suete
  An archebischop song his masse: in þe cite of Tolete
5 Riȝt atte sacring of þe masse: atte þulke holi dede
  A voiȝ he hurde of heuene: þat þuse wordes sede
7 Allas þe gywes trecherie: Allas þe liþere vode
  Þat among mie sones children: þat he bouȝte mid his blode
9 Þe schrewen schulle so vylliche: eftsone do him on þe Rode
  And so schendfulliche auyli: wiþ so liþere mode
11 Þe archebischop þo he hadde: his masse ibroȝt to ende
   He nom wiþ him folc ynouȝ: and to þe gywene gan wende

13 And let ofseche oueral: atte laste hi fonde
þe forme of oure louerd in a Rode: ibeten and ibounde
15 Inaïlled þurf fet and honde: as oure louerd wiþ vyf wounde
þat hadde þe gywes ido: god ȝyue hem harde stounde
17 And alle þat hem louye wel: for moche is þe vylte
And schame þat hi ofte doþ: oure louerd in priueite
¶ ȝut oure leuedi aliȝte: and warnede þe bischop fore
Moche godnisse heo haþ ido: siþþe heo was iboro
21 Nou, leuedi, for þe mylce: þat euere haþ mid þe ibeo
And for þe grete sorwe þat þu haddest: þo þi sone deide on þe treo
23 ȝeue ous grace þat we mote: such milce her iwynne
þat we mote to þe ioye: come. þat þu ert inne.

[*Seint Albon's* life follows.]

XII. ST. SWITHIN.
(Harl. MS. 2277, fol. 78.)

Seint swiþþin þe confessour: was her of Engelonde
2 Biside wynchestre he was ibore: as ic vnderstonde
Bi þe kinges day Egberd: þis gode man was ibore
4 þat þo was king of Engelond: and somwhat ek bifore
þe eiȝteteoþe king he was þat com: after kenewold þe kynge
6 þat seint beryn dude to cristendom: in Engelonde furst bringe
¶ Ac seint Austin hadde bifore: to cristendom ibroȝt
8 Apelbriȝt þe gode king: ac al þe londe noȝt
Ac siþþe hit was þat seint berin: her bi weste wende
10 And turnde þe king kenewold: as oure louerd him grace sende
So þat seint Egberd þat was kyng: þo seint swithin was ibore
12 þe eiȝteteoþe he was: after kenewold: þat so longe was bifore
¶ Seint swythin þe ȝunge man: swiþe ȝung bigan
14 Forto seruie ihesu crist: and bicom cristene man
Elmeston þe bischop ek: of wynchestre þat was þo
16 Seint swithin he makede preost: as he dude oþere mo
So þat fram on ordre to oþer: seint swiþin preost bicom
¶ Clene lyf he ladde and god: and to gret penance him nom

His godnisse was wide icud: aboute in eche side
20 Þo þat hit com þe king to ere: hit sprong aboute wide
Þe king him onourede swiþe wel: and louede him ynouȝ
22 And makede him his chiefe consailler: and mest to his consail drouȝ
Apulf his sone and eke his heir: he tok hem to loke
24 To norissie and to wardie wel: þat hi to gode toke
Þat he teiȝte him such portoure: þat to a such child bicome
26 Wel him wiste þis holi man: and god warde to him nom
¶ Þo kyng Egberd was ded: þis child Apulf his sone
28 After him was kyng ymaked: as lawe was and wone   .
Þis ȝunge king was god ynouȝ: as seint swithin him gan rede
30 After his consail al he drouȝ: and dude bi him his dede
Engelond was þo wel iwist: for þe king was god ynouȝ
32 And swithin his consailler: after wham he drouȝ
Elmeston þe bischop siþþe: of wynchestre was ded
34 Þe king and oþer heȝe men: þerof neme here red
¶ Þis holi man seint swiþin: bischop hi makede þere
36 Alle men þat him iknewe: ioyous þerof were
Bischop he was god ynouȝ: and alle gode he wroȝte
38 Þe king also to alle gode: holi churche brouȝte
So þat þurf þe heste of þe king: and þurf his wissinge also
40 Ech man wolde þurf þe lond: his teoþing wel do
Brokene churchen oueral: seint swithin let vp rere
42 And nue churchen in menie stede: þer neuerer none nere
Whan he halewede enie churche: bost ne kipte he non
44 Bi nyȝte afote myldeliche: he wolde þider gon
Aȝen him ne kipte he no ringinge: bobance ne prute
46 Þe bost of hors ne of squiers: for he tolde þerof lute
He poȝte on þat þe godspel. saiþ: þat me takþ of lute hede
48 Þat ho so doþ his dede mid bobance: him ne tyt non oþer mede
For he afongeþ his mede her: mid þe dede anon
50 Þat worþ habbeþ nou forȝute: þis heȝe meny on
¶ Seint swithin his bischopriche: to alle gode drouȝ
52 Þe toun also of wynchestre: he amendede ynouȝ
Þor he let þe stronge brugge: wiþoute þe est ȝate arere
54 And fond þerto lym and ston: to worcmen þat þer were
¶ Adai as þis worcmen: aboute here worke stode
56 And contrai men to chepinge: come mid moche gode

Mid a baggeful of eiren: a womman þer com
58 A masoun sone þis womman: to his folie nom
And biclipte hire in ribaudie: as foles doþ ȝut ofte
60 And brak hire eiren neȝ echone: he ne handlede hire noȝt softe
¶ Þo þe womman hire harm iseȝ: ruliche heo gan bigynne
62 For heo hem hadde igadered longe: sum siluer forto wynne
Heo makede deol ynouȝ: and cride also anheȝ
¶ Seint swythin com þo þerforþ: and þe deol iseȝ
Of þis womman he hadde reuþe: he nom vp his hond anon
66 And blessede þe eiren to-broke: and hi bicome hole anon
And sound as hi euere were: hi bicome atte laste
68 Glad was þo þis seli womman: and þonkede gost faste
Miȝte eirmongers nou fare so: þe baldelikere hi miȝte
70 Huppe ouer diches wher hi wolde: boþe wraxli and fiȝte
¶ Þe king Aþulf deide siþþe: þe kynges sone Egberd
72 And his sone was kyng after him: kyng Adelberd
Hit nas noȝt longe afterward: þat he was ymaked kyng
74 Þat þis holi man seint swithin: drouȝ to endyng
For he deide þe þridde ȝer: þat he was kyng ymad
76 And þo he schulde hunne wende: his men faste he bad
Þat hi ne scholde him burie noȝt: in churche wiþ prute
78 Ac sum war wiþoute in a stede: þat me tolde of lute
In a stede þat me tolde of lest: and lest ȝeme me tok
80 In alle manere þis holi man: bobance and prute forsok
He deide eiȝte hondred ȝer: and in þe sixteoþe ȝere
82 After þat oure louerd aliȝt: in his moder wombe here
¶ In a stede wiþoute þe churche: þis holi bodi hi leide
84 Þat me tolde of lute ynouȝ: as he him silue seide
Þer he lai an hondred ȝer: and neoȝe ȝer also
86 And almest fourtene nyȝt: er he were þanne ido
Bi þe kinges day Edgar: þat god was ynouȝ
88 Þat seint Edwardes fader was: þat his stipmoder a-slouȝ
Þis holi man seint swiþþin: schowede bitokeninge
90 Þat me scholde of þulke place: in heȝere stede him bringe
Þis Egdgar was þe noeȝþe kyng: þat after Adelbert com
92 Þat kyng was þulke tyme: þat seint swiþþin deþ nom
Þe bischop þat was at wynchestre: þo king Edgar was kyng
94 Þat was seint Athelwold: god and holi þurf alle þing

¶ Seint swithin þe holi man: a god tyme him gan biseo
96 Whan god kyng was and god bischop: ischryned for to beo
Aniȝt he cam to an holi man: in his bedes as he lay
98 In siknisse and sorwe ynouȝ: as he hadde ido meny a day
Arys, he seide, to morwe anon: and ne lef þu noȝt bihynde
100 To wynchestre þe olde Mynstre: and þere þu schalt fynde
þe gode bischop Athelwold: þat þe teoþe is·after me
102 And saye þat ich him grett wel: and sende him word bi þe
þat oure louerd hit haþ biseȝe: þat mie bodi schal beo ido
104 In churche in an heȝ stede: and nomore ligge so
And if þu doutest in enie poynt: þat þis beo duelsinge
106 And noȝt soþ þat ich telle nou: ic wole sende to þe kynge
For al so sone as þu wolt arise: forto do myn heste
108 þat vuel þat þu hast so longe ihad: ne schal no leng ileste
Ac þu worst þerof hol and sound: wordle wiþouten ende
110 If þe bischop ne leoueþ hit noȝt: oþer signe ic wole him sende
For whan ȝe comeþ to þulke stede: þer ic ligge ȝute
112 Anoneward þer liþ a ston: wiþ oþer prute wel lute
Ringes of yre þer beoþ on: ynailled þerto faste
114 Ac þer nis non so strong of hem: þat aȝen ȝou schulleþ ilaste
þat ȝe ne schulleþ riȝt liȝtliche: drawe vp þe ston
116 Wiþoute wem faste aȝen: fast sette hem on
¶ þis gode man of þis tokning: iolyf was ynouȝ
118 Wel bityme he aros: and toward þane wey drouȝ
And anon so he dude him on þe wei: hol and sound he was
120 Of þe vuel þat he bar so longe: neuereft igreued he nas
To þe bischop he wende Aþelwold: and tolde him of þis cas
122 þe bischop þo he hurde þis: wel was him þas
þe ring þat was on þe ston: faste as he seide er
124 Liȝtliche hi of nome wiþoute wem: and as faste sette hit þer
Wele þe ioye þat he makede þo: þe bischop Aþelwold
126 þis miracle was sone icud: and wide aboute itold
Seint Aþelwold wende sone: to Edgar þe gode king
128 And tolde him as wel was riȝt: þis holi teþing
¶ þis gode king was glad ynouȝ: hi nomen hem to rede
130 Hou hi miȝte mid mest honer: do þis holi dede
Hi assignede a dai þerto: as here consayl bisay
132 Bifore haruest in þe mounþ of Juli: þe ciȝteteoþe day

¶ Hi sumnede aȝe þis holi day: heȝe men ynowe þerto
134 Bischopes and Abbotes: þe holi dede to do
Þo hi come to wynchestre: þer þis bodie lay
136 In fasting and oreisouns: hi were niȝt and day
Þat oure louerd hem ȝeue grace: þis holi dede wel ende
138 Þo þe dai him was icome: to þe mynstre hi gonne wende
Ireuested faire ynouȝ: wiþ gret deuociouu
140 Wiþ tapres itend and þe croiȝ: wiþ gret processiouu
To þe tumbe hi wende sone: as þe bodi lay
142 As· hit ful in þe mounþ of Juli: þe vyfteoþe day
¶ Þis holi bischop Apelwold: as riȝt was to do
144 Let delue to þis holi bodie: and þo hi come þerto
Þer com smyte out a suete breþ: among þis gode men echon
146 Þat so gret suetnisse as hem þoȝte: ne smylde hi neuere non
Louerd moche is þi miȝte: soþ hit is ised
148 Þat a bodi scholde so suete smylle: þat so longe hadde ibeo ded
ȝe witeþ bi oþer dede men: þat hit was moche aȝe riȝte
150 A blynd womman anon mid þe dede: in þe place hadde hire siȝte
And menie oþere þer botnede ek: of vuel and of wo
152 And wiþ-inne þe tuey dayes: two hondred and mo
¶ Þis holi bodi was vp ynome: wiþ gret honour iwis
154 And into seinte peteres churche ibore: þer þe heȝe mynstre is
And ido in a fair schrin and noble: as hit liþ ȝute
156 Þe miracles þat of him comeþ: for soþe ne beoþ noȝt lute
Ischryned he was neoȝene and tuenti ȝere: in þon and tuenteoþe
ȝere
158 After þat oure louerd an vrþe aliȝte: in his moder here
Nou seint swithin þat was bischop: her in Engelonde
160 Bringe ous to þe ioye of heuene: þurf oure louerdes sonde.

[St. Kenelm follows.]

XIII. ST. KENELM.
(Harl. MS. 2277, fol. 80.)

1 Seint kenelm þe ȝunge kyng: þurf oure louerdes sonde
Kyng he was in Engelond: of þe March of Walis

3 Þe kyng kenulf his fader was: þat kyng was þer also
   Þat rerde abbai of wynchecumbe: & let þer monekes do
5 After his deþ he was þer ibured: & ȝut he lyþ þere
   In þe abbay þat ȝut stent: þat he him silue let rere
7 Gret Cite was þo wynchecumbe: & mest of ynouȝ
   In al þulke half of Engelond: as fur as his lond drouȝ.
¶ Vyf kynges þer were bi þulke tyme: in Engelonde ido
   For Engelond was god & long: & brod ynou þerto
11 Aboute eiȝte hondred mile: Engelond long is
   Fram þe souþ in to þe norþ: & two hondred brod iwis
13 Fram þe est in to þe west: also þere-inne beoþ
   Manye wateres goode ynowe: as ȝe alday iseoþ
15 Ac þreo wateres principales: of alle oþere beo iwis
   Humber & temese: seuerne þe þridde is
17 To þe norþ see humber goþ: þat is on of þe beste
   & temese into þe est see: & seuerne bi weste
19 Þis vyf kynges of engelonde: þat were bi olde dawe
   Hadde here part bi hem silue: as riȝt was & lawe
21 Þe kyng þat was of þe Marche: hadde þo þe beste
   Moche del he hadde of Engelond: þat on half al bi weste
¶ Wircestreschire & warewykschire: & also Gloucestre
   Þat is neȝ al o bischopriche: þe bischopes of Wircestre
25 He hadde also þerto shestreschire: & Derbischire also
   & staffordschire þat beoþ alle: in o bischopriche ido
27 In þe bischopriche of Chestre: ȝut he hadde þerto
   Schropschyre sum & haluendel: warewykschire also
29 Þis kyng hadde also herefordschire: þat o bischopriche is
   & Schropschire haluendel: þat falþ to þulke bischopriche iwis
31 & sum of warewykschire: & of Gloucestreschire also
   ȝut hadde þe king of þe marche: more lond þerto
33 Norhampte schire & bokingham schire: & þe schire of Oxenford
   Leicestreschire & Lincolneschire: & þe schire of hereford
35 & þat is o bischopriche: & þat of Lincolne is
   þat while was at Dorkcestre biside Oxenford iwis
37 ȝut hadde þe kyng of þe marche: Notingham schire þerto
   In þe bischopriche of Ouerwyke: ac þo nas hit noȝt so
39 Al þe lond was while icliped: þe march of Wales
   & of al was seint kenelm: & his fader kyng iwis

Nou of alle þoþerene kynedom: aȝen his non nas
42 At wynchecumbe of al his lond: þe chief Cite was
¶ Þe vif kinges þat were þo: þat on was of kent iwis
44 & þat oþer as ic seide er: of þe march of walis
Of westsex & of humberlond: & of estlond also
46 Þuse vyf kynges were þo: in Engelond ido
¶ Þe king of westsex hadde þo: al wilteschire iwis
48 & Dorsete & barrocschire: þat also bischopriche is
Þe bischopriche of salesbury: ac so nas hit þo noȝt
50 For þe chief of þe bischopriche was: at schireburne ibroȝt
ȝut was þe kynges of westsex: al souþsex also
52 Þe welde of al þe bischopriche: Cicestre þerto
& souþhampteschire & souþereye: þat o bischopriche is
54 Þe bischopriche of wynchestre: þat ȝut is þer iwis
& somersete þat to welles: þulke tyme drouȝ
56 Nou hit is þe bischopriche of baþe: ȝe witeþ wel ynouȝ
¶ ȝut hadde þe kyng of westsex: aldoneschir iwis
58 & Cornwaille þat in þe bischopriche: of Excestre is
¶ Þe kyng of kent was þo kyng: of al þe lond of kent
60 þat were in tuo bischopriches: & ȝut nis noȝt iwent
¶ Þe Archebischop of Canterbury: of Engelond is hext
62 & þe bischopriche of Roucestre: in þe west side is next
Þe kyng ek of estlond: king was of Norfolc
64 In þe bischopriche of Norþwych: & also souþfolc
& of þe bischopriche of Ely: þat þe ylle of Ely is
66 & of al Cantebrugge: þat þerto falþ iwis
¶ Of þis lond was seint Edmund: king bi olde dawe
68 Þat was in his owe lond: ȝe witeþ wel aslawe
¶ Þe kyng of Norþhumberland: was kyng ic vnderstonde
70 Of al þe lond biȝunde humber: anon into scotlonde
Of þe Archebischopriche of Euerwyk: & of Durham iwis
72 Seint Osewald bi olde dawe: kyng was ouer al þis
¶ Þus menie kynges þer were: while in Engelonde
74 & here londes departed were: þus ic vnderstonde
Þe kyng þat was þo of þe March: as ic telle bigan
76 Kenulf þe kyng was icleped: suyþe holi & god man
Seint kenelm his sone was: & his eir also
78 Bur wenylde & quendride: his douȝtren were tuo

d

In þe four & tuenti ȝer: of his kynedom
80 Kenulf wende out of þis wordle: & to þe ioye of heuene com
Hit was after þat oure louerd: in his moder aliȝte
82 Eiȝte hondred ȝer & neoȝentene: bi acountes riȝte
Seint Kenelm his ȝunge sone: in his souepe ȝere
84 Kyng was ymaked after him: þeȝ he ȝung were
¶ His o soster bur wenylde: louede him ynouȝ
86 & in eche manere to holi lyfe: & to alle godnisse drouȝ
Ac quendride þoper soster: of hire manere nas noȝt
88 For heo turnede to folie & to liperhede: al hire poȝt
Heo seȝ þat hire ȝunge broper: nas noȝt of soue ȝer
90 þat kyng was ymaked of al þat lond: þat hire fader hadde er
To him heo hadde gret enuye: þat he scholde so riche beo
92 & eir of hire fader lond: & ricchere þane heo
Heo þoȝte if heo miȝte bringe: þat child of lyfdawe
94 þat heo were of þe heritage: quene bi riȝte lawe
Al hire poȝt was nyȝt & day: to bipenche sum outrage
96 þat þis child were ibroȝt of dawe: & heo hadde þe heritage
Heo purueide hire felonye: poisoun streng ynouȝ
98 For to ȝyue þe ȝunge child: & slen him so wiþ wouȝ
Do þis poisoun was iȝcue: al for noȝt hit was
100 For þo þe child hit hadde idronke: no þe wors him nas
For oure louerd nold noȝt þat he scholde: so liȝtliche ymartred beo
102 If þe quene wolde spede: oper heo moste biseo
For þerof heo caste an ambesas: heo þoȝte anoþer poȝt
104 Do heo seȝ hit was for noȝt: þat þe poisoun was iwroȝt
¶ þis ȝunge child a maister hadde: þat his wardeyn was
106 Askebert he was icliped: strong traitour allas
For noman nemai þan oper: bet trecherie do
108 þat pulke þat is him next: & he trist mest to
¶ þis lipere quene bipoȝte hire: of alle liþer wrenche
110 For me saiþ þere nis no felonye: þat womman ne can bipenche
Mid þis Askebert heo spac: þat child forto aspille
112 And bihet him mede god ynouȝ: & of hire al his wille
So þat þis tuo lipere þinges: were at one rede
114 & bispeke hou hi miȝte best: do þis lipere dede
þe while hi speke boþe: þis ȝunge child to quelle
116 A sweueninge þat þe child mette: ich ȝou wole nou telle

¶ Him þoʒte þat þer stod a treo: riʒt tofore his bedde
118 þat anon to þe sterren tilde: & wel wide spredde
þis treo was fair & noble: & schynde briʒte ynouʒ
120 Ful of blosmes & of frut: & of menie a riche bouʒ
Brenninge wex & lampen ek: wel þikke brende & liʒte
122 So noble frut nas neuere non: ne þat schynde so briʒte
Him þoʒte he clemde vpon þis treo: to þe hexte bouʒ an heʒ
124 & bihuld aboute in to al þe wordle: & prute ynouʒ iseʒ
þe while he stod vpon þe treo: & bihuld aboute so
126 Him þoʒte þat on of his beste freond: þat he mest triste to
In þe grounde stod byneþe: & smot atuo þis treo
128 þat hit fil to grounde anon: þat deol hit was to seo
To a litel foʒel he bicom: non fairere ne miʒte beo
130 & bi-gan wiþ ioye ynouʒ: riʒt into heuene fleo
He awook & was in þoʒte: her-of nyʒt & day
132 þo þis child mette þus: at wynchecumbe he lay
He nuste what hit bitoknede: þe more was his þoʒt
134 Er he sumþing þerof wiste: he ne miʒte beo bliþe noʒt
His norice þat him hadde ifed: & mid hire mulc forþ ibroʒt
136 Tendre was of þis child: for heo him hadde deorest iboʒt
To hire þat child triste mest: wolwenne hire name was
138 þat child hire tolde priueite: of þis sweuening al þat cas
þo þe norice hadde ihurd: þat sweuening þat was so god
140 Heo bigan to sike sore: & in þoʒte stod
Allas heo seide þat ich scholde: þisne day euere abide
142 þat mie child mie swete hurte: scholde such þing bitide
Allas mie child mie suete fode: þat ich habbe forþ ibroʒt
144 þi soster bispekeþ þi deþ: & quelle þe haþ ipoʒt
Ac þe fowel þat þu bicome to: þat to heuene gan wende
146 þat was þi soule þat þider schal: after þi lyues ende
¶ þis sueuene bicom soþ ynouʒ: þat he fond atte laste
148 For his soster & Askebert: bispeke his deþ wel faste
¶ þis Askebert seide adai: þat þis child scholde wende
150 An huntiug forto pleyen him: bi þe wodes ende
& he wiþ him to wardi him: as hit was riʒt bi weye
152 He wende to þe wode of Clent: as hit were to pleye
As hi wende bi þe wode: as god ʒaf þe grace
154 A god wille þe child com on: to slepe in a place

Adoun he lay al softe þere: & bigan to slepe anon
156 Askebert ne þo϶te no϶t: þat he scholde þanne gon
Biside in a durne stede: he bigan to delue faste
158 Ane put forto sle þis child: & sippe þeron hit caste
¶ Þis child bigan to awake sone: as hit were bi cas
160 After his maister he bihuld: & ne se϶ no϶t whar he was
Ac oure louerd him ϶af þe grace: þc϶ he nuste no϶t of his dede
162 Þat he spac to his maister: & þuse wordes sede
Þu trauaillest þere aboute no϶t: & þi while þu dost spille
164 For in an noþer stede ic schal deye: whar so is godes wille
& þurf þis ϶urd þat her is: tokning þu schalt iseo
166 Whan þi liþere wille hit mai do: þat ich ymartred beo
For wende þis liþere maister: & þis child also
168 Forte hi come to anoþer stede: þat þis dede were ido
Askebert þis ϶urd nom: & sette hit on þe grounde
170 Hit bigan to leuy sone: & wexe in a stounde
& a gret asch bicom sippe: & stent in þulke place
172 To schewi þe mi϶te of seint kenelm: & oure louerdes grace
Þis liþere man nom þis child: in þe wode of Clent
174 & ladde him as me doþ ane þeof: to afonge his iugement
He ladde him in a priuei stede: al out of þe weye
176 Bitwene tuei hilles he϶e: in a dupe valeye
¶ Þis child þurf þe holi gost: þe϶ þoþer him nolde telle
178 Wiste wel his liþere þo϶t: & þat he þo϶te him aquelle
& þo he targede a lute while: þis liþere dede to done
180 Þat child seide wel myldeliche: þat þu dost, do sone
He bigan a song þat me singeþ: in holi churche a day
182 Þat was te domine laudamus: er he adoun lay
& þo he cam to an holi vers: þat þerinne was & is
184 A latyn iwrite as al þat oþer: þat an englische is þis
Þe white cumpaignye of martirs: louerd herieþ þe: Te mar-
                                    tirum candidatûs laudat exercitus
186 Ri϶t as he hadde þe vers iseid: as þe boc telleþ me
Þis liþere man smot of his heued: vnder an ha϶þorn treo
188 As hit godes wille was: þat he ymartrid scholde beo
A whit coluere as eni snow: out of him gan fleo teo
190 & ri϶t cuene was ise϶e: into heuene fleo
Vneþe he was soue ϶er old: er he ymartrid were
192 Al to soþ his sueuene was: as me mi϶te iseo þere

¶ þis liþere man þat him a-slou¡: bigan to delue faste

194 And makede a put deope ynou¡: & þerinne þe child caste

And burede hit faste ynou¡: þat hit ifonde nere

196 And wende ¡e forþ his wei: & let hit ligge þere

¶ To quendride his liþere soster: anon he gan wende

198 And tolde hire al þe liþere cas: fram bigynninge to þan ende

þis quene was þo glad ynou¡: aboute heo wende anon

200 Forto seisi al þe lond: & þe maners echon

And makede hir quene of al þe March: as hire broþer was kyng

202 & schrewe leuedi bicom ynou¡: & liþer þurf alle þing

& wende aboute into al þe lond: to fonge here manrede

204 & bicom sturne & huld hire men: in sorewe & wrechede

Nou in þe quedes part mote heo ride: fram toune to toune

206 And falsliche as heo com anhe¡: also heo ful þerdoune

Heo let hote in to al þat lond: þat no man so wod were

208 To nemne enes hire broþer name: for loue ne for fere

& if me mi¡te of enie wite: þat hit nere no¡t bileued

210 þat he nere anon ynome: & ismyte of his heued

þus furde þe liþere quene: & stirede hire wel faste

212 þat noman ne þerste hire broþere nempne: so sore hi were of gaste

¶ Euere lai þis holi bodi: ibured swiþe stille

214 þat noman ne þerste him enes nemne: a¡en þe quenes wille

So longe þat hit was al for¡ute: whan me nemi¡te of him speke

216 Ac hit nas no¡t so þat oure louerd: atte laste him nolde awreke

Whan no man nolde þat wittie was: of him þenche ene

218 Nolde oure louerd þat he were: allinge for¡ute so clene

Whan no man nolde þat witti was: of him habbe munde

220 A dombe best wiþoute witte: hadde a¡e cunde

For a widue hadde a whit cou: þat wonede þere biside

222 þat ¡eode adai to fecche hire mete: in þe wode wide

þer seint kenelm lai ibured: in þe valey þerdoune

224 Eche dai wolde þis white cow: whan heo com fram toune

Fecche hire mete mid oþer kyn: *renne heo wolde alone [*MS.k]

226 In to valeye al byneþe: & lete hire felawes echone

& sitte aboute þis holi bodi: forte eue al longe day

228 As hit were to honury him: for he alone lay

& so heo sat wiþoute mete: alday to þan ende

230 & whan þat hit eue was: homward he wolde wende

    & an eue whan heo hom com: fat & round heo was
232 & so ful of mulc heo was: þat me wondrede of þe cas
    For þer nas non of alle þe kyn: þat half so moche mulc ȝeue
234 As ful heo wolde a morwe beo: þeȝ heo wcre ymolked an eue
    Ho so hadde suche kyn ynowe: he nere noȝt to bymene
236 þeȝ his larder were neȝ ido: & his somer lese lene
   ¶ þat folc þat þe wonder iseȝe: gret gome mid alle hi nome
238 & awaitede wel adai: whar þis cou bicome
    & hi seȝe hire stitte adai: in þe valeye þerdounc
240 Meteles stille in one stede: forte heo ȝcode an eue to toune
    & whi heo leyc þer so: hi ne miȝte wite for noþing
242 Ac in here hurte him þoȝte wel: þat hit was sum tokning
    For þis cou wonede þer so: & ech dai drouȝ þerto
244 Coubache me clipede þis valeye: & ȝut me doþ also
    In coubache þis holi bodi: lay wel menie a ȝer
246 þere me nuste noȝt of him: as ic ȝou seide er
    For his soster was so fers: & in so gret prutc ibroȝt
248 & such pretninge for him makede: þat me ne þerste him nemne noȝt
    þo þis holi bodi ne moste: beo icud in Engelonde
250 Oure louerd þat wot alle þing: & þerto sende his sonde
    For as þe pope stod at Rome: & song his masse aday
252 At seint peteres weued in þe churche: as al þat folc isay
    A coluere whittere þan enie snow: com adoun fram heuene fleo
254 & leide vpe þe weued a litel writ: & siþþe gan to heuene teo
    & fleȝ vp an heȝ aȝe: as oure louerd hit wolde
256 þc writ was whit & schynde briȝte: þe lettres were of golde
    þe pope þonkede ihesu crist: & al þat folk also
258 þe pope nam þis holi writ: þo þc masse was ido
   ¶ He nuste what hit was to sigge: ne non ne couþe wite
260 For he ne couþe englisch non: & an englisch hit was iwrite
    He let clipie ech maner diuerse men: of eche diuerse londe
262 If enie couþe of þis holi writ: eni þing vnderstonde
    þo were þer men of Engelonde: þat wiste what hit sede
264 & vnderstode wel þat writ: po hi hit ihurde rede
    þc writ was iwrite an englisch: as me radde hit þerc
266 & to telle hit wiþoute rym: þuse wordes riȝt hit were
    In Clent in Coubache kenelm kinges bern liþ vnder a þorn
      heuede bireued

¶ Þis writ was nobliche: iwist & vp ido
270 & iholde gret relik: for jut hit is also
Þe nobleste relik hit is: on þerof of al Rome
272 As hit aujte wel ho vnderstode: rijt wel whannes hit come
For whan hit out of heuene com: & of oure louerdes honde
274 What noblerere relik mijte þer beo: y ne mai non vnderstonde
Þerfore seint kenelmes day: as þe pope makede his heste
276 At Rome hi holdeþ hejliche: & makeþ suyþe gret feste
¶ Þo þe pope to soþe wiste: what was þe tokninge
278 His messager into Engelonde: he sente wiþ pis tiþinge
To þe archebischop of Canterbury: wolfred þat was þo
280 Lettres he sende þat he scholde: such þing vndergo
& siche out of þe wode of Clent: if enie man mijte wite
282 `At such an haj þorn in Coubache: as hit was in þe write
And siche out þe holi bodi: þat durneliche lai þere
284 And do þat wiþ gret noblcy: þat hi ischryned were
¶ Þo þis lettre fram þe pope: to þe archebischop com
286 Of bischops & of Clerkes: his consail þerof he nom
So þat in þe wode of Clent: þat in Wircestreschire is
288 Hi lete siche þis holi bodi: & fonde hit out iwis
Vnder þe þorn of Coubage: as þe writ seide at Rome
290 & for þe erore miracle of þe toun: þe whatlokere þerto hi come
For þe contrai men þer-biside: þat vnder-jete þat cas
292 Ouertrowede wel whar hit lay: for þe miracle so fair was
Anon so hi holi bodi vp nome: a wil spring vp þere stod
294 Of þe stede þer he lai on: þat jut is cler & god
For þer is a wille fair ynouj: & euere eft haþ ibeo ·
296 In þe stede as he lai on: as me maj þer iseo
Þat me clepeþ seint kenelmes welle: þat menie men haþ isojt
298 And menie haþ of gret siknisse: þurf þat water ibeo ibrojt
Of þe Cite of Wynchecumbe: & of þe contrai þer biside
300 Þe men were mest þat sojte so: to make þe bodi abide
For þe bischop hadde iloked: þat hit scholde þider beo ibore
302 & ischryned þer his fader lay: þat arerde þe hous bifore
Þis men þis holi bodi: þat of Gloucestreschire were
304 & nobliche toward wynchecumbe: with processioun bere
¶ Þat folc of wircestre schire: þat wonede þer biside
306 Nome hem to rede menie on: to make þe bodi abide

Hi suore þat hi hit wolde habbe : þat no man ne scholde hit hem reue
308 For in þe schire þat hit was ifonde : þat hit scholde bileue
Bi þe watere of perschore : þis two schires hem mette
310 & conteckede for þis holi bodi : & faste to gadere sette
So þat hi nome a forme of pees : to do godes grace
312 Iff god wolde his wille schowe : er hi wende out of þe place
¶ Fortrauailled hy were sore : þat hi moste slepe echon
314 Hi makede a forme þat hi scholde : ligge & slepe anon
& wheþer of þuse tuei schires : whatlokest miȝte awake
316 Al sauf scholde wende forþ : & þe bodi mid hem take
Stille hi leye & slepe faste : þis schiren boþe tuo
318 & reste for here wirynisse : oure louerd hit wolde so
So þat hi of Gloucestre schire : bigonne to awaki echon
320 Al o tyme as god hit wolde : & of wircestre schire noȝt on
In pais hi wende forþ here wey : & þe bodi wiþ hem toke
322 Vyf myle wei hi were awend : er þoþere awoke
¶ Þis oþere iseȝe hem bigyled : anon so hi gonne awake
324 Hi bigonne to suy þis oþere faste : ac hi nemiȝte hem noȝt oftake
Þis men toward wynchecumbe : þis holi bodi bere
326 Er hi hit miȝte þider bringe : suyþe werie hi were
So þat hi come in a wode : a lute bi este þe toune
328 & reste þo hi were so neȝ : vp an heȝ doune
Apurst hi were for werinisse : so sore þat hit nas ende
330 For seint Kenelmes loue hi bede : som drinke oure louerd hem
                                                    sende
A cold welle & fair þer sprong : anoueward þis doune
332 Þat ȝut is þer fair & cold : a myle fram þe toune
Wel faire hit is iheled nouȝ : wiþ fair ston as riȝt is
334 And redi ech man to drinke þerof : þat comeþ þerforþ iwis
¶ Þe monekes sippe of wynchecumbe : arerd habbeþ þerbiside
336 A fair chapel of seint kenelm : þat men sicheþ wide
¶ Quendride þe liþere quene : at wynchecumbe þo was
338 He nuste hire broþer noȝt so neȝ : ne noȝt of þat cas
Heo sat in seint peteres churche : biside þe abbey ȝate
340 In a soler in þe est side : & lokede out þerate
Þo seȝ heo al þis grete folc : anoueward þe doune anheȝ
342 To-ward wynchecumbe come : riȝt vnder souþ leȝ
Heo of eschte what men hit were : & what hi poȝte þere
344 Me seide hire þat hi to churche wolde : & hire broþer bere

¶ Þo was þis quene sorie: iŋ gret deol & fere
346 Hire sautere heo nom an hondc: as heo witles were
Of þe sautere þe furste saume: tofore euesong iwis
348 Of cursing of liþere men: & of mansing ymaked is
Dominus laudem hit is icliped: þis saume þe quene radde
350 For acorsi hire broþer bodi: & þat him þider ladde
Þo heo com to þe neoȝenteoþe vers: as þe mansing endeþ iwis
352 Þat hoc opus eorum: a latyn icliped is
Þat saiþ what men hit scholde beo: þat scholde afonge such dede
¶ Vpe hire owe heued hit com: þo heo gan þat vers rede
For riȝt as heo þe vers radde: out berste aiþere hire eȝe
356 & fulle adoun vpe hire sautere: as manie men iseȝe
& þat was me þinȝþ wel ido: dai þat hire bymene
358 Heo ne biloȝ noȝt hire trecherie: hire biȝete was wel lene
þe sauter is ȝut at Malmesbury: & ho-so wole come þerto
360 Þerinne me mai iseo: whar þe dede was ido
Þis holi bodi was forþ ibore: wiþ gret honour atte fyne
362 To þe abbay as he liþ ȝut: & ido in noble schryne
¶ Þis liþere quene deide siþþe: in schindisse ynouȝ
364 Þis bodi as a corsed wrecche: in a foul dich me drouȝ
In þe fouleste þat þere was neȝ: & þerinne me hit slouȝ
366 Bote hire ending schindful were: iwis hit were wouȝ
Nou god for seint kenelmes loue: his suete grace ous sende
368 Þat we mote to þulke ioye: þat he is inne wende: Amen.

[St. Margaret follows; then St. Mary Magdalen; then St. Cristine; & St. James.]

XIV. A MIRACLE OF ST. JAMES'S.

(Harl. MS. 2277, fol. 100 b.)

In þe Cite of leouns: a ȝung man þer was also
2 Þat ofte to seint Jamé wende: & grete loue hadde þerto
O tyme as he þuder wende: he dude ane folie
4 Þat menie to helle bringeþ: þe sinne of lecherie
Toward seint Jame he wende forþ: er he ischcryue were
6 Þe deuel was wel ȝurne aboute: him to mislere

Aȝen him hi com in þe wei: swiþe mylde & softe
8 Riȝt as he seint Jame were: as he bigyleþ men ofte
Wostou euere ho ic am he scide: þoþer seide nai
10 Ich am þulke he scide þat þu hast: isued manie o dai
Seint Jame toward wam þu ert: y ne makie of þe no mone
12 þat þu nedost swiþ wel: of eche þing bote of one
þat þu dudest þe lecherie: er þu wendest to me
14 Among alle men if þat nere: mest ic preisi þe
¶ Seint Jame merci quath þis oþer: ic crie me milce & ore
16 Forȝif me þulke liþere sinne: y nele do so no more
A bean frere quaþ þis oþer: strong is þi misdede
18 þu ne miȝt me neuere paye wel: bote þu do as ic rede
þe membre þu most kerue of: wherwiþ þu isynewed hast
20 þe synne ic wole forȝyue þe þanne: whan he is fram þe icast
And neȝ me þu scholdest beo: in ioye in heuene aboue
22 & þu woldest beo ymartird: & þe silue matir for mie loue
A louerd, quaþ þis man, seint Jame: haue merci of me
24 & ic wole me martir for mi synne: & for þe loue of þe
¶ þis wrecche man carf of his membres: & awei fram him caste
26 & siþþe þurf his false red: him aslouȝ atte laste
Iredi was þe schrewe þere: þe soule he nom anon
28 & wel glad bigan in his manere: toward helle gon
Ne forget noȝt seint Jame his pelegrim: for cas þat hi gan bitide
30 Aȝen þe deuel he com adoun: & bad þe schrewe abide
þu berest he seide more þan þin owe: & þat ich wole cuþe þe
32 Hastou bitrayd mie pelgrim: moche schame dostou me
¶ ȝe al for noȝt quaþ þe schrewe: þu ert hider icome
34 In his synne him silf he slouȝ: & þerwiþ ic him habbe ynome .
Ne mai no manne in dedlich synne: to þe ioye of heuene wende
36 As wel þu miȝt go aȝen: he is myn wiþoute ende
þu liþere þing quaþ seint Jame: þu bitraidest him wiþ falshede
38 & wiþ trecherie to him come: þu let him go ic rede
Ich habbe leue quaþ þe schrewe: to bigyli & bitraye also
40 In eche quyntise þat mai: whi wolde he misdo
¶ þis strif ilaste bituene hem longe: ac þo seint Jame ne miȝte
42 Wiþinne þe schrewe wiþ resoun: come ne wiþ riȝte
þu schalt he seide wiþ me come: to an heȝere Justise
44 þat þe schal þe trecherie ȝulde: for whan þe schal agrise

To-fore oure leuedie swete & mylde: þane schrewe he gan lede
46 He ʒal & quakede dulfulliche: þo he iseʒ hire for drede
ʒe ʒulle moten hi euere mo: & wo ʒou mote bitide
¶ þe schrewe fond his macche þo: ic wot he scholde abide
þu liþere þing quaþ oure leuedi þo: whi fondestou in alle wise
50 To bynyme ous & bitraye hem: þat beoþ in oure seruise
þu ne schalt neuere þis soule broke: for þi trecherie
52 Leoue leuedi quaþ þe schrewe: merci ic þe crie
Vnderstond þat ich habbe leue: to bigyli men ynouʒ
54 & þat ich him fond in dedlich synne: & þerinne him silue a-slouʒ
& þat neuere noman in such cas: to heuene come ne miʒte
56 As he myn mid alle lawe: hold me ic bidde to riʒte
¶ þu liþere best oure leuedi seide: to moche ʒoure poer is
58 Allas þat man nele beo war: er he do amis
As þu mid trecherie: his lyf him bynome
60 Al so ic wole him ʒyue aʒe: his lyf bi riʒte dome
& þanne he mai cheose as he wole: god man oþer vuel beo
62 Oure leuedi makede þe soule aʒe: to þe bodi fleo
. Fram depe to lyue he aros: þurf oure leuedi lore
64 & god lyf ladde afterward: & þe deuel doutede þe more
His membres þat he of carf: euere he dude misse
66 Bote a lute wharþurf he miʒte: whan he wolde pisse
& þe deuel ʒeode awey: & huld him a-gyled sore
68 Nadde þe schrewe neuere so moche schame: þat he nere worþe
more
For he doþ men euere schame: sorewe him mote bifalle
70 And liþer þrift vpon his heued: amen siggeþ alle
Nou seint Jame for þe holi stede: þat þu hast in Galiʒ
72 Hel alle þi pelegrims & ous: & bring ous to heuene blis. Amen.

XV. ST. CRISTOPHER.
(Harl. MS. 2277, fol. 101 b.)

Seint Cristofre was saraʒin: in þe lond of Canaan
2 In no stede bi his daye: ne fond me so strong a man
Four & tuentie fet he was long: & þicke & brod ynouʒ
4 Such man bote he were strong: me þinʒþ hit were wouʒ

Al a contrai where he were: for him wolde fleo
6 þerfore him þoȝte þat noman: aȝen him scholde beo
Wiþ no man he seide he nolde beo: bote wiþ on þat were
8 Hexist louerd of alle men: & vnder non oþer nere
He wende to siche such a man: so þat me him tolde
10 Of þe hexiste þat an vrþe was: & mest poer dude wolde
¶ Seint Cristofre him soȝte fur: atte laste he com him to
12 þe kyng him eschte what he were: & what he wolde also
þis oþer seide what he was: & þat he seruise wolde
14 þe hexte man þat owhar were: & to noman abowe ne scholde
If he euie such fond: þe king aȝe sede
16 þat he ne huld of no man: ne nescholde of noman beo in drede
Here aiþer was of oþer glad: Cristofre him seruede longe
¶ þe kyng louede melodie: of harpe & of songe
So þat his iugelour adai: to-fore him pleide faste
20 & anemnede in his rym: þe deuel atte laste
þo þe kyng ihurde þat: he blescede him auon
22 Seint Cristofre nom gode ȝeme: ane fot he nolde gon
Er he wiste whi hit were: þe kyng was loþ to telle
24 þoþer seide bote þu telle me: no lenger bileue y nelle
¶ þo þe kyng ne seȝ non oþer: leoue Cristofre he sede
26 Hit was for he nemnede þane: deuel: for ic haue of him drede
Eke he is quaþ Cristofre: heȝere maistre þan þu
28 þat ne mai ic noȝt quaþ þe kyng: wel wiþsigge nou
Haue god dai ek quaþ þis oþer: y nele neuere wiþ þe beo
30 Ich wole siche þane deuel & seruie him: if ic him mai iseo
¶ þe kyng was sorie & alle his: for he nolde abide
32 To siche þe deuel he wende forþ: ac napeles noȝt wel wide
For þe schrewe is euere prest: þat to him habbeþ ynome
¶ þo Cristofre com wiþoute þe toun: gret folc he seȝ come
Wiþ grete noblei wel anhorse: swise firse & proute
36 Cristofre hem mette baldeliche: of noman he nadde doute
þe maistre þat was firs ynouȝ: com & ymette him anon
38 Beau sire he seide what ertou: & whoder wostou gon
Ich am he seide in mie seruise: & noman scruie y nelle
40 Bote mie louerd þat ic siche: þane heȝe deuel of helle
Beau frere quaþ þis oþer ic hit am: wolcome ertou to me
42 þe beste seruise þat þu wolt cheose: ic wole delyurie þe

Cristofre ise꜡ his grete folc: & þat he was of gret poer
44 Of such a louerd he was glad: & of such a mestier
⁋ þe maister het alle his men: awei bote hem tueye
46 To teche his mester priueiliche: as hi ꜡eode bi þe weye
As hi ꜡eode tellinge forþ: of þis liþere seruise
48 A croi꜡ þer stod in þe wei: þe deuel him gan agrise
Fur in breres & in þornes: al aboute he drou꜡
50 ꜡e ne come he neuere in betere stede: for þulke was god ynou꜡
& þerinne were he alto-drawe: forte ic wolde him bymene
52 & þo he þe croice ipassed was: he tournde a꜡e to þe clene
Cristofre eschte whi hit were: him was loþ to telle
54 Certes he seide bote þu me telle: neuere serui ic þe nelle
Cristofre quaþ þe deuel: ic wole þe seruie vayn
56 Wiþ þat þu seruie me þe bet: afterward wiþ al þi mayn
Wiþ a suche croice as þu ise꜡e: þe he꜡e god þat was here
58 Ouercom & in sorwe brou꜡te: me & alle myne fere
Ek he is he꜡ire þan þu quaþ Cristofre: & haþ poer more
60 I ne mai hit no꜡t ofsake quaþ þoþer: & þat me rueþ sore
⁋ Sai þat þanne quaþ Cristofre beo leng in þi seruise
62 If ic of þulke he꜡e manne ou꜡t iwite eny wise
Forþ he wende to siche oure louerd: wide he gan gon
64 Atte laste he fond an hermyte: þuder he wende anon
He tolde him clanliche hou hit was: & hou he such man so꜡te
66 I-hered beo he quaþ þe heremyte: þat in such wit þe brou꜡te
For he is þi louerd leoue sone: to man he þe wrou꜡te
⁋ & mid his owe flesch & blod: in þe croi꜡ þe bou꜡te
þu most sumwhat for him þolie: & faste eche friday
70 I ne faste neuere quaþ þis oþer: ne ꜡ut y ne may
þu most quaþ þis oþer to churche go: & þi beden bidde also
72 I not quaþ Cristofre what hit is: ne y ne mai hit no꜡t do
No quaþ þis hermyte þu ert strong: & her is a water biside
74 þat noman ne mai þerouer come: bote he þe he꜡ire ride
þu most in lisnisse of þi synne: þer habbe þi woninge
76 & whan enie man haþ to þe neod: þu most him ouer bringe
In for꜡yuenisse of his misdede: he grantede þis anon
78 þe ermyte him ꜡af cristendom: & let him þider gon
Cristofre biside þulke watere: & lute hous makede þere
80 In his hong [sic] he bar a long perche: his staf as þe꜡ hit were

Whan enie man wolde ouer þat water: vpe his rug he him caste
82　& nom his parche & bar him ouer: & step hardeliche & faste
For he was so long & so strong: þat þer ne com so heuy non
84　þat he nolde wiþ him wel baldeliche: ouer þe deope gon
¶ A niȝt in þat oþer half of þe water: a voiȝ come & gradde
86　Cristofre hale hale: þat he him ouer ladde
Cristofre anon vp aros: his parche an honde he nom
88　Wod forþ & ne fond no man: þo he to londe com
He nas bote vneþe atom: þat he ne gradde also þer
90　He wod forþ & ne miȝte fynde: namore þan he dude er
ȝut he gradde þe þridde tyme: þo he com hom to londe
92　Wiþ his rod he wod oȝe: a lute child he fond stonde
þat child him bad par charite: þat he him ouer bere
94　ȝe com herforþ quaþ Cristofre: y nuste wher þu were
Wel liȝtliche þis child he nom: & in his armes him caste
96　Eucrec as he bar þis child: hit gan to heuye faste
& þat water him wax also: Cristofre him sore agaste
98　To adrenche so heuy þat child was: þat vneþe he stod atte laste
He nas neuere so neȝ ouercome: at eche tyme he grunte & blaste
100　& leste þat child were adreynt: he ne þerste hit adoun caste
¶ þo he was to londe icome: as him þoȝte longe er　　　·
102　þat child he sette adoun to grounde: forto kele him þer
What ertou he seide so lute: & so heuy bicome
104　So heuy þat ic was vpe þe poynte: to adrenche ilome
þeȝ al þe wordle hadde ileye vpe me: me þinȝþ so heuy nere
106　No wonder Cristofre quaþ þat child: þeȝ ic heuyere were
þan al þe wordle for ic am more: þan al þe wordle iwis
108　& al þe wordle ic makede of noȝt: & al þing þat is
& þat þu þat soþe iseo: piche þi staf on þe grounde
110　& leuy he schal & bere frut: & blowe in a stounde
¶ þo nuste he whar þat child bicom: Cristofre his staf nom
112　& piȝte in þe grounde: & also hit bicom
þo was he sikerere þan he was: & oure louerd louede more
114　Forþ he wende to schewi him: & to prechi godes lore
He ihurde sigge wher cristene men: in tourment were ibroȝt
116　To confortie hem he wende þider: þat hi ne flecchede noȝt
Beoþ hardi he seide & stedefast: & doþ as ic ȝou lere
.118　þe iustise sturte vp anon: & smot him vnder þe ere

Sitte wel stille quaþ Cristofre: ic rede ne smyt no more
120 Ertou he seide of þulke: þu hit schalt acore sore
For if ic nere cristene man: ic wolde me awreke auon
122 ʒe bileoueþ on þis Maumetʒ: ymaked of treo & ston
þat no miracle ne mowe do: namore þan so moche treo
124 Of mie louerdes Miracles some: bi mie staf þu schalt iseo
His rod he piʒte in þe grounde: & he gan anon
126 Leuie & blowe & bere frut: bifore hem echon
On such god he seide ʒe schulde bileoue: þat such virtu mai do
128 Hi ue þerste for he was so moche: o bold word speke him to
For his faire miracle of his staf: & for his preching also
130 To god tournde in þe place: soue þousend & mo
To-ward a maner wyldernisse: seint Cristofre wende
132 In Godes scruise to lede his lyf: as oure louerd him grace sende
¶ þe Justise tolde þe kinge fore: þat such a man he seʒ
134 Tourne þat folc & he ne þerste: for his strenʒþ come him neʒ
þe kyng het tuo hondred knyʒtes: siche forto hi him fonde
136 þat hi him nome & sone ladde: to him faste ibounde
Forþ wende þis tuo hondred knyʒtes: wel yarmed anon
138 Toward Cristofre his come a lute: hi bihulde him echon
Hi alle ne þerste come him neʒ: ac hanward gonne fleo
140 & tolde þo hi come hom: þat hi ne miʒte him noʒt iseo
¶ What ʒe cowardʒ quaþ þe kyng: nabbe ʒe him noʒt ifounde
142 Ich wole if he is alyue: habbe him faste ibounde
He sende oþer tuo hondred knyʒtes: þat hi him wide souʒte
144 & þat hi ne come neuere aʒe: bote hi him wiþ hem brouʒte
Wel yarmed hi wende forþ: & þo hi Cristofre iseʒe
146 Hi stode & ne þerste come no ner: ne vneþe him loke wiþ eʒe
For he was so gastliche & so moche: þat hi þerste vneþe him iseo
·148 He miʒte wiþ a lute lupe: wel sone habbe ymaked hem fleo
¶ þis gode man hadd god game of hem: & eschte what hi wolde
150 We ne þore noʒt þis knyʒtes seide: do bi þe as we wolde
For þe kyng ous het þe bringe him: þyn honde faste ibounde
152 If þu wolt we wolleþ him sigge: þat we nabbeþ þe noʒt ifounde
¶ Nai for gode quaþ Cristofre: ʒe ne schulle noʒt beo iblamed so
154 Ich wole go wiþ ʒou to loke fawe: what he wole habbe ido
He makede hem al aʒen hire wille: his honden faste bynde
156 & ladde him forþ harde ynouʒ: his honden faste bihynde

Bi þe wei as hi him ladde: he gan hem so lere
158 þat er hi come hom to þe kyng: alle icristned hi were
Ac napeles hi ladde him forþ: to þe king faste ibounde
160 Lo sire he seide godes kniȝt: nou we him habbeþ ifounde
℞ þe kyng sat an heȝ vpe his sige: & anon þo he him iseȝ
162 For fere he ful to grounde anon: þat his necke to-berste neȝ
þis kniȝtes anon to him come: & þo his wit aȝe com
164 Cristofre he seide tourn þi poȝt: & bilef cristendom
Gode man þu miȝt quaþ þis oþer: as wel beo stille
166 Mi bodi þu hast faste ibounde: do bi me þie wille
Certes sire quaþ þis knyȝtes: þat him hadde þider ibroȝt
168 We habbeþ itake cristendom: we nulle bileue hit noȝt
℞ þe king let þo in grete wrappe: þis Cristofre in prisoun do
170 & þis kniȝtes bynde faste: & smyte of here heuedes also
℞ þo þe kniȝtes biheueded were: þe kyng him biþoȝte
172 & tuo faire wymmen mid alle: seint Cristofre he broȝte
Nite het þat on & þoþer Aquiline: forto tourne his mod
174 þo þis wymen iseȝe Cristofre: as he in prisoun stod
Hem þoȝte his face briȝtere was: þan sonne oþer mone
176 Merci Cristofre loude hi gradde: cristendom ȝef ous sone
℞ Cristofre teiȝte here bileue: & cristnede hem þere
178 þe king hem let amorwe fecche: & loke hou hit were
& wende hi hadde þane gode man: in lecherie ibroȝt
180 þis wimmen ȝeue him liȝt answere: as hi ne ȝeue of him noȝt
What, hou goþ þis, quaþ þe king: habbe ȝe itournd ȝoure þoȝt
182 Honoure oure godes ich ȝou rede: while ȝou is wel idoȝt
ȝoure godes beoþ worþie quaþ þis wimmen: in faire stede
honoured beo ⁚
184 þerfore swopeþ þe stretes: þat alle men hit mowe isco
& we hem wolleþ onoure iwis: as riȝt is & lawe
℞ þe king let do al as hi sede: sone & wel fawe
þo þis maumetȝ were ibroȝt: in þe stret atte laste
188 þis wymmen nome here gurdles boþe: & teide to hem wel faste
And drowe hem into al þe stret: & hewe hem to douste þere
190 Goþ hi seide & fecche hem leches: þat hi iheled were
℞ þe king was þo for wrappe wod: þat o womman he let honge
192 Heuye rekkes bynde to hire fet: þat hire deþ þrowes were
stronge

Þo þis womman was vp idrawe: hire lymes burste wiþ-inne
194 Necke & synuen & oþer ek: wel auȝte heo heuene iwinne
In strong fur he let poþer do: ac no fur ne com hire neȝ
196 Siþþe he let smyte of hire heued: þo he þat iseȝ
Þis holie wimmen boþe þus: to þe ioye of heuene wende
198 Þurf þe grace þat oure swete louerd: þur Cristofre hem sende
Þe king let fecche Cristofre: '& eschte of him anon
200 Wheder he wolde his maumetȝ seruie oþer to deþe gon
⁋ Cristofre forsoc here maumetȝ: & here seruise also
202 Þe king het þat me scholde anon: vpe a gridire him do
And roste him wiþ fur & pich: & þo he was þerinne idon
204 Awei þe gridire mylte: þat fur queynte anon
& he aros vp wiþoute harme: wroþ was þe king þo
⁋ To a piler he let him bynde: & knyȝtes aboute him go
Hi schote him to stronge deþe: wiþ wel kene flo
208 Þer schute wiþ bowe & arblestes: tuo hondred kniȝtes & mo
Ac non arewe neȝ him ne com: ac alle abide biside
210 In þ'eir hi honge aboue him: as hit were forto abide
⁋ Anon so þe kyng hit iseȝ: for wrappe þider he wende
212 Ouer Cristofre an arewe heng: þat toward þe king kende
Boþe his eȝe smyte al out: fur vp in his heued
214 Þe king stod þo for angusse: as his wit were bireued
Þu vnseli wrecche quaþ Cristofre: what is worþ þi miȝte
216 Aȝen him þat þu hast bigonne: þu ert wel feble to fiȝte
Of þi wrecchede ic habbe reuþe: & þat ich wole cuþe þe
218 For mie louerd to morwe wole: þat me martir me
Smyre þanne þin eȝen wiþ mie blod: & þe tit siȝt god
⁋ Þis blynde kyng hadde þerto hope: & wel hit vnderstod
Amorwe he let smyte of his heued: & smyrede wiþ þe blod
222 & hadde his eȝen gode & clere: & tournde sone his mod
Þis holi man he let burie faire: & bileouede on god anon
224 And afeng cristendom: & his men echon
& to þe ioye of heuene wende: & so hem was bet
226 Þan wende to helle pyne : & seruie here maumet
Þus seint Cristofre atte laste: þe hexte king out souȝte
228 Nou god ous bringe to þulke ioye: þat he his soule brouȝte: Amen:

[St. Martha follows; then St. Laurence, the Assumption of St.
Mary, St. Bartholomew the Apostle, St. Giles the Confessor,

the Holy Rood and its miracles, St. Matthew, Seint Michel
þarcangle; then the pit of hell &c., printed at the end (p. 132–140)
of Mr. Wright's edition of Popular Treatises on Science written
during the Middle Ages, London 1841; then St. Jerome, St.
Denis, and St. Luke.]

XVI. THE 11,000 VIRGINS.
(Harl. MS. 2277, fol. 137.)

Ellene þousend virgines: þat fair cumpaignie was
2 Imartred were for godes loue: ic wole telle þat cas
A king þer was in Britaigne: Maur was his name
4 A douȝter he hadde Ourse: a mai of noble fame
So fair womman me niste non: ne so god in none poynte
6 Cristine heo was & al hire cun: swiþe noble & queynte
Of hire fairhede & godnisse me tolde in eche side
8 þat þe word cam in-to Engelond: & elleswhoder wide
¶ A king þer was in Engelond: a man of gret poer
10 Of þis maide he hurde telle: gret noblei fur & nher
To spouse hire & his sone: to-gadere he hadde ipoȝt
12 Ac þer nas þe ȝut in Engelond: no cristendom ibroȝt
¶ To þe king of britaigne he sende worþ: his douȝter þat was so fair
14 þat he hire lete marie: to his sone þat was his heir
If he were þer aȝen: þat þe dede were ido
16 Destruye he wolde al his lond: & him silue also
¶ þo þis message was: to þe king ised
18 Sorie & dreorie he was: he ne couþe þerof no red
For þe king of Engelond: was heþene & alle his
20 & he wiste wel his douȝter nolde: beon iwedded iwis
& for þe kyng of Engelonde: was man of grete miȝte
22 & þat he nadde poer non: aȝen him forto fiȝte
& naþeles trues of answere: aȝe þe message he nom
24 Deol & sorwe & lute ioye: in his hurte þer com
He ne tolde noȝt his douȝter fore: of þis reuful cas
26 Ac naþeles heo hit vnderȝet: for he so sorie was
ȝurne heo bad god day & a niȝt: þat he scholde hire rede
¶ A angel þer com to hire a nyȝt: & þuse wordes sede
¶ Ne beo þu noȝt aȝe þis sonde: ac þi fader forto paye
30 Grante iwedded forto beo: aȝt a certeyn daye

Wiþinne þreo ȝer þat þu mowe: þi maidenhod honoure
32 & þer wonye mid þe: clene maidenes in þi boure
þat þe kynge sone & þi fader: beo at one rede
34 To cheose þe ten maidenes: wiþoute enie wikhede
Whan ȝe to-gadere beoþ: þat hi fynde ȝou ek þerto
36 A þousend maidenes to ech of ȝou: to seruie ȝou also
þat whan alle ȝe to-gadere beoþ: þat ech mowe in his side
38 Honoure here maidenhod & þyn: þat hit beo couþ wide
So þat me nute maide non: alised aȝe þe
40 & þat he wole cristene beo: þi louerd þat schal beo
In þisse foreward grante him: in þe þridde ȝere
42 Iwedded to beo in godes lawe: naue þerof no fere
¶ Þo þis maide ihurde þis: heo was glad of þis lore
44 Þat heo wiste wharwiþ hire fader: bringe out of sore
To hire fader heo wende anon: & bad þat hire telle scholde
46 Whi he mournynge ȝeode so: & he seide he nolde
Ich wot wel þi þoȝt quaþ þis maide: þeȝ þu hit holde stille
48 Of þi message naue þu no doute: ic wole don al þi wille
Þo gan heo sigge in whiche manere: as þ'angel hadde ised
50 Heo wolde habbe þis heȝe man: if hit were his red
¶ Wele þat þe king was glad: þo he hurde þis
52 Þe message he ȝaf an answare: mid gode hurte iwis
Þo þe teþinge to him com: wel he him paide
54 Sone he let,him cristinie: for loue of þis maide
& þurf his fader red: & þurf þoþer kynge
56 Elleue þousend maidenes clene: to þis maide hi lete bringe
Wher me miȝte fynde nou as sone: as me miȝte þo
58 I ne wene noȝt wher me scholde: in al þis toun fynde mo
¶ Þis maide was glad of þe cumpaignye: þat to hire com
60 Sone heo gan in priueite: teche hem of cristendom
Þat for hire loue & hire prechinge: alle cristene hi were
62 Louerd which a cumpaignye: of clene maidenes was þere
So glad was þe king of his douȝter: & of hire faire ferede
64 Þat he hem let makie a schip: of gret lengþe & brede
Þat hi scholde aboude in þe see: pleye wher hi wolde
66 Þat ech man a londe & a watere: here maidenhod preisi scholde
Hi songe ofte a londe & a watere: & tresches gonne lede
68 & oþer maner faire pleyes: & alle of faire dede

Mete & drinke stilleliche: to schipe hi gonne bringe
70 To þreo ȝeres sustenance: wiþoute leue of þe kynge
A day hi furde to þe see: & pleide vp & doun
72 For ioye þer bihulden hem: men of menie o toun
¶ As hi were in mest pleye: oure louerd a wynd sende
74 þat drof hem fur in-to þe see: me nuste whoder hi wende
Wel glade weren hi þo: þe wynd hem drof wel blyue
76 Atte Cite of Coloigne: hi gonne furst aryue
To damaisele Ourse: an angel þer com þere
78 And hire maidenes bad lede wel: forte hi ymartred were
& seide hi schulde furþere fare: & alle aȝe wende
80 & in þulke toun ymartred beo: for godes loue attan ende
Glad was þis maide þurf þis word: forþ hi wende anon
82 Atte Cite of Basilie: hi aryuede þo echon
Fram þulke euerechone: afote hi wende to Rome
84 þe pope hem makede ioye ynou: þo hi þider come
For menie of hem him were isibbe: & for he was of britaigne
86 Ciriac his name was: hi were wiþ him wel fawe
¶ To þe pope an angel þer com a niȝt: & seide þat he scholde
88 Mid þis maidenes ymartred beo: for oure louerd hit wolde
After þis tyme þis holi man: honourede hem þe more
90 & prechede hem of clanniesse: & of oure louerdes lore
Tuelmonþ & elleue wyke: alle þis maidenes were
92 At Rome wiþ þis holi pope: þat he dude wel lere
Ac þe pope þo seint Ciriak: his consail clipie bigan
94 His clerkes & his Cardynals: & menie anoþer man
Tofore hem al his dignete: he tok vp attan ende
96 & seide he wolde into anoþer lond: mid þis maidenes wende
His Cardynals were þeraȝen: þat he his dignete gan reue
98 Wiþ wenclen forto go: & his dignete bileue
Napeles he wende forþ wiþ hem: al aȝen here rede
100 His Cardinals & his clerkes: gret schame þerof him sede
¶ Tuei liþere princes: Maximin & Affrican
102 þoȝte þat þis maidenes wolde: tourne menie man
To here prince of Coloigne: hi sende for þan one
104 þat he whan hi þider come: hem martrede echone
¶ þis child þat schold þis maide wedde: as hi hadde ised
106 King was ymaked in Engelond: þo his fader was ded

þat ladde swiþe chast lyf: & langede wel sore
108 Wiþ þe clene maide speke: þurf strenþe of godes lore
⁋ An angel þer com to him: & bad him in alle wise
110 þat his moder & his junge soster: he lete baptize
    & þat he to Coloigne wende: wiþ him wiþ al his mayn
112 & afonge cristendom: er hi come agayn
    þat he bounde hure to him faste: in word & in dede
114 & endede to-gadere here lyf: as he hem wolde rede
    þe junge king fawe dude: as þangel him gan lere
116 He nom his moder & his soster: & þo hi ibaptised were
    & þe bischop Clement ek: þat hem ibaptised hadde
118 Toward Coloigne forþ wiþ him aje: þis maidenes he ladde
    Wel glad was þe junge kyng: þo he to his lemman com
120 As glad was þis maide: þo heo sej him in cristendom
    Gladdest he was wiþ his soster: þat het Florentine
122 þat heo scholde so jung & so clene: suffrie deþes pyne
    Ourse of Britaigne þe junge king: of gret ioye him gan lere
124 þat he huld him faste to hire: & þat he ne flecchede for no fere
    þat hi mijte in true loue: togadere ymartred beo
126 & in heuene beo mid ihesu crist: þat hen boujte on þe treo
    þis junge kyng grantede al þis: þis womman nojt ne wornde
128 His furste pojt to true loue: of clannisse he tournde
⁋ þe heþene prince jare was: þo hi to Coloigne come
130 & liþere men menie on: & þis cumpaignye nome
    Hi suede & cride on hem aschame: to grounde hi hem slowe
132 As so fele wolues among hem: here flesch hi to-drowe
⁋ þo hi come to þis clene þing: Ourse of britaigne
134 þo hi fonde such a creatoure: so fair & so fayne
    þe prince hire nom & hire bihet: to lete hire go alyue
136 & for hire noble gentise: habbe hire to wyue
    þis maide seide þat heo nolde: non vrþlich spouse take
138 þe prince was þo wroþ ynou: þo he was forsake
⁋ Archers he let hire schute anon: to deþe attan ende
140 & þo heo & hire cumpaignye: to þe blisse of heuene gonne wende
    & þe junge kyng of Engelond: & his moder also
142 & his junge soster Florentine: to deþe were ido
    & þe pope Ciriac: & bischopes menie on
144 þat for hope of martirdom: wiþ þo maidenes dude gon

Ou, louerd, þe grete ioye: of þis swete ferrede

146 þat martirdom for þi loue: afonge wiþoute drede

In þe tuo hondred: & ciȝte & prittie ȝere

148 After þat god an vrþe com: þis maidenes ymartred were

þis elleue þousend maidenes: & al þe cumpaignye

150 Ibured were sippe iu Coloigne: in a nonnerie

An abbod þer was þer biside: þat hurde of þis cas

152 & ofte of þis clene maidenes: gret miracle þer was

He bad þ'abbot of Coloigne: þat he him granti scholde

154 A body of þis clene maidenes: & he hit wolde do in golde

¶ þo þis bodie him was bitake: tuelfmonþ he let hit beo

156 Wiþoute siluer oþer gold: in a chiste of treo

þo þe tuelf monþes were ido: as þe monekes echone

158 At matyns were a niȝt: þe bodie aros vp alone

& enclynede hire to þe heȝe weued: & wende myldeliche

160 Out þurf al þe couent: faire & stilleliche

þis monekes þo hi þis iseȝe: adrad & sorie were

162 To þe tumbe hi wende þer heo was: & ne fonde hire noȝt þere

¶ þis quaþ þ'abbot is oure wreche: for we nadde hire ido

164 In golde riȝt as hit hadde ibeo: for we bihete hire so

To þ'abbesse of Coloigne: þ'abbot wende anon

166 & tolde þe cas hou hit was: of þe maide agon

Hi wende to þulke stede: þer as heo was ileid er

168 & heuede vp þe lid of þe þrouȝ: & fonde hire ligge þer

Faire & euene as heo dude er: so lute lyme þer nas

170 þat ne lai as he furst dude: fair miracle þer was

þ'abbasse was þo glad ynouȝ: & þe nonnen echon

172 & for þe miracle songe an heȝ: & þonkede god anon

¶ þ'abbot bad þat he moste habbe: þo holi bodi eftsone

174 & he hit wolde honoury fawe: as riȝt was to done

Ac þ'abbesse hit nolde granti noȝt: no þe couent noþer

176 þat he hit scholde eft lede aweie: þeȝ hit were here broþer

For hi seȝe hit was godes wille: þat hit scholde bileue þere

¶ þis abbot wende hom aȝe: wiþ wel dreorie chere

Nou god ous grantie for his grace: þat we mowe iwinne

180 þe heȝe ioye of heuene: þat þis maidenes beoþ inne: Amen:

[Seint Simon & Seint Jude follow; then St. Quintin the Martyr,
All Saints Day, All Souls Day, St. Leonard the Confessor, &
St. Martin.]

XVII. ST. EDMUND THE CONFESSOR.

(Harl. MS. 2277, fol. 155.)

   Seint Edmund þe confessour: þat liþ at Ponteneye
2 Of gode men & true he cam: þeȝ hi nere noȝt wel heye
   Ibore he was in Engelond: in þe toun of Abyndone
4 Glad·miȝte þe moder beo: þat bar such a sone
   Mabille þe riche his moder het: þat god womman was ynouȝ
6 For boþ wyf & widne: to holi lyf heo drouȝ
¶ A seint Edmundes day þe king: þe gode child was ibore
8 So clene he cam fram his moder: wiþoute enie hore
   & so drie þat no cloþ: þat neȝ þe moder was
10 Ne neȝ þis ȝunge child ibore: noþing isoilled nas
   A seint Edmundes dai he was ibore: þo hit was furst dai
12 Fram þe morwe forte hit was neȝ niȝt: as ded þing he lay
   Riȝt as he were ded bore: for no lyf on him ne say
14 Aȝen eue he cudde furst his lyf: to churche he was ibore
   & for seynt Edmundes day hit was: Edmund icleped þerfore
¶ þis child wax & wel iþeȝ: elles wonder hit were
   þo hit was of enie elde: þe moder hit let lere
18 & Robert ek hire oþer sone: for sones heo hadde hem two
   & tuei maidenes clene ynou: hire douȝtren were also
20 Dame Margerie & dame Alice: þat at Kattesby were ido
   & þat in ordre nonnes were: & liggeþ þer boþe tuo
¶ Dame Mabille þe gode moder: þis children louede ynou
22 & wissede hem to clene lyue: & to godnisse drouȝ
   þe wile children ȝunge were: ofte heo ȝaf hem mede
24 For to faste þane fridai: to watere & to brede
   þurf mede & þurf faire biheste: hi wer so þer-on ibroȝt
26 þo hi were in grettere elde: hit ne greuede hem riȝt noȝt
   þe moder werede harde here: for oure louerdes loue
28 Fram þe schuldre to þe hele: & harde hauberk aboue
   In suche penance heo ladde hire lyf: þis widue þat was so wys
30 Wel ȝung heo sende boþe here sones: to scole to Parys
   & bitok hem spense lute ynouȝ: as heo miȝte biseo
32 Hi seide aȝe þat hi ne miȝte noȝt: bi so lute beo
   Leoue sones, quaþ þis moder: ic mai beo ȝut wel hende
34 If ȝe wolleþ don after me: ic can ȝou more sende

& hit schal ȝut likie wel: bi þan ȝe wite þan ende
36 If ȝe þore mid so lute: out of londe wende
¶ Leoue moder, quaþ þe sones: we schulle don after þi lore
38 Ac þu wost we ne mowe noȝt libbe: bote þu ous sende more
¶ Þe moder tok wel stilleliche: ech of hem an here
40 Þat hi werede hem eche wike: tueye oþer þrie þere
& heo wolde hem sende spense ynou: þe while hi at scole were
¶ Þis children ȝeode to scole þo: & dude here moder heste
& werede here here þrie a wyke: oþer tueye atte leste
44 So longe hi hem vsede perto: þat hi hem nome oftere mo
So longe þat noþer dai ne niȝt: hi nolde hem noȝt forgo
46 Hi vseden hem so wel perto: þat hi werede hem dai & niȝt
Þis was lo a god moder: þat teiȝte hire childrene ariȝt
48 And euere as heo hem sende clopes: as heo hem miȝte iwynne
Þerwiþ heo wolde heren sende: isued stille wiþ-inne
¶ Seint Edmund þe gode clerc: to eche godnisse drouȝ
Þat euerech clerc þat him iknew: hadde of him ioye ynouȝ
52 For oure louerd & his holi grace: mid him was wel ryue
& þat oure louerd cudde him wel: in his ȝunge lyue
¶ For as he ȝeode a dai: in a mede for to pleye
His felawes he bileuede echon: & ȝeode biside þe weye
56 & alone ȝeode vp & doun: & his beden sede
Þer cam go a fair whit child: to him in þis mede
58 Felawe, he seide, hail þu beo: þat gost þe silue alone
¶ Seint Edmund stod in gret[e] þoȝt: wannes þis child cone
60 Ne knoustou me noȝt, quaþ þis child: seint Edmund seide no
Nam ic þi felawe, quaþ þis child: whoder þu euere go
62 At scole ic sitte ek bi þe: euere bi þi riȝt side
& wiþ þe ic go in eche stede: ne go þu noȝt so wide
64 & þi pleyfere ic am: & if þu nost noȝ ho ic beo
¶ In mie foreheuede iwrite: mie name þu schalt iseo
66 Signe þerwiþ þi forcheued: & þi breost also
An eue whan þu to bidde gost: & aday whan þu risest perto
68 Euerech niȝt er þu slepe: as in munde of me
& þe deuel ne tit poer non: forto greuy þe
¶ Seint Edmund nuste mid þis word: whoder þis child bicom
He kneu wel þat hit was oure louerd: gret ioye to him he nom

72 He nolde forȝete noȝt o niȝt: his lore forto do
   To croici þrie his foreheued: & his breost also
74 & sigge ihesu cristus nazarenus: as he hit iseȝ iwrite
¶ Wiþ noþing ne scholde a man bet: wiþ þe deuel him wite
76 In penance & in his lore: þat child dude al his poȝt
   For godes loue he þolede moche: þat deore him hadde iboȝt
78 In penance he was so wel yused: & þeron ȝung ibroȝt
   þat þo he was of grettere elde: hit ne greuede him riȝt noȝt
¶ At Parys he was at scole longe: & at Oxenford also
   He ne dude neuere lecherie: ne neuere ensentede þerto
82 As his schriffader wolde telle: ofte in priueite
   He ne miȝte neuere fynde non: of so gret chastete
84 Pryuciliche at Oxenford: þerfore a dai he com
   To þe ymage of oure leuedi: & bi þe hond hire nom
86 And forhet bifore hire: truliche wommanes mone
   And wiþ truþe holde al his lyf: clanliche to hire one
88 þe ymage he weddede wiþ a ring: as man doþ his wyf
   Clanliche to holde in spoushode: to hire al his lyf
90 Aue maria gracia plena: þuse four wordes were ido
   & igraued in his ring of golde: for hit acordeþ þerto
· 92 Wel he huld his truþe siþþe: & his wedding also
   & true spouse was ynou: & nolde noȝt misdo
94 Ich wot me miȝte fynde: ho so soȝte blyue
   Som man þeȝ hit selþe beo: vntruere wiþ his wyue
96 & as ful beo of þe mariage: & as fawe hit vnbynde
   Wele whar enie of ȝou couþe: such an hosebonde fynde
¶ His osteste had a douȝter: þer he was at inne
   þat louede moche þis holi child: if heo miȝte of him enie loue
                                                    awinne
100 Heo ne couþe neȝ non oþer wit: heo fondede forto do
    Folie bi niȝte & bi daye: if heo miȝte come þerto
102 Heo bad him þat heo moste a niȝt: to his bedde wende
    þis holi child ne wornde hire noȝt: ac dude as þe hende
¶ þis maide was þo glad ynouȝ: for er heo bad wel ofte
   A nyȝt þo heo seȝ hire tyme: to his bed heo com softe
106 Hire cloþes he dude of anon: as hit is lawe of bedde
    & makede hire redi to kreopen in: ac wel febliche hire spedde

108 For seint Edmund hadde a smeort ȝerd: þis womman adoun he
                  redde
 & leide vp hire nakede rug: þat heo neȝ awedde
110 He ne sparede rug ne side noþer: er heo to grounde bledde
 Quenche miȝte hire fole poȝt: mid blod þat heo schadde
112 & euere seide þis holi man: as he leide on hire faste
 Maide þu schalt lurny þus: awei forto caste
114 Þi fole wil of þi flesch: wiþ suche discipline
 Heo þoȝte lute of fol poȝt: er þis gode man wole fyne
 ¶ Þis wenche wende softe aȝe: hire rug smurte sore
 Heo biȝat so lute þo: þat hire ne longede þuder no more
118 Clene womman heo bicom: wiþoute flesches dede
 & clene maide sippe deide: as hire schriffader sede
120 Þis maidenes þat beoþ wilful: folie to do
 Ich wolde hi fonde such a lemman: hem to chaste so
 ¶ Þo Mabille his swete moder scholde: of þis wordle go
 Seint Edmund hire holi sone: neȝ hire was þo
124 Þe moder him ȝaf hire blescing: þo heo schulde hunne fare
 Blesce ek mis broþer, quaþ þoþer: þeȝ he beo elleswhare
126 Leoue sone, quaþ þe moder: boþe ȝe come of me
 & he is whan þe beoþ o blod: iblesced forþ wiþ þe
 ¶ Ac ic bidde þe for þe loue of god: & of seinte Marie
 Þat þu somwhar þi sostren do: in a nonnerie
130 Þat hi mowe lede clene lyf: in godes seruise
 Þat þu ne suffrie þat hi beo: iwedded in none wyse
132 Þis catel þat ich biqueþe: þis dede forto do
 Al ic bitake in þyne warde: & hem þerwiþ also
134 Þis gode womman deide þo: & of widuen was flour
 & in seint Nicholas churche at Abyndone: ibured was wiþ gret
                 honour
136 Vnder a ston bifore þe Rode: in þe souþ side iwis
 A lute wiþoute þe abbay ȝate: þe chapel arered is
138 Aboue hire hit is iwrite: her lyþ on þe ston
 Mabille flour of widuen: & lesing nis hit non
140 For heo was womman of gode lyue: as me miȝte bi hire iseo
 & menis miracle sippe at Abyndone: for hire haþ ibeo
 ¶ Nou ne forȝet noȝt seint Edmund: þat his moder him hadde ibede
 Þo his poer was iwoxe: he pourueide him a stede

144 & his sostren were ido: in a nonnerie
    Ac wel vneþe he miȝte hit do: wiþoute symonye
146 Atte laste he com to Cateby: in Northamte schire
    Igranted him was þer anon: al þat he wolde desire
148 Boþe his sostren a godes name: nonnen he makede þere
    & lyuede þer al here lyf & holie wymmen were
                                        [Margeria
150 þe vlþere was sippe priorasse: of þe leuedies echou
    For hem haþ sippe god ido: miracles meuie on
152 & bifore þe wcued an heȝ: ibured hi beoþ þere
    In a chapel of seint Edmund: þat hi lete arere
  ¶ þis holi man seint Edmund: werede stronge here
    In strongere manere he was ymaked: þan oþer manes were
156 He nas isponne ne iweue: ac ibroide of strenges longe
    & sippe as me knyt a net: iknyt harde & stronge
158 Of hard hors-her ymaked: þe knottes deope wode
    þat moche del his bodi orn: in quitoure & in blode
160 Herof he hadde brech & scherte: fram necke to þe hele
    Vneseliche he miȝte ligge: & lutel ese ifele
162 A strong rop þer was sippe aboue: fram þe schuldre ido
    To his buttok of hors her: to holde hit faste to
164 & sippe he was byneþe his brech: igurd faste ynouȝ
    Wiþ a strong corde aboue þe here: þat faste to-drouȝ
166 So faste was in eche side: þe here to him ibounde
    þat vneþe he miȝte bye his rug: oþer lokie to þe grounde
168 & whan he byde him enie þyng: his flesch was so ignawe
    þat wonder hou he þolede hit: to beo so to-drawe
170 Fet & honde þat nere noȝt: itourmented wiþ þe here
    Necke & heued & al his face: þat wiþoute were
172 He ruddede a niȝt wiþ his here: whan no man ne miȝt hit iseo
    For he nolde þat no lyme: vnypyned scholde beo
  ¶ A dai he toc al priueiliche: his man his olde here ˙
    þat he hem forbrende stilleliche: for hi forolþed were
176 He cast hem in gret fur: ac hit ne com noȝ þer neȝ
    Ac euere hi were iliche sounde: as þis man iseȝ
  ¶ þo he seȝ hit ne brende noȝt: he bond þerto faste
    Heuye stones to drawe hit adoun: & þe water hit vp caste
180 Nadde þat fur poer non: to tuochi þe holi here
    Ac naþeles he tolde his louerd: þat hi forbrende were

¶ Seint Edmund & his felawe: as hit was ofte here wone
   In a day fram Lenkenore: wende to Abyndone
184 As hi come in a gret faleye: blake monekes he se꜔
   As hit crowen & cho꜔en were: fleo bi þ'eir anhe꜔
186 A lute blac sac as þe꜔ hit were: among hem þis fowcles bere
   & caste hit vp fram on to oþer: as hi hit to-tere
188 þat was a soule for his wickednisse: þat hi to helle bere
   His felawe stod & bihuld: & was ne꜔ wod for fere
¶ Seint Edmund ꜔af him god confort: & tolde what hi were
   Deuelen of helle he seide hit beoþ: & þat hi bereþ iwis
192 A manes soule of stafgrene: her bifore hit is
   þat nou ri꜔t deide late: he ne comeþ neuere in blis
194 He mai singe welewei: þat euere he dude amis
   Forþ hi wende to staf-grene: þat soþe hi fonde þere
196 þe man ded a lute bifore: & ligge hot in a bere
   No þe gladdere ne mi꜔t he beo: þat þe deueles him so to-tere
¶ Seint Edmund þis holi man: louede wel his lore
   For his loue he louede ꜔ut: godes seruise þe more
200 Mest he louede an oreisoun: þat was of ihesu crist
   & of oure leuedi his swete moder: & of seint Johan þ'ewangelist
202 þat .o. intemerata: bigynneþ a latyn
 . þe bigynnyng is wel god: & also þe fyn
204 Eche dai bi custume: he seide þis oreisoun
   He nolde hit bileue for no scole: ne for no lessoun
206 Ane dai he hit for꜔ot: he hadde so moche to done
¶ Seint John þ'ewangelist: com to him wel sone
208 A pameri he brou꜔te on his hond: gret & strong ynou꜔
   Seint Edmund he nom bi þe hond: & his pamerie drou꜔
210 So he꜔e & wiþ so gret eir: as he him wolde altodryue
   Seint Edmund lay & quakede: & dradde of lyue
212 For if he him hadde ismyte: as he drou꜔: he hadde ibeo ded anon
   He quakede & cride dulfulliche: louerd merci seint John
¶ Ich wole for-꜔eue þe, quaþ seint Johan: þu criest so sore
   & þench bet on oure oreisoun: & ne for꜔et hit nomore
216 He ne for-꜔at after þulke tyme: nomore þis oreisoun
   For no studie ne for no neode: ne for þo꜔t of lessoun
¶ So wel lurnede þis holi man: & suche grace hadde
   þat he bigan at Oxenford: & of art þer radde

220 Of art he radde six ȝer: contynuelliche ynouȝ
    & siþþe for beo more profound: to arsmetrike he drouȝ
222 & arsmetrike radde in cours: in Oxenford wel faste
    & his figours drouȝ aldai: & his numbre caste
¶ Arsmetrike is a lore: þat of figours al is
    & of drauȝtes as me draweþ in poudre: & in numbre iwis
¶ A niȝt in a visioun: his moder to him wende
    Sone heo seide to what figours: wostou nou entende
228 Leoue moder, quaþ þis oþer: suche as we iseoþ
¶ Leoue sone, quaþ þe moder: betere figours þer beoþ
230 Wherto þu most þin hurte do: & þenche her-on nomore
    Heo nom forþ his riȝt hond: & wrot þeron his lore
232 þreo rounde cerclen heo wrot: in þe paume amidde
    In þe tueye heo wrot fader & sone: & holi gost in þe þridde
¶ Sone heo seide her-afterward: entende to þis lore
    To heuene aȝe þe moder wende: he ne seȝ hire no more
¶ þo iseȝ seint Edmund: þat hit was al of þe trinite
    & þat god wolde þat he schulde: ihure diuinite
238 To diuinite as god wolde: þis gode man him drouȝ
    þer ne spedde non in Oxenford: so wel of ynouȝ
240 Hit nas noȝt longe þer afterward: þat þe Chanceler ne sede
    & þe hexte maystres of þe toun: þat he schulde bigynne & rede
242 He wiþsede & longe seide: þat he nas noȝt worþie þerto
    So þat moche aȝen his wille: nede hi makede him hit do
244 So þat he bigan at Oxenford: of diuinite
    So noble a losed þer nas non: in al þe vniuersite
246 Of redinge he hadde so gode grace: þat menie on to him drouȝ
    His scolers þat ihurde of him: gode men were ynouȝ
248 So pitousliche he wolde rede: & so gode grace hadde þerto
    þat his scolers þat ihurde of him: nuste ofte what to do
250 Ac sete as in anoþer wordle: & ofte hudde here eȝe
    & wepe þat þe teres vrne adoun: þat men hit al aboute iseȝe
252 Vneþe enie ihurde of him: þat þe betere ne bicom
    & menie bileuede al þe wordle: & to religioun nom
¶ A dai as þis holi man: in diuinite
    Desputede as hit was his wone: of þe trinite
256 In his chaire he sat longe: er his scolers come
    A lutel he bigan to swondrie: as a slep him nome

258 Þo þoȝte him in his swondringe: þat a whit coluere com
Fram heuene mid oure louerdes flesch: & þe wei to him nom
260 & þat swete flesch pulte in his mouþ: & sippe fleȝ vp anlicȝ
Heuene opencde hire aȝen: as þis gode man iseȝ
262 Þe sauour of oure louerdes flesch: him þoȝte was in his mouþe
And al þe clergie him þoȝte of god: þo he awok he couþe
264 Of þe pure stat of crist: & of his mageste
As angel him þoȝte he couþe: & of his priueite
  ¶ He bigan so deope desputie: of þe trinite
Þat gret wonder me hadde: þurf al þe vniuersite
268 Þat þe gretteste clerkes þat were: in Oxenforde þo
Ne þoȝte þat enie vrþlich man: so furforþ miȝte go
270 Ne wite so moche of godes stat: bote hit angel were
Þer nere none maystres inOxenford: þatin gret wonderþerofnere
272 Ac he miȝte of ihesu crist iwite: more þan was in boc
Whan he vsede oure louerdes flesch: & in his mouþe toc
  ¶ Ne þoȝte noȝt þis holi man: so moche in his lessoun
Þat euere among his þoȝt nas mest: in godes passioun
276 O tyme he was in grete studie: of his lessoun a nyȝt
Þat longe he sat þer aboute: forte hit was neȝ dailiȝt
278 Þo hit was toward þe dai: anapped he was sore
He lynede adoun vpon his boc: þo he ne miȝte studie nomore
280 So þat he ful aslepe: & vnywar also
& ne þoȝte nóȝt on þe passioun: as he was iwoned to do
282 Þe deuel com to him wel sone: noþing to siche he nas
Seint Edmund of him was iwar: in swondring as he was
284 He wolde him blesci wiþ þe deuel: his riȝt hond he gan forþ drawe
Þe deuel him nom þerbi anon: he ne miȝte him noȝt wawe
286 Þo nom he forþ his lift hond: to blesci him wiþ also
Þe deuel him nom þerbi faste: þat he ne miȝte noþing do
288 Vpe him he laie as a sak: þat he was al ouercome
He ne miȝte him wawe fot ne hond: his poer him was binome
290 Ac delyure he hadde al his þoȝt: so þat he þoȝte sone
Of oure louerdes passioun: as he was woned to done
  ¶ Þe deuel ne miȝte þo bileue: vpe him none þrowe
For drede he ful sone adoun: bituene him & þe wowe
  ¶ Seint Edmund aros vp anon: & þe deuel ouercom
Strangliche & harde ynou: bi þe þrote he him nom

296 Þurf oure louerdes passioun: tel nou he seide me
    Ich axie þe hou cristene man: mai best him witie fram þe
298 Me ne schal wiþ noþing quaþ þe deuel: schulde fram mie poer
    So wel as þurf his passioun: þat þu nemnedest er
¶ þer lurnede þis holi man: as we mowe ek echon
    In whiche manere we mowe best: þe deueles poer forgon
302 For he hatieþ godes passioun: as man doþ his fon
    & whan a man hit haþ in munde: he wole him fleo anon
¶ Eche tyme of þe dai & of þe niȝte: seint Edmund him gan biseo
    þat he diȝte him wel to godes wille: þat he nolde idel beo
306 Oþer he was in oreisouns: oþer at his boc
    Oþer he et oþer he slep: oþer to oþer þing he toc
¶ þreo tymes him poȝte he forles: whan he com þerto
    Whan he rod & whan he slep: & whan he et also
310 For he nas þanne in studie: ne in bede no þe mo
    Ech oþer tyme him poȝte: to som prou scholde go
¶ So longe þis gode man: to eche godnisse drouȝ
    þat his godnisse was wide couþ: & me spac þerof ynouȝ
314 þe beste prechour he was iholde: þat me owar vnderstode
    For ho-so haþ wiþ him godes grace: his dedes mote nede beo gode
¶ þo þat of þe croserie: þe pope sende fram Rome
    To bischops of Engelond: þat hi a wysman nome
318 To prechi of þe croserie: aboute in þe londe
    þat me wende to iherusalem: & sende here sonde
320 Procuracies hi ȝeue hem ek: þer hi wende aboute
    Of persones to nyme largeliche: þat non nere wiþoute
¶ Seint Edmund was þerto ichose: þis prechinge forto do
    For he was prechour god ynou: & holi man þerto
324 He nolde of persones nyme noþing: ne no spense take
    Ac whan persones him bode ouȝt: he hit wolde forsake
¶ For whan he seruede ihesu crist: of his owe spense he toc
    & of persones & of oþer men: ȝiftes he forsoc
328 He ne furde noȝt as þis Arcedeknes: ne þis oþere no þe mo
    þat persones & pouere preostes: oueral doþ wel wo
330 As he prechede a dai: of þe croiȝ wel longe
    A ȝung man wende among þoþere: þe croiȝ to afonge
332 A womman þat him louede: anon þo heo iseȝ þis
    Hente him bihynde hasteliche: & aȝen him drouȝ iwis

334 As stif as cnie bord: hire honden bicome anon
Þat heo nemiȝte hem awolde noȝt: noþer synues ne bon
336 Þat þe hond was ek forcroked: heo makede reuliche bere
Seint Edmund bihuld aboute: & eschte what hit were
¶ Sire merci quaþ þis womman: wrecchede ic am ynouȝ
As þis man wolde afonge þe croiȝ: a lute ic him wiþdrouȝ
340 & myn hond is al-forcroked: wharwiþ ic him nom
In ale wrecchede ic am ibroȝt: allas þat ich euere her com
342 Womman quaþ þis holi man: woltou þe croice take
If ic miȝte louerd quaþ þis oþer: y nolde hire noȝt forsake
344 Þis womman sat adoun a kneo: & of him þe croice nom
& þe crokede hond streiȝte forþ: & anonriȝt hol bicom
346 Heo cride & herede ihesu crist: þis was couþ anon
For þis miracle þer toke þe croiȝ: men menie on
¶ In o tyme of þe roueisouns: þis holi man also
Prechede a dai at Oxenford: as he hadde ofte ido
350 In alle halewe churchȝerd: in þe norþ side
Mid þe baners at vnderne: as men doþ a londe wide
352 As þe holi man amidde al þe folc: in his preching was best
Þe grislikeste weder þat miȝte beo: com fram þe west
354 Swart & durc & grislich: & ouercaste al þan toun
Þe wynd bleu ek so grisliche: as al þe wordle scholde adoun
¶ So durk hit was ek þerto: þat vneþe me miȝte iseo
Grislikere weder þan hit was: ne miȝte an vrþe beo
358 Þat folc for drede of here cloþes: faste gonne to fleo
Abideþ quaþ þis holi man: oure louerd is god & freo
360 Þis weþer þe deuel brinȝþ: to desturbie godes lore
Oure louerd is strengere þan he: ne drede ȝe noȝt so sore
362 He bihuld to god an heȝ: & cride milce & ore
To schulde hem fram þe deueles miȝte: þat he ne greuede hem
nomore
¶ Þo he hadde iseid his oreisoun: þat weþer bigan to glide
In anoþer half of þe churche: al in þoþer side
366 Þer hit gan dasche adoun: hit nolde no leng[er] abide
Þat vneþe þurf þe heȝe strete: me miȝte go oþer ride
368 Ac in þe norþ half of þe churche: þer þis gode man stod
Þer ne ful noȝt a reynes drope: to desturbi a manes mod

370 Ac in þe souþ half of þe heȝe strete: hit leide on for wod
Þat al þe stret a watere orn: as hit were a gret flod
372 Þat folc þat fram þe prechinge: for doute of reyn drouȝ
Hi þat wende bi þe heȝe strete: hadde þerof ynouȝ
374 Ac hi þat bileuede þere: drie & clene were
¶ Louerd, moche is þi miȝte: fair miracle was þere
375* In þe toun of wircestre: ful þulke silue cas
376 As þis holi man seint Edmund: in his preching was
Such weþer þer com ouer him: þat hem drof hit awei also
378 Me þingþ as bi his lyue: fair miracle þer was ido
So wide sprong his holi lyf: aboute fur & nher
380 Þat me ne huld of holinisse: in Engelond his per
Imaked he was at Salesbury: Canoun seculer
382 Prouendre he hadde of þe hous: & was tresourer
Þo he was auanced: he tolde þerof lute
384 He spende aboute pore men: þat opere dude in prute
He spende so moche for godes loue: aboute in almesdede
386 Þat vneþe he miȝte half a ȝer: bi his rente his lyf lede
¶ To þ'abbei of Stanleghe: he wende þanne ilome
388 & soiournede þer for defaute: of his crop
For maistre steuene of Laxingtone: þat abbod was þo þere
390 His disciple hadde ibeo: while hi at scole were
His fille ne et he neuere mo: þat enie man hit miȝte iseo
392 Ne as moche as man nede moste: in god poynt forto beo
Of him wondrede euerech man: þat him iseȝ ete
394 Hou he miȝte holde his lyf: bi so lutel mete
Of god mete nolde he noȝt: þeȝ me wolde him bringe
396 Hit was what lutles þat he et: al of grete þinge
Þane dai þat he masse song: flesch ne et he non
398 Ne þe dai þer bifore: for noþing þat miȝte gon
Fram þat me lek allan: forte com ester day
400 He ne est noþing þat þolede deþ: as al þat folc isay
Ne in þe aduent no þe mo: ac þat was lute ynouȝ
402 Aȝen his oþer penance: þat he al day forþ drouȝ
Hit biful þat þe Archebischop: of Canterbury was ded
404 Seint Edmund was ichose: perto þurf þe comun red
Þo þe ellectioun was ymaked in þe Court of Canterbury
406 Anon hi sende here messager: to him to salesbury

f

He wende toward salesbury: ac þer nas he noȝt
408 He fond him in þe toun of Calne: þo he was al isoȝt
In his chambre he was priueiliche: at his boc wel stille
410 Ne þerste noman to him go: forto wite his wille
Ac napeles on þat was him next: as hit were his chamberlayn
412 God tepinge wende to him bringe: þerto he was fayn
He tolde him þat he was ichose: archebischop to beo
414 Þis holi man him chidde anon: & het him þanne fleo
Beo stille, fol, he seide, ich hote þe: & go out hunne anon
416 Make faste þe dore after þe: & ne let no man in gon
To desturbi me of mie studie: ac let me in pays beo
418 Of þis tepinge he told lute: þerbi me miȝte iseo
So fareþ ȝut þis clerkes: hi ne wilnyeþ no maistrie
420 Ne beo ichose to heȝe men: for gode ich wene ic lie
¶ Þis messagers bileuede wiþoute: & carefulle were of þoȝt
422 For þe dai wende forþ: & here message ne dude hi noȝt
Hi wende for here gode tepinge: to beo nobliche vnderfonge
424 So murie hem þoȝte here semblant: þat he þoȝte þer wel longe
Here ȝiftes hi miȝte epe bere: þat seint Edmund hem caste
426 Hi bimende & ofþoȝte sore: þat hi hiȝede þider so faste
He n'aros ane fot fram his boc: er god þanc tyme sende
428 As he was iwoned anoþer dai: ac so forþ wel softe wende
¶ Þo he cam out of his chambre: þe messagers come
430 & seide here erande hou hit was: he toc þerof lute gome
¶ Þo þe lettres were irad: beau freres he sede
432 Ich wole loke what mie felawes: of þis þing wolleþ rede
In þe chapitre of salesbury: as riȝt is þat ich do
434 Hi nadde of him non oþer ansuere: þo hit alles com þerto
¶ Þe chapitre of salesbury: amorwe was plener
436 Alle þe Canouns of þe queor: þer come fur & ner
To consailli him of þisse þinge: þe red was sone ido
438 For gladliche at one worde: hi radde him alle þerto
¶ Beoþ stille, quaþ þis holi man: what schal þis ised
440 Worþi nam y noȝt þerto: nymeþ anoþer red
Certes, quaþ þe bischop, þo: & þe Canouns alle also
442 Nou þu ne miȝt noȝt þer aȝen beo: þu most hit nede do
¶ Þe bischop al wepinge: cride on him faste
444 And in obedience: him bet atte laste

þat he ne scholde noȝt bileue: godes wille to do
446 To buxom to holi churche: & to al þe lond also
¶   Þo bigan þis holi man: to wepe & sike sore
448 Nou god he seide ous ȝeue his grace: his milce & his ore
      & ic take god to witnisse: & seinte Marie also
450 Þat if y ne wende synewi dedliche: y nolde neucre hit do
¶   Þo hi ihurde þis word: ioyful ynou hi were
452 Hi nome him vp wiþ ioye ynou: & to þe heȝe weued him bere
      & te domine laudamus: songe muric & heȝe
454 Euere wep þis holi man: as þis Canouns iseȝe
      So þat hi come to Canterbury: & dude as riȝt was þere
456 & Archebischop was ymaked: vnþonkes þeȝ hit were
      Ne þer no man eschte þer: whar he toke on wel ynouȝ
458 & wel wissede holi churche: & to alle godnisse drouȝ
      If his lyf was holi er: wel betere hit was þo
460 In penance he was strong ynouȝ: in fastinge & oþer wo
      He hadde euere of seli men: pite & deol ynouȝ
462 For him þoȝte þat heȝe men: dude hem al dai wouȝ
¶   O tyme on of his pore men: wende of lyfdawe
464 His beste best to heriet: me brouȝte as hit [was] lawe
      Þo cam þis seli manes wyf: þat careful widue was
466 & mette wiþ þis holi man: as oure louerd ȝaf þat cas
      Heo cride on him deolfulliche: merci & his ore
468 & seide bote þat o best: lute god heo hadde more
      Ne heo nuste in whiche manere: for meseise lyue
470 Heo bad him for godes loue: þat he þe best aȝeu hire ȝyue
¶   Gode womman, quaþ þis holi man: þu wost wel lawe hit is
472 Þe chief louerd to habbe þe beste eiȝte: whan a man ded is
      To his clerkes he seide a latyn: þat heo hit noȝt ne vnderstod
474 Me þinȝþ hit is a liþer lawe: & noþer riȝt ne god
¶   Þis gode wyf haþ forlore hire louerd: þat hire god forþ drouȝ
476 & to leose after hire beste best: me þinȝþ hit were wouȝ
      Nis þat on liþer ynouȝ: þeȝ heo ne lore þat oþer also
478 Þurf þe deuel of helle hit is: & þurf god noȝt ido
¶   Gode wyf, he seide, if ic take þe: aȝe þi best to lone
480 Woltou hit witie to myne bihoue: of ic hit esche eftsone
      Aȝe sire, quaþ þis widue: god ȝulde þe þyn ore
482 Þis widue nom hom hire best: & ne ȝuld hit no more

f 2

¶ Þis cas biful menie o tyme: whan men bede him ouȝt
484 Heriet of pore men: ne wilnede he riȝt nouȝt
    We ne mowe nowhar neȝ: rekene al his gode dede
486 For in penance strong ynouȝ: his lyf he gan lede
    & truliche huld vp holi churche: & schulde hire fram wouȝ
488 Þerfore hadde þe deuel of helle: enuie gret ynouȝ
    He bigan to rere contek: bituene hem anon
490 & kyng Henrie þat was: þe kynges sone Johan
    þe kyng & moche del of þe lond: aȝen holi churche was
492 As þe kyng er his grandsire: was aȝe seint Thomas
    & þe Couent ek of Canterbury: aȝen seint Edmund hulde faste
494 Ofte hi nome a louedai: ac þe Contek euere ilaste
¶ A Legat was þo in engelonde: þat aȝen him was also
496 Stedefast was þis holi man: peȝ he lute help hadde perto
    Hi ne miȝte acordi for noþing: ac þe leng þe wors hit was
498 Ac þis holi man euere nam: his ensample bi seint Thomas
    Wel ofte he bad þe king & his consail: if hit were here wille
500 Holi churche werrie noȝt: ac in pees lete hire beo stille
    Hire franchise as hit was: as hit hadde ibeo ȝare
502 Þe king him pretnede faste anon: bote he bileuede his fare
¶ Of þi pretnynge ic drede lute: seide þis holi man
504 For if þu me dryuest out of londe: anoþer red ic can
    For ic can go to parys: as ic habbe er ido
506 & wynne me þer mete ynou: & cloþinge þerto
    If þu letest me to depe bringe: þu payest me wel ynouȝ
508 Þu ne miȝtest do me nomore honour: þan quelle me wiþ wouȝ
¶ ȝut eft as he dude ofte: to þe king he sende
510 He answerede him þe leng þe wors: & nolde noþing amende
    Þo þis holi man iseȝ: þat hit non oþer nolde beo
512 Þurf holi churche he gan to fiȝte: & amansede alle þeo
    Þat werrede þe churche of Canterbure: & eke dude schame
514 & somme þat he gulti wiste: he amansede bi name
¶ To þe king & his consail: þe worþ wel sone drouȝ
516 Ne þer noman esche þo: whar hi were wroþ ynouȝ
    Þretinge þer was & bost ynouȝ: seint Edmund him huld stille
518 & fast huld vp þe sentence: & let hem speke here wille
¶ Seint Thomas com & spac wiþ him: & fram heuene aliȝte
520 & bad him holde vp stabliche: holi churche riȝte

For non vrþlich anuy ne for deþ: ne flecche þu noȝt
522 Ac nym ensample of me & of oþere: þat so deore hire habbeþ iboȝt
¶ Seint Edmund ful adoun a kneo: & huld vp his hond also
524 To cusse þis holi manes fet: ac he ne moste hit noȝt do
Þo bigan he to wepe sore: louerd he seide þin ore
526 Beo nou stille, quaþ seint Thomas: ne wep þu so no more
Whi wilnestou to cusse mie fet: hit nere no riȝt to do
528 Þu schalt nu ene þi wille habbe: & cusse mie mouþ also
¶ Seint Edmund after þulke tyme: stedefast was ynouȝ
530 To deye raþere for holi churche: þan me dude hire wouȝ
He þoȝte on seint Thomas: hou he out of londe weude
532 Þe while þe king was in mest wraþþe: if he wolde amende
Ensample he nom of him: & priueiliche ynouȝ
534 Wende him out of Engelond: & into france drouȝ
He þoȝte ek þat at Ponteney: he was faire vnderfonge
536 & isustened in his anuy: þat ileste swiþe longe
& also steuene of Langetone: þat Archebischop was
538 Six ȝer was at Ponteney: in þulke silue cas
So þat seint Edmund vnderstod: of his ancestres ynowe
540 Whan contek was of holi churche: þat to Ponteney drowe
¶ Also dude seint Edmund: to Ponteney he wende
542 To abide þe stat of holi churche: when oure louerd hit wolde
amende
Honoured he was þer ynouȝ: of alle þat þer were
544 & euere abod amendement: fram ȝere to ȝere
¶ Hit biful þat seint Edmund: as god wolde atte laste
546 Velde his bodi heuy ynouȝ: & febli wel faste
So longe þat he was so feble: þat me ne radde him noȝt beo þere
548 Ac to soiourny elleswhar: where betere eyr were
¶ Þis holi man his leue nom: elleswhoder to wende
550 Þe monekes makede so moche deol: þat hit·nas non ende
Beoþ stille, quaþ þis gode man: fare ic wole þurf alle þinge
552 & come aȝe hider to ȝou: a seint Edmundes day þe kynge
Louerd in such siknisse: which word þer was ised
554 Ac whan he ne miȝte noȝt alyue: foreward he huld ded
¶ Forþ he wende wiþ his men: þer god eyr were
556 To þe toun of soycie: & bileuede þere

þer heo ȝeode so longe as hit was: in siknisse ynouȝ
558 So longe þat he lai adoun: & to þe depe drouȝ
  ¶ So þat he eschte oure louerdes flesch: & hit was him ibrouȝt
560 He sat & bihuld hit faste ynouȝ: in studie & in poȝt
  Longe hit was er he spac enie þing: & þo he seide myldeliche
562 Louerd, he seide, þu hit ert: þat ich habbe iloued truliche
  & truliche on þe bileoued: & ipreched of þe also
564 And þu truliche at myn endedai: ert icome me to
  Ich take þe louerd to witnisse: þe while ic haue her an vrþe ibeo
566 Noþing elles y ne wilnede: louerd bote þe
  Louerd þat þis was an heȝ word: & he þat þus sede
568 God & holi moste he beo: & holi lyf lede
  ¶ Þo he hadde ynome oure louerdes flesch: he sat longe in þoȝte
570 & al laȝinge an englisch: þuse wordes forþ broȝte
  Me saiþ game goþ a wombe: & ic sigge game goþ an hurte
572 & in his bed þer he lai: vpriȝt he sturte
  In oure louerd þat he had ynome: wel ioyful he was þo
574 & al his game was in hurte: for his bodi was wel wo
  Þe more his bodi pynede :þe nher he was his ende
576 & whan he were of þisse lyue: he wiste whoder wende
  Þerfore þe more he was: in siknisse & in wo
  ¶ Þe gladdere he was for he wiste: whoder he scholde go
  & þe more he loȝ in ioye ynouȝ: & þe muriere him gan like
580 Me nuste him noȝt enes ligge adoun: ne gronye ne sike
  & sat euere glad ynouȝ: & lynede wel ofte
582 Vpe cloþes oþer vpe his hond: as þeȝ he deide softe
  So fair semblant ne makede he non: as þo he was at an ende
584 In þe morweninge as þe sonne aros: out of þis wordle he gan wende
  He deide tuelf hondred ȝer: & two & fourti riȝt
586 After þat oure suete louerd: in his moder was aliȝt
  Me let him openie anon: & his guttes take
588 & burie þer as he was ded: in þe Minstre of seint Jake
  & his holi bodi me nam: & faire let hit lede
  ¶ To þe abbai of Ponteney: as he him silf sede
  A seint Edmundes dai þe king: þider he was ibroȝt
592 Foreward he huld þis monekes: & ne faillede hem noȝt
  For þo he ne com noȝt aȝe alyue: ded he com iwis
594 & þer he was ibroȝt an vrþe: & also ischryned is

& lyþ þer faire ynou: & wiþ gret honour also
596 Menie is þe faire miracle: þat god haþ for him þer ido
Nou for his loue we biddeþ god: þat ous deore bouȝte
598 Bringe ous to þe heȝ blis: þat he his soule to brouȝte: Amen:

XVIII. ST. EDMUND THE KING.
(Harl. MS. 2277, fol. 162 b.)

Seint Edmund þe holi king: of wham we makieþ gret feste
2 Of þat on ende of Engelond: kyng he was her bi este
For of soupfolc he was kyng: & of þe contray wide
4 For þer were in Engelond: kynges in eche side
Swiþe fair knyȝt he was & strong: & hardie in eche poyute
6 Meok mylþe & ful of milce: & swiþe curteys & quoynte
Tuei princes of anoþer lond: þat were of liþer poȝt
8 Faste here red to-gadere nome: to bringe Engelond to noȝt
Hubba was þoþer ihote: & þoþer het Hyngar
10 Wiþ grete furde hi come to Engelonde: er enie man were iwar
In norþhumberland hi bigonne: & þer hi sloȝe to grounde
12 Robbede also & brende to noȝt: & destruyde al þat hi founde
¶ þo hi hadde norþhumberland: clenliche to noȝt ibroȝt
14 Also hi þoȝte al Engelond: hi ne þoȝte raþer bileue noȝt
Hyngar þat o maister was: his felawe bileuede þere
16 & her bi este wende him silf: to sle þat þer were
Of þe godnisse of seint Edmund: he hurde moche telle
18 In to his lond he wende anon: to fondie him to quelle
¶ In to his hexte toun he com: er enie man were iwar
20 & robbede al þat he fond: & makede þane toun bar
þat folc he sloȝ al to grounde: al þat he miȝte ofgon
22 ȝung & old wyf ne maide: he ne sparede non
Children fram here moder breost: he drouȝ & let hem quelle
24 & alto-drawe tofore here moder: þat reuþe hit is to telle
þe modres he let siþþe quelle: þat reuþe hit was ynouȝ
26 þe toun he brende al to douste: & þat folc aslouȝ
He of-eschte of þat folc: where here kyng were
28 & hi him teiȝte wher he was: hi ne þerste non oþer for fere

¶ For in þe toun of Eglesdone: a god wei þannes hit was
30 Þo þe liþere prince þis ihurde: he ne makede noȝt softe pas
Ac wende þider hasteliche: wiþ his men echone
32 Hi come &mette wiþ seint Edmund: wiþoute þe toun alone
¶ Þo Hyngarwiste þat he hit was: he nom him anon þere
34 & bisigede alle þe men: þat wiþinne þe toun were
Seint Edmund was faste ynome: in a lute stounde
36 & ilad to-fore þe prince naked: his honden faste ibounde
As me ladde oure louerd tofore Pilatus: forto afonge his dom
38 Þo his dom was iȝuue: faste me him nom
& ladde him to a þicke wode: & makede him menie wounde
40 & beote him sore wiþ harde scourgen: & to a treo him bounde
So þat þis liþere tourmentours: þat beote him so sore
42 Þoȝte þat þeȝ hi him schame dude: þat hi him wolde do more
Hi stode afur & bende here bowes: & here arewes riȝte
44 And as to a merke schote to him: as euene as hi miȝte
Þe arewes stode on him þicke: & al his bodie to-drowe
46 & euere stod þis holi man: stille as þeȝ he lowe
As ful as an illespyl is: of pikes al aboute
48 As ful he stikede of arewen: wiþ-inne & wiþoute
So ful þat in none stede: ne miȝte an arewe in wende
50 For oþer bote he his bodi corue: & him dude torende
As þe holi man imartred was: þe holi seint Bastian
52 Also hi rende his holi bodie: & schote þis holi man
Þat eche pece ful fram oþer: wonder hit was of his lyue
54 Euere he stod as him ne roȝte: & cride on god wel blyue
¶ Þo Hyngar iseȝ þat he ne miȝte: him ouercome noȝt
56 He let smyte of his heued: þat he were of lyue ibroȝt
¶ As þis holi man his bedes bad: me smot of his heued
58 Ac his bodi was er alto-rend: þat noþing n'as bileued
& for hit was alto-drawe: hi lete hit ligge þere
60 Ac his heued for me ne scholde hit noȝt fynde: forþ mid hem hi bere
¶ In þe wode of Eglesdone: a durne stede hi fonde
62 Among þicke þornes hi caste hit: & hudde hit in þe grounde
¶ Þo hi hadde of þis holi kyng: al here welle þere
64 Glade & bliþe hi wende forþ: liþere men as hit were
Þat heued hi hudde durneliche: þat noman þerto ne come
66 If enie were bileued alyue: & þat heued wiþ hem nome

A wyld wolf þer com sone: & to þe heued drouȝ
68 & þer vppe sat & wiste hit faste: aȝe cunde ynouȝ
For his cunde were betere to swolewe hit: he lickede hit ofte
& custe
70 & as he wolde his owe whelp: wiþ wylde best hit wiste
Sippe þo come cristene men: & in som poer were ibroȝt
72 þe holi bodi hi fonde sone: for hit nas ihud noȝt
Ac for hi ne fonde noȝt þat heued: aboute hi wende wide
74 & longe hi soȝte in eche stede: euerech in his side
¶ Hi ne miȝte hit finde for noþing: so þat hi come a day
76 Biside þulke þicke stede: þer as þe heued lay
Hi nuste noȝt þat hit was þer: þat heued bigan to grede
78 As hit among þe þornes lai: & þuse wordes sede
Al an englisch. her: her: her: as þeȝ hit were alyue
80 Þo þat folc ihurde þis: þider hi vrne blyue
Þat heued hi fonde in þulke stede: þer as hit him silue sede
82 Louerd ihered beo þi miȝte: þat þer was a fair dede
Þat heued hi bere to þe bodie: & sette hit euene þerto
84 & bere forþ boþe wiþ gret honour: as riȝt was to do
& þe wolf makede þo deol ynouȝ: þo hi þat heued forþbere
86 He ȝal & furde pitousliche: as þeȝ he witles were
He suede hem euere while he miȝte: ȝullinge wel sore
88 Atte laste he wende al aweie: þer me ne seȝ him no more
Hi ladde him to seint Edmundesbury: as me clepeþ þane toun
90 Þis holi man al isound: & leide him þeradoun
In noble schryne hi him brouȝte: as riȝt was to do
92 Þer he lyþ al hol & sound: as hi seoþ þat comeþ him to
For his bodi þat was so to-drawe: bicom al hol anon
94 As þe while he was alyue: boþe in flesch & bon
His heued as faste to þe bodie: as hit was euer er
96 In al his bodi þer nas wem: as menie man iseȝ þer
Bote as his heued was of ismyte: as oure louerd hit wolde
98 A smal red lyne al aboute: schyninge of golde
Wele whiche fair pelrynage: is þider forto fare
100 To honoury þat holi bodie: þat haþ ibeo þer so ȝare
Nou god for þe loue of seint Edmund: þat was so noble kyng
102 Grante ous þe ioye þat he is inne: after oure ending: Amen:

[*Seint Clement* follows, & then *Seinte Katerine.*]

XIX. ST. KATHERINE.

(Harl. MS. 2277, fol. 171.) [The & of the MS. is printed and.]

Seinte katerine of noble cunne: com bi olde dawe
Hire fader kyng hire moder quene: boþe of olde lawe
King Cost hire fader het: gret clerc þat maide was
þer nas non of þe soue artȝ: þat heo gret clerk of nas
5 þulke tyme heo was old: eiȝtene ȝer vneþe
And ic wene in þulke vlþe: heo was ibroȝt to deþe
Maxent þemperour: meche londe let crie
þat eche kinriche vnder him: come to Alisandrie
And of hem þat bileuede: to do stronge gywise
10 Ech man to do for his stat: to here god sacrefise
¶ þo alle þe men were þider icome: to don here lawe
Seinte katerine baldeliche: þiderward gan drawe
Heo stod bihalues and bihuld: here gydihede
Heo seȝ honoure þe maumetȝ: menie cristene men for drede
¶ þo hadde heo gret deol in hurte: heo blescede hire anon
16 And forþ anon to þemperour: baldeliche gan gon
Sire riche Emperour heo seide: þu ert noble and hende
þu scholdest þi poer and þi wit: to som wysdom wende
For þe folie ic sigge þat: þat ich iseo her do
20 So moche folc of furrene londe: þat þu clipest herto
¶ In gret ioye and wonder in ȝoure hurte: of þis temple ȝe doþ so
þat is ymaked of lym and ston: and of ȝoure maumetȝ also
Whi ne biholde ȝe þe heȝe temple: þerof ȝou wondri maie
Of heuene þat goþ aboute: aboue ȝou niȝt and daie
25 Of sonne and mone and of þe steires: þat fram þe est to þe west
Wendeþ and neuer werie beoþ: and neuer hi nabbeþ rest
Biþench þe bet and turn þi þoȝt: to som wysdom ic rede
And whan þyn owene inwit þe saiþ: þat no whar nis such a dede
Al-miȝtie god þu him holde: þat such wonder can make
30 To fore alle oþre honoure him: and ȝoure maumetȝ þu forsake
Mid oþer reisouns of clergie: þat maide preouede also
þat here godes noþing nere: þat hi aourede hem to
¶ þemperour stod and ne couþe: answerie in none wise
Him wondrede of hire fairhede: and of hire queyntise

35 Maide he seide abyd her wiþ: forto oure sacrefise
 And we schulle anoþer wiþ þe speke: ic oþer mie Justise
¶ Þis heʒe man after his sacrefise: ʒeode and sat in his tronc
 And al his folc aboute him: me brouʒte þis maide sone
 Maide, quaþ þis Emperour: þu þenchest gent and freo
40 Of what kyn ertou icome: wonder me þinʒþ of þo
¶ Sire Emperour, quaþ þis maide: ic wilnie swiþe lute
 Of mie kyn to telle þe: for hit were sinne and prute
 For in his boc þe wise man: Catoun saiþ also
 Þat man ne schal him silue preise: ne blame no þe mo
45 For so doþ foles þat beoþ idreiʒt: wiþ veyne glorie and prute
 Ac naþeles ic wole wiþ oute prute: of mi kyn telle a lute
¶ Ich am þe kinges douʒter Cost: þat þu wost wel which he is
 Hider ic com to speke wiþ ʒou: þat ʒe bileoueþ amis
 For me clepeþ him godes wiþ wrong: þat ane fot ne mowe go
50 Ne noman helpe in none wise: ne hem silue no þe mo
 Maide seide þemperour: if þat þis soþ were
 Al þe men of þe wordle were in gydihede: and þu one hem
              scholdest lere
 And me schal leoue alle men: and more hit wole beo note
 Þan a fol womman as þu ert: ʒoure bolt is sone ischote
55 Sire, quaþ þis maide þo : þeʒ þu lute telle of me
 As god mai þe resoun beo: of me as of þe
 For Emperour me saiþ þu ert: and ech man is also
 Þat mai hote and his men mote: nede his heste do
 Of bodi and soule þu ert ymaked: as þu miʒt þe silf iseo
60 Mid riʒte þi soule maister is: and þi bodi hire hync schal beo
 If þanne þi bodi maister is: and þi soule his hyne
 Aʒe cunde þanne hit is and þu worst: þerfore in helle pyne
 Þurf clergie þis holi maide: resouns makedc so quoynte
¶ Þat þemperour ne non of his ne couþe: answerie hire in none
              poynte
65 Maide he seide þu schalt abide: in warde her mid me
 And bityme ic wole fynde: þat scha answerie to þe
 Þis emperour sende anon: wel wide aboute his sonde
¶ To þe heʒiste clerkes: þat were in enie londe
 And bihet hem mede gret: to do a lute maistrie
70 To sustenie vp here lawe: þurf strenʒþe of clergie

So þat vyftie maistres come: þe gretteste þat me fond
As wide as me miȝte siche: o whar in enie lond
þemperour he seide anon: whi he after hem sende . : Retores
74 Aȝen a womman to desputi: þat al here lawe schende
¶ Nou is þis scide þat on: gret schame ic vnderstonde
An Emperour to siche aboute: so wide in eche londe
After maistres to plaidi: aȝen a ȝung wenche
Whan on of oure knaues miȝte: hire resouns sone aquenche
¶ Nai seide þemperour: heo is wisere þan ȝe wene
80 If ȝe mowe oȝt aȝen hire do: hit worþ sone isene
For ich wole bet þat ȝe hire ouercome: mid resouns a somme
                                                        wise
þan we hire mid strenȝþe makede: to do sacrefise
Let bringe hire forþ, quaþ þat on: and heo schal sigge anon
þat heo ne spac neuere wiþ wisere men: er heo fram ous gon
85 An angel to þis maide com: and bad hire noþing drede
For heo scholde hem alle ouercome: and to cristendom lede
þat þurf hire resouns hi scholde alle: afonge martirdom
¶ þo þis maide ihurde þis: gret ioye to hire heo nom
Wel baldeliche heo wende forþ: þo meste hire to com
90 Sire, heo seide to þemperour: ȝyfstou a wys dom
þus fole maistres of clergie: bringest and settest a benche
To desputie aȝe me one: þat nam bote a fol wenche
And if hi ouercomeþ me: þu bihotest hem grete prute
And mid strenȝþe makest me wiþ hem speke: and bihotest me lute
95 And þinȝþ me vnriȝt whan ic am: one aȝen hem alle
Ac ic wole whan god is myn help: afonge what me wole bifalle
¶ Sai me quene what ertou: þat o maister seide [primus retor
Aȝen oure clergie þenȝpstou speke: turn þi poȝt ic rede
þu saist þat god almiȝtie: deþ an vrþe þolede here
100 Ich wole preouie þat hit ne miȝte: beo soþ in none manere
Ho so deyeþ he ne maie: neuere to lyue come
Whan al þe vertu of his bodi: þurf deþ him is bynome
¶ If þu saist þat god is ded: þu ne miȝt libbe noȝt
104 If he þat lyf þe scholde ȝeue: is to deþe ibroȝt
¶ Nai seide þis holi maide: þu faillest of þyn art [Katerina
þe ne tit bote þu speke bet: of þe maistere no part

God hadde euere and euere schal: wiþ his godhede
And for loue of ous in oure flesch: he nom his manhede
Of two þinges he was ymaked: aiþer moste his cunde afonge
110 For in cunde of manhode ous to bugge: he þolede deþ stronge
Ac to bileue ded hit was: aȝe cunde of godhede
þerfore he aros from deþe to lyue: þo he hadde ido al his dede
þurf þe stronge deþ þat þurf Adam: we were on ibroȝt
þurf godhede ymengd in oure kunde: nede moste beo iboȝt
115 If þu wiþsaist þis reisoun: anoþer ic wole þe make
þat clerkes seide of ȝoure lawe: ȝe ne mowe noȝt forsake
Platon þe grete philosophe: þat was of ȝoure lawe
Seide þat god wolde iscourged beo: and eke to-drawe
Loke hou hit miȝte beo soþ: in oþer manere
120 Bote þat þe mochele god for ous: bicom a lute man here
As god balaham ȝoure prophete: þat heþene was also
¶ In his boc seide ȝe witeþ whar: if ȝe wolleþ loke þerto
þat þer scholde of Jacobes cunde: a sterre arise briȝte
* þat boþe kinges and Dukes scholde: bynyme here miȝte
125 þat was þat oure louerd wolde: of Jacobes cunde beo ibore
And ouercome alle þat euer were: sippe oþer bifore
¶ ȝut þreo kynges of ȝoure lawe: of þulke sterre þoȝte
For þe sterre þat god was ibore: and þerfore lok him broȝte
¶ þo þe maistres ihurde here speke: of so gret clergie
130 Ne couþe hi answerie noȝt o word: ac ȝiue hire þe maistrie
Certes sire, quaþ þis maistres: so gret cler non þer nis
þat to hire reisouns hire scholde answerie: for hi beoþ soþe iwis
We scoþ þat þe holi gost is mid hire: and in hire mouþe
We ne conne answerie hire noȝt: ne we ne þore þeȝ we couþe
135 þerfore bote oure lawe: þe betere we iseo
Alle we siggeþ mid one mouþe: icristened we wolleþ beo
¶ Hei traitours, quaþ þemperour: beo ȝe icome herto
Certes ȝe schulle to stronge deþe: alle beon ido
Amidde þe toun he het anon: forbrenne hem echone
140 And hi þane deþ for godes loue: afonge wiþoute mone
Ac mest reuþ hi hadde of alle: þat hi ifulled nere
þis maide hem gan to conforti: and of cristendom lere
And seide here stronge deþ: þat hi þolede þere
Scholde beo here cristendom: if hi stedefast were

¶ Þis maistres were igladed þo: gladliche forþ hi ȝeode
146 And nome þane deþ for godes loue: þat me wolde hem beode
Hi makede þe signe of þe croiȝ: and in þe fur me hem caste
Þo hi hadde longe ibrend: and ded were atte laste
And þat fur was aqueynt: al hol hi leye þere
150 Whyttere and fairere in heu: þan hi euere were
Þer nas non so lute wem: noȝt þe leste of hare here
Oþer of cloþ apeired were: hi leye wiþ faire chere
Þemperour let fecche anon: þat maide katerine
Haue reuþe, he seide, of þe silue: and schulde fram pyne
155 Haue reuþ of þi ȝunge bodi: þat so fair is and hende
Þu schalt libbe in gret noblei: if þu wolt þi þoȝt wende
In mie paleys ic wole þe make heȝist after mie quene
And after þi forme lete make: an ymage briȝt and schene
Ouergult and hire sette: amidde þe Cite
160 And ech man him schal honoure: for honour of þe
As me schal a god do: þu ne schalt mid al þi lore
So moche noblei biþenche: þat y þe nele do more
¶ Sire Emperour, quaþ þis maide: bilef þi fole þoȝt
Þu nast no more while to spille: þan to speke so embe noȝt
165 God almiȝtie-es spouse ic am: and al þi blandisinge
Ne þi tourmentz ne schulle ene: fram him myn hurte bringe
¶ Þemperour hire let stripe al naked: to a piler faste ibounde
And bete hire sore wiþ stronge scourges: and make hire harde
                                                        wounde
Þo hi seȝe þat hi ne miȝte: þermid turne hire þoȝt
170 In durke prisoun and in deope: sone heo was ibroȝt
Þat noman ne ȝaf hire mete ne drinke: for heo scholde for
                                                        hunger deye
Oþer turne hire þoȝt to here lawe: and beo ibroȝt out of treye
In prisoun þis maide lai: tuelf dayes and tuel niȝt
Þat heo noþer ne et ne dronk: ne seȝ non vrþlich liȝt
¶ A whyt colure fram heuene: com to hire eche dai
176 And broȝte hire fram heuene mete: as heo in prisoun lai
¶ A dai as þemperour: fram home was afare
Þemperice þoȝte on hire: and hadde of hire grete care
Of hire bed wel priueiliche: heo aros at midniȝt
And nom wiþ hire sire porphirie: þat was hire priuei kniȝt

180 Þo hi to prisoun come: hi seȝe þer gret liȝt
¶ Hem wondrede wharof hit were: þat þulke stede was so briȝt
Þo seȝen hi katerine: in þe prisones grounde
And an angel of heuene: smyrie hire wounde
¶ Þemperice cride anon: katerine þyn ore
185 Mi riȝte bileue tech þu me: y nele beo fol namore
Þe kniȝt als god sire porphirie: loude cride also
Þat moche folc þat þer aboute was: sone com þerto
Sire porfirie ful adoun to hire fet: and loude he gan to crie
Anon þis maide hem prechede of god: and of seinte Marie
190 So þat porphirie and þemperice: þurf þis maide þere
And tuo hondred knyȝtes ek: ibaptiȝed were
Oure louerd him silf com adoun siþþe: to seinte katerine
Lo here he seide ic hit am: for wham þu ert in pyne
Beo stedeuast in þi tourmentz: and ic wole beo mid þe
195 Þi sige is ymaked in heuene: þer þu schalt wone wiþ me
¶ Anoþer dai þis Emperour: after þis maide sende
Þat heo were for hunger ded: swiþe wel he wende
Þis maide was tofore him ibroȝt: swiþe fair and round
What he seide hou goþ þis: is heo ȝut hol and sound
200 Whar beoþ þis traitours: þat hire in prisoun wiste
Hi habbeþ ifed hire stilleliche: þat noman hit miste
Bi þe fei ic owe Mahoun: hi ne schulle nomore
He let nyme his Gailers: and turmenti sore
¶ Sire Emperour, quaþ þis maide: is þis god iugement
205 Gultelese men for mie gult: to bringe in such tourment
Ho þat me haþ þer ifed: he ne dredeþ þe noȝt
For an angel of heuene hit is: þat mete me haþ ibroȝt
Do me what tourmentz so þu wolt: and let hem quite gon
For certes of þat þu hem saist: gult nabbeþ hi non
¶ Hei, hende maide katerine: seide þemperour
211 Þench on þi noble gentrise: for of maidenes þu ert flour
Turn þi þoȝt and þu schalt beo: þemperesse peer
Heo ne schal habbe noȝt tofore þe: bote þat heo is mie fer
¶ Gode man, quaþ þis holi maide: þu spext al embe noȝt
215 Mid al þi poer þu ne schalt: fram ihesu wende mie þoȝt
Alle þe tourmentȝ þat þu miȝt þenche: of pynes swiþe stronge
Þu miȝt do me if þu wolt: iredi ic am to afonge

For noþing ne wilny ic so moche: as mie flesch and blod iwis
To ȝyue for mie lordes loue: þat for me ȝaf his
¶ Þo was þemperour so wroþ: þat he was neȝ iswowe
221 Four wheles of ire he let fulle: of rasours kene ynowe
And makede hem mid gynne turne aboute: þe tuei wheles vpward
And oþer tueie euene hem aȝene: in þoþer side doneward
Þat ho þat bituene were: in þoþer half ne scholde wende
225 Þat þe rasours nolde al his flesch: todrawe and torende
¶ Þo þis maide was: ido þeron to schende
Oure louerd crist fram heuene: an angel gan þider sende
Þis angel wiþ a drawe swerd: þis wheles alto-heu
And þe peces flowe aboute: as corn whan me hit seu
230 And smyte on þis liþere men: wel harde to þe grounde
Þat four þousend þer were aslawe: in a lute stounde
ȝe for gode þat was wel: þer hi miȝte lurne
To fiȝte aȝe ihesu crist: mid here false querne
To wende aboute here rasours: þe holie maide to drawe
235 Hi nemiȝte hit noȝt wel biliȝe: þat were ibroȝt of dawe
¶ Þo nuste þemperour noȝ what do: for deol ne for sore
Þemperesse nolde þo: hire stat hele nomore
Sire heo seide hou goþ þis: for godes loue þyn ore
Ich iseo þis maide is god: and of holi lore
240 ȝoure maumetȝ ic forsake: y ne bileue for no fere
Þo gan þemperour for wraþþe: loude ȝulle and rore
Him þoȝte he ne miȝte for noþing: fram ihesu hire þo wende
He het þat me scholde hire lede: to þe tounes ende
And hire breosten fram hire bodie: wiþ kene hokes rende
245 And after smyte of hire heued: hire þe more to schende
¶ Wiþ gode hurte þemperesse: þane deþ gan afonge
Þe quellers heo bad hiȝie faste: and n'abide noȝt to longe
Hi nome kene hokes of ire: and hire flesche to-gnowe
As me draweþ wiþ combes wolle: here breostes hi todrowe
250 Fram hire bodi mossel mele: and siþþe smyte of hire heued
Þe bodie for houndes hit scholde ete: vnbured hit was bileued
Ac porfirie burede a niȝt: þis holi bodi and god
¶ Þo þemperour þat bodi miste: he was wraþ and wod
He turmende menie men: þat nemiȝte hem noȝt skere
255 Þo seide porfirie anon: lo sire whar ic am here

Ich burede þyn holi wyf: þat was cristes make
And to ihesu crist ich haue also: al myn hurte itake
For no poer þat þu miȝt do: y nele him noȝt forsake
¶ Þo gan þemperour for sorewe: alle his lymes to schake
260 Mahoun, he seide, what schalt þis beo: hou schal ic nou do
Nou ic haue mie wyf forlore: and sire porfirie also
Whi nas porfirie al myn hurte: neltou me noȝt rede
¶ Þo wende þis oþer kniȝte forþ: and loude gonne grede
And we beoþ cristene bicome: euerechone hi sede
265 We nulleþ þane deþ for godes loue: leue for no drede
Þemperour þo gan drawe his her: and sore sike and grone
Mahoun he seide hou schal ic do: schal ic bileue alone
¶ Whi neltou raþere fecche mie men: after mie leoue wyue
Ac þeȝ þu nulle helpe me: y nelle forsake þe noȝt
270 Þis foles þat habbe forsake þe: to deþe schulle beo ibroȝt
He let nyme porfirie anon: and his felawes echone
And let smyte of here heuedes wiþ þe toun: as Mahounes fone
¶ Þo let he fecche katerine: Damaisele he seide
Ich wole if þu tourne wolt: forȝyue þe þi misdede
275 And wiþ gret noblei as Emperesse: oueral wiþ me þe lede
And alle þing ic wole do: also after þie rede
¶ Certes sire, quaþ þat maide: þis wordes beoþ for noȝt
Þu ne schalt me neuere fram him bringe: þat haþ me deore iboȝt
Do what þu wolt and haue ido: and bring þi wille to ende
280 For þu ne schalt mid no tourment: mie þoȝt fram ihesu crist
           wende
¶ Whar beo ȝe mie quellers: þemperour þo sede
Þis wicche ȝe schulle faste bynde: and wiþ-oute þe toun lede
And smyte of hire heued anon: and do þe gode dede
Þat heo ne bringe ous neuereft: in sorwe ne in drede
¶ Þo þis maide was ibroȝt: to sle wiþoute þe toun
286 To god heo makede hire preyere: a kneo heo sat adoun
Louerd, heo seide, grante me: þat ech man þat haueþ mone
In enie neode oþer anuy: in myne passione
Þat he mote to his wille: help habbe sone
290 Þo com our louerd silf and sede: ic granti þe þi bone
Com her forþ mie lemman: mie leoue spouse also
Heuene ȝat yopened is: þat þu schalt come to

           g

¶ þe quellere smot of hire heued: as þe men aboute stode
Whit mule þer orn out of þe wounde: and noȝt o drope of blode
295 þat was signe of maidenhod: þat þe mule out com
þat clene was wiþoute synne: and wiþoute swikedom
¶ An angel com and nom þe bodi: among alle þe manne
And bar hit to þe hul of synay: tuentie iourneyes þanne
And burede hit þer nobliche: and faire ynou also
300 þer ȝut to þis dai: þe bones beoþ ido
Of hire tumbe þer vrneþ ȝut: holi oylle wel blyue
Wher-þurf menie sik men is ibroȝt: to hele and to lyue
Wide a londe hit is ilad: ho so hit habbe mote
Noble relik hit is: sike men to habbe of bote
305 þreo hondred ȝer and twentie: after þat god was ibore
Imartred was þis holi maide: of wham we tolde bifore
Noon ihesu crist for þe suete loue: of seinte katerine
ȝyue ous þe ioye of heuene: and schulde ous fram helle pine.

XX. ST. ANDREW (follows St. Katherine).
(Harl. MS. 2277, fol. 174 b.)

Seint Andreu þ'apostle: was seint peteres broþer
2 Oure louerd silf to cristendom: him brouȝte and non oþer
For fischeres hi were boþe: and as hi fischede aday
4 Bi þe se oure louerd com: and here fisschin isay
Come, he seide, after me: and ic wole ȝou make
6 Manfischers, and þis opere: here nettes gonne forsake
And suede him mid þis word: and ne chose noȝt amis
8 Hem was so betere þan to pasken: in þe water iwis
While oure louerd an vrþe was: mid him boþe hi were
10 And siþþe hi wende wide aboute: cristendom to lere
¶ In þe lond of patras: seint Andreu siþþe com
12 He tournde þer wel faste: þat folc to cristendom
Churchen he rerde al aboute: and teiȝte me perto
14 Egeas wyf þe Iustise: he makede cristene also
þerfore he iustise was wroþ: and wende to patras
16 To þe cite in gret wraþþe: as seint andreu was

Cristene men þat he þer fond: sone he let take
18 To make hem wiþ his tourmentȝ: cristendom forsake
¶ Seint Andreu sone to him com: sire he seide nym ȝeme
20 Þu þat ert so gret iustise: seli men to deme
Þe heȝe Iustise of heuene: þu haddest neode to knowe
22 Þat in-to þe put of helle: þe schal deme wel lowe
¶ What ertou Andreu, quaþ þe Iustise: þat menie dai haþ igo
24 And idrawe men to þi false god: þu ne schalt neuereft mo
Ich drawe men, quaþ seint Andreu: to god þat soþ is
26 Ac wrecches and false ȝoure beoþ: and deue and dombe iwis
Whi saistou so, quaþ þe iustise: þu wost wel mid alle
28 Þat þu þerof loude lixt: hou miȝte hit so falle
For þe god þat þu of telst: þe gywes while nome
30 And slowe him as he worþie was: bi pur riȝt of dome
¶ Nai certes, quaþ seint Andreu: riȝt nas hit noȝt
32 Ac þurf godes wille ous to bugge: he was to deþe ibroȝt
¶ Hou miȝte hit beo, quaþ þe Iustise: þat his wille were þerto
34 For þe gywes him wiþ strenȝþe nome: and him slowe also
¶ Ich wot to soþe, quaþ Andreu: aȝen his wille hit nas
36 For ic was wiþ him þulke tyme: and iseȝ hou hit was
For er wel longe he tolde ous fore: hou hit scholde beo
38 Tyme and stede and euerech poynt: as we miȝte siþþe iseo
If þu woldest þat soþe ihure: and if þu riȝt vnderstode
40 Gret vertu ic wole þe telle: of þe suete holi rode
Ich wole herkny, quaþ þis oþer: and bote þu do after me
42 In þe Rode as þi louerd deide: ic wole sette þe
If ic doutede, quaþ þis oþer: y ne prechede þerof noȝt
44 Ac þeron is al myn hope: mie ioye and al mie þoȝt
Þis þu miȝt telle, quaþ þe Iustise: men þat luueþ þe
46 And for y nelle hit ileoue noȝt: oþer þing þu schalt telle me
Bote þu bileoue on oure godes: miȝtie of alle þinge
48 In þe Rode þat þu of spext: to deþe me schal þe bringe
Al miȝtie god, quaþ þis oþer: ich herie niȝt and day
50 Ich bileoue on him and herie wole: þe while ic speke may
¶ Þe Iustise was þo wroþ ynouȝ: seint Andreu he let caste
52 In strong prisoun and he lai þer: þe while hit ilaste
As þe iustise sat amorwe in his siȝe: to him he was ibroȝt
54 Andreu, he seide, ic hopie wel: þat þu beo bet biþoȝt

g 2

And þat þou habbe fram folie: þi poȝt itournd to niȝt
56 To libbe wiþ ous in ioye gret: and leue þin vnriȝt
¶ Þu lipere bern, quaþ seint Andreu: þu huntest aboute noȝt
58 Þe more tourment þu me dost: þe gladdere is mie poȝt
For þe mo tourmentȝ þat ich þolie for mie louerd: er þat ich deye
60 Þe more worþ mi ioye wiþ him: in þe ioye of heuene heye
Ich doutie more of þe pan of me: for mie pyne nele ileste
62 Bote o dai oþer tueye her: oþer þreo atte meste
Ac þe tourment þat þu schalt habbe: wharto þu schalt wende
64 In tuenti þousend ȝer ne mo: ne worþ ibroȝt to ende
Þo was þe Iustise swiþe wroþ: he het his men anon
66 Seint Andreu scourgi so: þo þat him oke ech bon
And sippe bynde him honde and fet: to þe Rode faste
68 Wiþ stronge corden for his lyf: scholde þe lengore ilaste
And he þe more in pyne beo: and þe more schede of his blode
70 Þe tourmentours wel ynouȝ: his heste vnderstode
Anon to þe bon hi beoten him furst: wiþ stronge scourges gode
72 In to þe vrþe hi pulte faste: þe tuei endes of þe Rode
¶ Þo seint Andreu iseȝ þe Rode: adoun he sat a kneo
74 Hail beo þu swete Rode he seide: swettest of alle treo
Þat þu wiþ mie louerdes lymes: ihalewed mostest beo
76 And of ȝymmes preciouses: wel glad ic þe iseo
And wel glad ic come to þe: wel glad afong þu me
78 For euere sippe mie louerdes deþ: ic habbe þe
Nym me nou al fram þis men: to mie louerd þu most me sende
80 For al myn hope and mi wil is: þurf þe to him wende
Þo he strupte of him silf his clopes: atte bigynnynge
82 And bitoc þe tourmentours: þat scholde him to depe bringe
Faste boþe fet and honde: to þe croiȝ hi bounde
84 Þe honden boþe aboue þe heued: þe fet toward to grounde
Þat folc com þicke aboute him: he gan to prechi faste
86 Tuei dayes and tuei niȝt: þe while his ly ilaste
Þat folc pretnede þe iustise: and þicke aboute him come
88 And wolde him alto-drawe anon: bote he him adoun nome
¶ Þe Iustise him wolde nyme adoun: seint Andrew him forbed
90 I nele noȝt he seide come adoun: er þan ic beo ded
For ic iseo mie swete louerd: and erwhile ic iseȝ
92 Þat abydeþ me til ic come: he is her wel neȝ

Whan me wolde him nyme adoun: he þoȝte he was anheȝ
94 No man ne miȝte him areche: for euere vpward he steȝ
Here armes whan hi vpward reiȝte: bicome as stif as treo
96 So gret liȝt þer com aboute him: þat noman ne miȝte him iseo
Hi hurde him and ne seȝe him noȝt: þat liȝt ileste iwis
98 Forte þe holi soule wende: þerwiþ to heuene blis
Þo þe soule was forþ iwend: and þe holi bodi bileuede þere
100 Maximille þe iustises wyf: and oþer þat þer were
Wiþ gret honor hi hit neme adoun: and to buringe bere
¶ ȝut nolde þe iustise ileoue noþing: þat he gan him lere
Þerfore amidde þe wey: as he homward wende
104 He ful ded to fore þe men: and his soule to helle sende
Ac seint Andreu was sippe: heȝe ilad iwis
106 To þe lond of Constantinople: þer as he ȝut is
Swiþe glad þat lond is: þat he euere þer com
108 In þisse manere seint Andreu: þolede martirdom.

[The Miracles of St. Andrew follow; and then St. Nicholas and his
Miracles.]

XXI. SEINTE LUCIE.
(Harl. MS. 2277, fol. 183.)

Seinte Lucie þe holi maide: in Cisille was ibore
Wel ȝung heo gan to scruie god: & bilcuede synne & hore
Dame Entice hire moder het: þat hire to womman brouȝte
4 Of such a child wel glad heo was: as heo wel ouȝte
¶ So þat hire moder cam an vuel: swiþe greuous & longe
For four ȝer heo hadde mid grete pyne: þe meneisoun[1] stronge
In fisciciens heo hadde ispend: moche del of hire gode
Ac þer nas non þat miȝte hire hele: þat heo ne bledde blode
So þat wel wide in þe lond: me tolde of seint Agace
10 Of miracles þat at hire schryue: come þurf godes grace
In þe Cite of Attenes: þer þis holi womman lay
þat folc wende þider þicke: boþe niȝ[t] & day

---

[1] *menisoun*, la dyssenterie, le flux de ventre.

Bi menie þousend to-gadere: of eche lond aboute
¶ Þo seinte Lucie isej al dai: of folc so gret route
15 Moder, heo seide, þu hauest an vuel: swiþe greuous mid alle
And we hureþ aldai miracles: of seint Agace falle
Go we forþ þider mid opere: to þe holi seint Agace
And þu schalt þer to hele come: þurf oure louerdes grace
¶ Nou was Lucie stilleliche: itournd to cristendom
20 Ac hire moder heþene was: and al þat folc þat heo of com
To an heþene man Lucie was: iwedded in junghede
Ac napeles clene maide he wa: wiþoute ech foldede
Hire moder heo nom stilleliche: & mid opere forþ wende
To þe tumbe of seint Agace: hire moder lyf to amende
25 Þo hi were þider icome: hi leuede a stounde þere
And hurde þe masse þer adai: wiþ opere þat þer were
So þat þe godspel: was adai as Lucie vnderstod
Of a womman þat while hadde: þe meneisoun of blod
And come & tuochede þe lappe: of oure louerdes cloþ ene
30 As he wende in grete presse: and was hol anon and clene
¶ Leoue moder, quaþ Lucie: if þu leouest in holi churche
And þe wordes of þe godspel: & wold þerafter wurche
Þurf tuochinge of seint Agace Tumbe: þu worst hol anon
As þe womman was þurf oure louerd: þat after him gan gon
35 Þo þat folc was al iwend: seinte Lucie com
To seinte Agace holie Tumbe: & hire moder wiþ hire nom
Þer hi leye in hire bedes: hi nolde þanne gon
So þat Lucie þis maide: werþ aslepe anon
Þat holi maide seint Agace: fram heuene to hire alijte
40 Wiþ gret cumpaignie of angles: hire croune schynde brijte
Lucie heo seide leoue soster: whi trauaillestou so
Whi biddestou me so jurne þing: þat þu þe siluc mijt do
Þi bileue þat is so god: helpeþ þi moder iwis
Anon þurf þe and þi godnisse: þi moder iheled is
45 And also as þis Cite: is moche ihered þurf me
Also schal þi contrai: beo ihered þurf þe
¶ Þo seinte Lucie awok: heo gan to quake sore
Moder heo seide þu ert hol: þe neþer drede namore
For þe loue of þe holi maide: þat þe haþ to hele ibrojt
50 Ne fonde þu neuere to bringe me: of mie clene þojt

Ne let neuere mie spouse in folie: mie maidenhod aspille
Ne let me noȝt leose þe longe lyf: for a lute fol wille
Ac al þat þu igranted hast: to mie spouse ȝyue mid me
54 Let me hit ȝyue pore men: moder ic bidde þe
¶ Þe moder þo heo hol was: god womman heo bicom
And þe douȝter þurf þe moder wille: al hire god nom
And delde among pore men: while hit ilaste oȝt
To him þat hire spouse was: þe teþinge was ibroȝt
¶ To seinte Lucie norice he wende: and eschte hire faste
60 What Lucie were so onbicome: hire god awei to caste
And whi heo dude hit so awei: and whoder heo dude hit bere
Þe norice quenteliche: ȝaf þerof answere
And seide to sulle heo haþ ifounde: dureworþe þing iwis
Þat is such a þousend worþ: as al hire þing is
65 Þe beste cheffare hit is ibouȝt: þat euere man to drouȝ
Woldestou enter þerinne in per: þu were riche ynouȝ
Þe cheffare was heueneriche: þat þis maide hadde ibouȝt
Þoþer wondrede of þanswere: and stod in gret þoȝt
So þat þoþer vnderȝat: þat heo cristine was
70 In grete wrappe he tolde fore: þe Iustise þat het pascas
¶ Lucie was wel sone ifet: and tofore þe iustise ibroȝt
Maide seide þe iustise: what hastou iþoȝt
Bilef he seide þi folie: ic rede in alle wise
And to oure godes as riȝt is: þu do sacrefise
¶ Ich haue, quaþ þis holi maide: al þis preo ȝer ido
76 Mi sacrefise to ihesu crist: and ȝut ic wole also
Al þat ic hadde ic haue isold: and itake am to his lore
And nou ic wole mie bodi perto take: whan þer nis bileued nomore
Ich ȝulde him vp al mie bodi: sire Iustise atfore þe
80 To spene ech lyme in his seruise: do what þu wolt bi me
¶ Nou ic wot, quaþ þe iustise: wharto þu tournest þi mod
For in hordom and in lechours: þu hast ispend þi god
And whan þu nast nomore to spene: þu saist in þi speche
Þeron þu wolt spene al þi bodi: and þerof þu dost þreche
85 For þu spext as an hore strong: whan þu wold forsake
Þi louerde to wham þu ert iwedded: & to lechours take
¶ Iwedded ic was to ihesu crist: þis holi maide tolde
Þo ic ifulled was: þulke weddin ic wolde holde

Ac to hordom þu woldest me bringe: whan þu woldest me make
90 Mi swete spouse ihesu crist: for enie oþer forsake
¶ Þu him schalt forsake, quaþ þe iustise: haddestou hit iswore
Oþer to comun bordel: beo ilad oþer ibore
And þer schal menie a moder child: go to licame
And ligge bi þe ech þat wole: in hordom & in schame
¶ Ne mai no womman, quaþ þis maide: of hire maidenhod beo ido
96 For no dede þat me do þat bodi: bote hire hurte beo þerto
For þe more aȝe mie wille: mie bodi defouled is
þe cleunere is mie maidenhod: & þe more mie mede iwis
¶ Þe Iustise let aboute wide: into al þe contrai crie
100 Þat alle þat wolde bi such a fair womman: do enie folie
¶ To hire come alle þat wolde: for alle heo scholde take
For in bordel heo scholde beo ido: & non of hem forsake
He het his men hire nyme faste: & to bordel hire lede anon
Alle þat miȝte neȝ hire come: hi droȝe faste echon
105 Hi schoue & droȝe al þat hi miȝte: hi nemiȝte hire a fot awinne
Ne make hire icche anne fot: of þe stede þat heo was inne
¶ Þo nome hi ropes stronge ynou: & to fet & honden tyde
And alle þat miȝte þer neȝ come: faste hi drowe & breide
A þousend men mid al here mayn: hire one gonne drawe
110 And euere heo lai stille as ston: hi nemiȝte hire enes wawe
¶ What, hou goþ þis, quaþ þis Iustise: what reisoun mai þis beo
Þat a þousend men nemowe hire enes: of þe stede teo
Sire Iustise, quaþ þis maide: þu huntest aboute noȝt
¶ For þeȝ þu haddest ȝut to hem: ten þousend ibroȝt
115 ȝut ic wolde beo for ȝou alle: ic fele bi me her
þe holi vers þat seint Dauid: saiþ in þe sauter
Þat a þousend men scholde in mie side falle: & to grounde beo
                                                          ibroȝt
And ten þousend in mie riȝt half: and me aprochi noȝt
Þerfore hit is al for noȝt: þat þu huntest aboute
120 God is strengere þan þu beo: þerfore nabbi no doute
¶ Þu ert wicche, quaþ þe Iustise: þerof me mot þe bringe
Mi clerkes & myne enchantours: bynyme schulle þi wicchinge
His clerkes he let bringe forþ: and his enchantours echone
And hi dude here enchantementz: aboute hire alone

¶ Þo hi hadde ido þat hi couþe: þat folc gan eft drawe
126 And euere heo lai stille as an hul: hi nemiȝte hire noȝt cues wawe
    Þo Iustise þo he iseȝ þis: for wrappe was wel neȝ wod
    Certes, he seide, hire wicchinge: ne schal do hire no god
¶ Stronge temes he let fecche: of Oxen menie on
130 And bringe þer þat maide was: and teye to hire echon
    He let hem prikie and harli faste: hi gonne to drawe & tuicche
    And euere lai þis maide stille: hi nemiȝte hire enes icche
    Wel ic wene wher me miȝte: þurf enie lasse drawinge
    Enie womman an vrþe nou: to suche folie bringe
135 Ac for alle meu nabbeþ noȝt: of oxen so god won
    Summe þeȝ hit fewe beo: mid lasse drawinge wolleþ gon
¶ Certes, quaþ þe iustise: oþer what we mote do
    Wiþ oþer þing we schulle hire welde: whan we ne mowe noȝt so
    Makieþ vpe þe hore as heo lyþ: whan we ne mowe iwynne hire
                                           henne
140 As strong fur as ȝe mowe make: þat heo al forbrenne
¶ Þo þis fur was strong ymaked: he sat amidde wel stille
    Ne miȝte þat fur hire enes brenne: ne harmie worþ a fille
    Þo nomen hi & walde pich: and brinston wel faste
    And vpe hire tendre bodi naked: al seoþinge gonne hit caste
145 And euere sat þis maide stille: hit ne greuede hire noþing
    Ac prechede euere wiþ glade hurte: of ihesu heuene king
¶ Þo nuste þe liþere Iustise: what he miȝte do more
    Whan he nemiȝte þis clene þing: ouercome mid his lore
    A scherp swerd he let & kene: þurf-out hire þrote do
150 To bynyme hire speche: and hire holi lyf also
    Þo heo was þurfout þe þrote ismyte: þe bet heo spac ynouȝ
    And prechede ȝurne of ihesu crist: & wel smere louȝ
¶ ȝe, heo seide, þat cristene beoþ: glade & bliþe ȝe beo
    Nou ne beo ȝe adrad of noþing: for gret ioye ic iseo
155 A ioyful teþinge ic ȝou telle: þat soþ is and les noȝt
    Þat riȝt nou is holi churche: in god pees ibroȝt   .
    For oure tuei wiþerewynes: þat habbeþ ibeo so ȝare
    Deoþ riȝt nou to noȝt ibroȝt: ȝe ne þore of hem noȝt care
    For þe liþere Dioclician: þat so moche harm haþ ido
160 Ipult is out of his kynedom: he ne comeþ neuere more þerto

And also Maximian: þat so liþer haþ ibeo
Riȝt nou deide in liþere depe: ȝe ne scholle hem nomore iseo
Þis glade teþinge ic ȝou bringe: þeȝ hi fur hunne beo
Ihered beo god þat ic moste þis dai alyue iseo
165 Ich wole ȝou non bitake ihesu crist: for ic wole fram ȝou wende
Bringeþ me oure louerdes flesch: for þat schal beo myn ende
Preostes wende forþ anon: and þat folc þat þer stod
And fette to þis holi maide: godes flesch and his blod
Þo heo hit hadde vnderfonge: and hire riȝtes also
170 And þe orcisouns were alle iseid: þat bifulle þerto
Wiþ þe laste word heo ȝaf þe gost: as hi amen sede
Angles al ȝare were: hire soule to heuene lede
Þer heo is wiþ ihesu crist: in ioye wiþouten ende
Nou god for þe loue of hire: ous lete þider wende: Amen.

> [Seint Thomas follows; then Seinte Anastace, Seint Stephene,
> Lucian, and Seint Iohan þ'ewangelist and his Miracles.]

XXII. ST. EDWARD.—A Miracle of St. John's.
(Harl. MS. 2277, fol. 195 b.)

Seint Edward þat was nou late: in Engelond owre kyng
Seint Iohan þ'ewangelist: louede þurf alle þing
Me ne scholde him noþing bidde: for loue of seint Iohan
Þat he miȝte do wiþoute blame: þat he ne grantede anon
5 A dai þer eom a pore man: wiþ wel dreorie mod
And bad him for seint Iohnes loue: þat he him ȝeue som god
Seint Edward biþoȝte him þo: he nadd neȝ him noþing
For to ȝyue þis pore man: wiþ a goldene ring
Þis ring he louede wel ynouȝ: and for þe loue of seint Iohan
10 He ȝaf him: ȝut þe pore man: & he ȝeode forþ anon
¶ Þer after ward sippe seint Iohan: com to a kniȝt of Engelond
As he was biȝunde see: auentoures to afonde
Wend, he seide, whan þu hom comest: to Edward ȝoure kyng
And sai him þat he for was[1] loue: he ȝaf þisne ring   [1 whose
15 Him sende here his ring aȝen: and þonkede him also
¶ Þo þis kniȝt com to Engelonde: his erande he gan do

Seint Edward ikneu þaue ring: and ynderstod anou
þat þe pouere man þat he him ȝaf: was þe louerd seint Iohn
þulke ring is ȝut at Westmynstre: for relik ido
20 As me scheweþ pelegrims: þer ofte comeþ þerto
Nou seint Iohn þ'ewangelist: if þi wille is
Bidde for ous þat we mote: come to heuene blis.

[Gilbert's and Beket's lives (Percy Society,) follow.]

XXIII. JUDAS ISCARIOT.
(Harl. MS. 2277.)

Incipit vita Iude cariote:

Iudas was a liþer brid: þat ihesu solde to Rode
2 Sum-what me maiȝ of him telle: ac lute of enie gode
For me ne schal no whar: of him wite bote ho so wole lie
4 Ruben was his fader icliped: his moder Thiborie
þis ruben in ierusalem: wonede mid his wyue
6 þeȝ here sone a schrewe were: hi were of gode lyue
As þis Ruben bi his wyf: aniȝt ileye hadde
8 Harde metinge his wyf mette: whar of he sore adradde
Hire poȝte heo hadde ibore a child: þat al þe wordle was loþ
10 And al þe wordle him a-cursede: and was wiþ him wroþ
And þat acursed he schulde euere beo: while þe wordle stode
12 And al his cun me cursie wolde: for such a liþer vode
þis wyf was wel sore adrad: to hire louerd heo tolde anon
14 ȝe, he seide, hit is þe mase: and also hit wole gon
Wel ic wot, quaþ þis gode wyf: if ic am mid childe
16 þat hit is tokning of a bern: liþer and vnmylde
þis wyf rekenede þe tyme: and swiþe heo gan iwite
18 And yfele þat he was mid childe: and þulke tyme biȝite
Sorie heo was and sore of drad: hire freondes heo tolde fore
20 Hi nuste what hem was to done: þo þat child was ibore
Loþ hem was to murþrie: here flesch and here blod
22 And loþ a bern to norischie: so liþer and vngod
¶ So þat he seȝe: a barayl atte laste
24 þer inne hi dude þis liþer child: and amidde þe see hit caste

Þe see him hurlede vp and doun: as a liþer clot
26 Siþþe hit caste him alond: vpe þe yle of Cariot
Þerfore Iudas cariot: euere icleped he was
28 For in þe yle of Cariot: ifonde he was bi cas
Þe king and þe quene of þe lond: togadere were longe
30 Ac hi no child for no þing: bituene hem nemiȝte afonge
So þat þe quene ȝeode adai: and pleide bi þe stronde
32 In þe yle of Cariot: þe liþere bern heo fonde
Þo heo seȝ hit was a child: manlich and fair
34 Glad heo was and hopede: of him to habbe an heire
Heo let hit witie in preuite: mid childe heo hire makede
36 Þe king and al þe lond also: þerof were wel glade
Sone þe tyme heo nom forþ: þat þe child scholde beon ibore
38 Me schowede forþ þe liþere bern: glad was þe king þerfore
¶ Þo he seȝ hit fair and hende: he let hit nemne Iudas
40 Hit nis noȝt al god þat is fair: isene per hit was
Þat child was ido in gode warde: as kinges sone scholde
42 Sone hit ful perafterward: as oure louerd hit wolde
Þat þe quene mid childe was: of hir louerd biȝite
44 Glad were boþe king and quene: þo hi hit miȝte wite
So þat heo hadde a knaue child: þat fair and gentyl was
46 Þe quene vpe him hire hurte dude: and þe lasse vpe Iudas
¶ Þe children waxe swiþe wel: Iudas bigan sone
48 To do liþere and qued ouer al: as him was to done
Children þat he com to: he wolde smyte and bete
50 And breke here armes and here heued: and þat god lete
To þe kinges sone he hadde enuie: for he was iloued more
52 Of þe quene þan he were: hit of þoȝte him sore
Þerfore he alto-beot þat child: whan he miȝte hit one wite
54 Ac þe quene him beot sore aȝen: whan heo hit miȝte vnderȝite
Ac perfore nolde he neuere bileue: for neuere ichasted he nas
56 So þat þe quene vpbreid adai: þat he fyndling was
After þulke tyme þis liþere þing: þat child haſede ynouȝ
58 He awaitede his tyme wel: and priueliche hit slouȝ
¶ Þo ne þerste he no leng abide: leste he hadde his dom
60 Stilleliche he wende to ierusalem: me nuste whar he bicom
Þer was pilatus: of þe lond Iustise
62 Þis Iudas anon vnder him: leuede in seruise

    So wel he louede him anon: þat styward he him made
64 Of al his þing, and het his men: do þat he bade
    Þat o schrewe wiþ þat oþer: maister was as riȝt is
66 For ech þing loueþ his iliche: so saiþ þe boc iwys
    For þeȝ in al a contray: bote tueie schrewes nere
68 ȝut hi wolde felawes beo: if he to-gadere were
¶ So þat þis tuei schrewen: þe louerd and þe stiward
70 Adai ȝeode alone pleye: vnder an orchard
    Swiþe faire aples: pilatus iseȝ þerinne
72 Clembe ouer he bad Iudas: and some þerof iwinne
    Iudas brac þe ȝard anon: and sone was in ibroȝt
74 His owe fader orchard hit was: ac napeles he nuste hit noȝt
    Com þe gode man þat was his fader: and eschte him what he were
76 And bi was leue he brac his ȝard: and what he dude þer
    Iudas seide ic wole her beo: maugre þi teþ bifore
78 And of þis applen habbe and bere: þeȝ þu hit haddest iswore
¶ Þis gode man was anuyed: of þis liþer answere
80 Þe schrewe he misdude aȝen: he nemiȝte noleng forbere
    So þat hi neme aiþer oþer bi þe top: and makede stronge wounde
82 Þe schrewe was strengere þan his fader: and broȝte him sone to
                                                        g[r]unde
    So þat he smot him wiþ a ston: bihynde in þe pate
84 Þat al þe sculle to-daschte: þe brayn ful out þerate
    So þat he slouȝ his owe fader: and þo me miȝte wite
86 Þat his moder mette of him soþ: þo he was biȝite
    ȝut were his fader betere: habbe ibroȝt him of dawe
88 As sone as he was ibore: þan he hadde him aslawe
    Of þ'aplen þat þe schrewe whan: and of þe peren also
90 And bar pilatus and tolde him: hou he hadde ido
¶ Pilatus wende anoþer daie: to þe gode manes house
92 And ȝaf Iudas al his god: and makede him wedden his spouse
    For he was maister & Iustise: he miȝte do vnriȝt ynouȝ
94 Þo weddede þe schrewe his owe moder: and his fader aslouȝ
¶ As þis gode wyf lai aniȝt: bi hire schrewe louerd þere
96 Heo gan to sike swiþe sore: he eschte whi hit were
¶ Certes, sire, quaþ þis wyf: wel aniȝte ic sike sore
98 Wo and sorewe me comeþ to: none womman more

Glad ne bliþe ne worþe ic neuer: whan ic me biþenche
100 For ic nadde neuere sone bote on: and him ic let adrenche
Sippe ic fond mie louerd aslawe: y not in whiche wise
102 And myn vnþonkes ic am iwedded: wiþ strengþe of þe iustise
Þo Iudas ihurde þis: sorie he was ynouȝ
104 Certes, he seide, ic am þi sone: and mi fader ic aslouȝ
Þo was þis gode wyf soriere: þan heo euere were
106 Sone, heo seide, what mowe we do: þat we ischryue nere
¶ Iudas ihurde of oure louerd telle: þat he an vrþe ȝeode
108 Þat he halp menie man: in siknesse and in neode
Þurf his moder red to schrifte: to oure louerd he wende
110 Repentant he was and wilnede: his lyf to amende
So þat he suede oure louerd longe: to wite of his manere
112 Oure louerd him makede his disciple: to beo apostles ifere
Sippe oure louerd him makede apostle: to fondi his mod
114 And sippe pursberer of his pans: to spene al his god   .
For meni men ȝyue oure louerd god: þat were of gode þoȝt
116 To susteynie his apostles: oþer nadde he noȝt
Ac þo Iudas wiþinne was: and his miȝte founde
118 Of oure louerdes god þat he wiste: he stal al to grounde
Whan he miȝte of eche þing: þe teoþing he wolde stele
120 A schrewe he was al his lyf: y ne maie no leng hele
Wel wiste oure louerd þas: and al his liþer dede
122 Ac naþeles he moste fulfille: þat þe prophetes sede
¶ Seinte Marie Magdaleyne: to oure louerd com
124 To-fore his swete passioun: and moche oignement wiþ hire nom
His fet heo wosch wiþ hire teres: and wipede wiþ hire her
126 Wiþ þis swete oignement: heo smired oure louerd þer
Iudas of þoȝte þis ille: for hit moche worþ was
128 And seide þat hit was vuele ido: þat hit isold nas
Þreo hondred pans hit was worþ: and þermide me miȝte fille
130 Menie pore man afingred: ho so hit moste sille
Þat he seide for he wolde: if þe boxes hadde ibeon isolde
132 Habbe ispend and to him: þe teoþing iholde
Þe teoþing þerof was þrettie pans: sore him of-þoȝte þerfore
134 Þat so menie pans of his þeofþe: scholde fram him beo ilore
Þerfore oure louerd for þrettie pans: he solde mid vnriȝte
136 Þat he þe teoþing of þulke boxes: to him keouerie miȝte

Him suede eche liþeri þewe: for he louede barct and stryf
138 He was strong þeof and man quellere: and also he endede his lyfe
And suche men schulde anhonge beo: and þo noman hit nolde do
140 Him silf he heng vp a treo: for such deþ he scholde to
His wombe to-berste amidde atuo: þo he schulde deye
142 His gvttes fulle to grounde: menie men hit iseye
þer wende out a liþer gost: atte mouþ hit nemiȝte
144 For he custe er oure louerd: þerwiþ mid vnriȝte
Nou swete louerd þat þurf Iudas: isold wer to þe treo
146 Schuld ous fram þe liþere stede: þer we weneþ þat he beo: Amen.

XXIV. PILATE.
(Harl. MS. 2277.)

Pilatus was a liþer man: and com of liþer more
Bituene a king and a fol wonman: in spousbreche ibore
þe king Tirus was an heȝ man: and of grete fame
Bi a melewardes douȝter he lai: Pila was hire name
5 And biȝat on hire vnder þe querne: þe liþere bern bi cas
þe meleward þat hire fader was: atus ihote was
For þe douȝter þat het Pile: and þe fader Atus
Of here beire name me makede anne: and clipede him pilatus
þe child wax and wel iþeȝ: and þo hit was of þreo ȝere
10 þe moder hit sende to his fader: for he was of gret poer
þe king hit louede swiþe wel: and let hit wel lere
· Bi þe quene he hadde anoþer child: boþe in one ȝere
þat child þat was riȝt biȝute: and pilatus also
To norisschi and to lere wel: to-gadere were ido
15 As hi wexe hi toppede ofte: þer nas bituene hem no loue
Ac þat child riȝt biȝute: euer was aboue
¶ Pilatus awaitede his poynt: and þoȝte to ȝulde his while
He stal adai stilleliche: and slouȝ þat child wiþ gyle
¶ þo þe king þis ihurde: he was sorie ynouȝ
20 He nuste what do wiþ þe schrewe: þat his riȝt sone so slouȝ
He þoȝte if he hit slowe: þat hit were doble wo
And þat he nemiȝte bliþe beo: whan he him iseȝe owhar go

¶ Þ'emperour to him sende: after truage of his londe
Þe king him biþoȝte hou he miȝte best: paye him of his sonde
25 Pilatus he sende þider: as hit were in ostage
For þ'emperour him scholde sle: whan him faillede of his truage
He sende him word þat he nadde: children bote him on
And for al þe god alyue: he nolde his lyf forgon
And bote he at his daye: sende his truage
30 Hi his sone do what he wolde: as riȝt is bi ostage
¶ Þemperour him louede moche: ac of his schreuhede nuste he noȝt
Þe kinges sone of france ek: was in hostage þider ibroȝt
He was bet biloued þan pilatus: þeȝ hi felawes were
And for þat on was god and þat oþer schrewe: gode felawes
neuere hi nere
35 Þe schrewe awaitede wel his tyme: for he was fel ynouȝ
Bituene hem silue stilleliche: his felawe he slouȝ
Þemperour him nom anon: he nuste what wiþ him do
He wolde him sle, ac his consail: ne ȝaf him noȝt þerto
And seide he was toward: swiþe hardie man mid alle
40 Of a such man miȝte moche god: in to al þe contray bifalle
¶ Schulle we lete quaþ þ'emperour: a manquellere alyue go
Sire sire quaþ þis oþer: þu hast menie a fo
And such man if he bileueþ forþ: gret god maie þe do
And if lawe of londe nele: þat þu him lete so go
45 Wel þu wost þat in þe yle of Ponce: schrewen þer beoþ ynowe
Þer com neuere Iustise: þat hi sone ne slowe
Þerfore þu miȝt him sende þider: to beo Iustise of þulke yle
And bote he beo queyntere þan enie oþer: he ne scapeþ noȝt a
gyle
And if he þat lond chasteþ wel: and bringeþ vnder fote
50 He worþ man wiþoute peer: if he duri mote
¶ Þo pilatus was þider isend: he wiste wel þe gyle
And þe maner enquerede of þe lond: þo he cam in to þe yle
He spac faire and mylde: and was euere stille
Wiþ fair speche and quentise: he hadde of hem his wille
55 Hi dude al after his wille: and hulde him euere Iustise
Þer nemiȝte so neuere non: beo in none wise
¶ Þo þ'emperour ihurde þat he miȝte: þat liþere folc so þewe
He ne huld non so queynte man: as he huld þe schrewe

Of his queyntise me spac wide: bi daye and bi nyȝte
60 Hou he amaistrede þe yle of ponce: as neuere no man ne miȝte
60* For he amaistrede and ascapede: þe yle of ponce so wel
Ponce pilatus me him clipeþ: in crede and godspel
¶ Þe king herodes þat was: þo king bi kynde
Of þe lond of ierusalem: and of Galilee and ynde
Of pilatus he hurde ynouȝ: of his wit and his queyntise
65 Glad and bliþe he wolde beo: to habbe such a Iustise
Noble ȝiftes he him ȝaf: and fondede in alle wise
If he wolde out of þat lond: and leue in his seruise
So þat pilatus com to him: and such consail hi toke
Þat more þan half his kynedom: he tok him to loke
70 To beo maister of ierusalem: and also of ynde
In his owe lond he athuld: Galilee of his kynde
Þo pilatus hadde þer longe: þe maistrie fur and nher
He gan to cuþe what he was: þo he seȝ his poer
For ech schrewe wole abide his tyme: to cuþe his felonie
75 He gaderede tresour and oþer god: ynouȝ in his baillie
And wende to Cezar þemperour: þat was maister ouer þe kinge
Of tresour and oþer god ynouȝ: largeliche he gan him briuge
And ȝaf him wiþ þat he moste: þe baillie holde pere
Of him as he dude of herodes: his kynedom þeȝ hit were
¶ Þemperour þat was þe kinges louerd: sone him biþoȝte
81 And gladliche nom þe tresour: þat pilatus him broȝte
And grantede pilatus al þat lond: to holde bi maistrie
Þat he huld er of herodes: þer was gret trecherie
He wende aȝe to ierusalem: and to ynde also
85 As louerd he dude alle his hestes: þo he cam þerto
Herodes sende after him: to accountie after wille
Pilatus spac þurf þemperour: and ne ȝaf noȝt worþ afille
Þo herodes iseȝ þe trecherie: and þe liþere falshede
He huld him bitrayd þurf felonie: he nuste what to rede
90 Þo he seȝ þat he ne miȝte: vndo þemperoures dede
Pilatus he acursede ilome: for his liþere falshede
And þo he ne miȝte him oþer do: bote wraþþe him bar mid riȝte
So gret wraþþe hem was bituene: þat no tonge hit telle ne miȝte
Þe wraþþe ilaste forte oure louerd: to deþe scholde go
95 Ac for aiþer to oþer sende: acorded hi were þo

h

¶ Þe while pilatus in his lond: louerd and sire was
Iudas þat oure louerd solde: to him com bi cas
His steward he him makede anou: gode freond hi were
For tuei schrewen wolleþ freond beo: þeȝ no mo men nere
100 Iudas was þer his steward: forte he his fader aslouȝ
And forte he wedde his owe moder: wiþ grete strenȝþe and wouȝ
¶ Suþþe god was ynome: and schulde beo to deþe ido
Pilatus þurf þe gywene wille: him demde þerto
For þe gywes in ierusalem: in here poer him nome
105 Þerfore hi ne miȝte him quelle noȝt: bote þurf his dome
Longe after þat he was ded: he repentede him ilome
He ne þerste noȝt for þemperour: þerfore come at Rome
Ac euere him huld at Ierusalem: among þe gywes faste
Ac sore he dradde þemperour: þat he him slowe atte laste
110 Longe hit ful þerafterward: þat þemperour was sek
In strong vuele and wel long: þat he nas noman ilek
Leches he let fecche wide: ac him ne miȝte hele non
So þat his o messager: to ierusalem com gon
Longe and wide he eschte þer: after sum god leche
115 To a womman he com þat het veronike: þat heo scholde him to
                 sum on teche
Allas, quaþ þe womman: if þu haddest hider igon
Þe while þe prophete her was: þi wille hadde beo idon
¶ A whar, quaþ þe messager þo: þe prophete beo bicome
Certes, quaþ veronike: þe gywes him habbeþ ynome
120 To deþe him hi brouȝte on þe rode: þurf pilatus dome
Þerfore he ne þerste neuer eft: bifore ȝou come at Rome
Þe while þe prophete her was: gret ioye ic hadde midde alle
Him to neȝ beo: if hit miȝte so bifalle
And þo y ne miȝte neȝ him beo: ic him bad a bone
125 Þat ich miȝte ofte his forme iseo: he me grantede sone
¶ Mi keuerchief ic him bitok: and he wond hit aboute his face
Þat ech man miȝte wel iseo: his miȝte and his grace
For þer he leuede his owe forme: þat in his face was
In ech poynt þo he hit me tok: þat no defaute þer nas
130 Þulke forme is me bileued: þat ich miȝte igladed beo
Þurf þe siȝt þat is him so iliche: whan y ne mai him silue iseo
Hadde þi louerd þemperour: þe forme iseȝe ene
Ich wot he were hol anon: and of his vuel clene

Dame, mercie, quaþ þe messager: maie þulke ymage oʒt
135 For enie gold oþer siluer [1]: to þemperour beo ibroʒt
Þat nis noʒt, quaþ þis wyf: for al his gold iwis
Bugge ne miʒte þe leste hurne: þat þeron is
Ac ic wole, quaþ þe wyfe: wiþ þe to him wende
If oure louerd him wole bote: þurf his forme him sende
¶ Heo wende forþ wiþ þis messager: and þo heo com to Rome
141 Þemperour hi tolde al þis: þo hi to him come
¶ Anon þo he þe ymage iseʒ: he was ol anon
He honourede wel veronike: heo ne moste fram him gon
Þe ymage he athuld þat hit ne com: neuereft out of Rome
145 In seint peteres churche hit is: as men iseoþ ilome
¶ Þo eschte he whar oure louerd were: and whar he siþþe bicome
Veronike him seide hou þe gywes: to stronge deþe him nome
And hou pilatus his Iustise: þe dom ʒaf þerto
¶ Ou liþere man, quaþ þemperour: haþ he itake on so
150 Assentede he to þe gywes: and nas noʒt of here lawe
Ich wole if ic maie to him come: anhonge him oþer todrawe
Allas þulke holi man: þat he let bringe of dawe
Ich wot þe gywes beoþ wel liþer: hi wolde beo þerof fawe
In faire manere he let sende: after pilatus sone
155 Þat he come to him as to his louerd: as riʒt was to done
Ac pilatus sende ane lettre: to his louerd er
Þat he forʒeue him his wraþþe: þat he to him ber
And þat he was gulteles of þe deþ: þat me vpe him sede
And þat þe gywes him slowe: al wiþoute his rede
160 Ac a strong tempest in þe see: his messager gan dryue
In-to þe lond of galilee: and þer he gan ariue
Ac vaspasian þat was þer maister: þe messager faste nom
So þat neʒ þemperour: þe messager neuere ne com
¶ Þo þemperoures messager: to pilatus was icome
165 And pilatus hadde of him: his erande ynome
He wende þat his owe messager: to þemperour hadde iwend
And þat he hadde forʒeue him his wraþþe: and after him isend
Oure louerdes curtel he dude on: þat he wiste euer wel
Þat vnsued was of þred: as hit saiþ in þe godspel

---

[1] siluer: is repeated in the MS.

170 Wiþ wel glade chere: he wende to þemperour
And grette him þo he com him to: wiþ wel gret honoure
¶ So wroþ wiþ noman vnder sonne: þemperour nas bifore
As he wiþ pilatus was: for his deþ he hadde iswore
And for he hadde oure lordes curtel: on whan he bifore him com
175 His hurte was al swaged: wiþ grete ioie he him nom
He makede mid him al þe ioye: þat man miȝte mid oþer do
For virtu of þe holi curtel: and his men also
Anon so he was out of his siȝt: his oþ he swor anon
Þat to stronge depe he wolde him bringe: if he miȝte him ofgon
180 Ac gret ioye he makede mid alle: whan he to him com
And euere whan he fram him was: he iuggede him stronge dom
Þis maner ileste longe: þat alle þat ihurde þis cas
Wondrede moche of þemperour: þat he vnstable was
So atte laste þis pilatus: as oure louerde hit wolde
185 His curtel he stripte of bi cas: as he neuere ne scholde
And com so bifore þemperour: and he anon him nom
He swor his more oþ anon: þat he to wroþere hele þer com
Sai, he seide, þu wrecche man: sai what hastou ido
Slowe þu þe holi prophete: to wroþere hele dudestou so
¶ Certes sire, quaþ pilatus: y ne dude him noȝt to depe
191 Beo iknowe, quaþ þemperour: for þu miȝt as eþe
Bote þe lipere gywes, quaþ pilatus: to þe depe him broȝte
Wiþoute þe, quaþ þemperour: neuere such þing hi ne wroȝte
¶ Certes sire, quaþ pilatus: y ne maie noȝt ofsake þis
195 Þat y ne demde him to depe: ac ic moste nede iwis
For þenqueste vpe him seide: þat he destruyde oure lawe
And lawe ȝifþ þat alle suche: me scholde bringe of dawe
And ic þer þat þi iustise was: þurf þin heste and þi rede
Moste nede ȝyue þe dom: whan þenqueste sede
¶ Whan þu vnderȝete, quaþ þemperour: þe gywene falshede
201 Whi naddestou ispeke þer aȝe: and desturbed þe lipere dede
God hit wot, quaþ pilatus: and ierusalem also
Þat ic was þer aȝen bi mie miȝte: þat he nere to depe ido
Ac hi were vpe him alle so faste: þat me ne miȝt mid no lawe
205 Whan þenqueste passede: bote he were ibroȝt of dawe
¶ If þu ne miȝtest mid riȝte him sauue: þemperour þo sede
Hou þerstestou wiþoute mie red: do such a lipere dede

Certes sire, quaþ pilatus: y ne maie wiþsigge noȝt
þat ic þerof ne misdude: in gulte ic am ibroȝt
210 And me schal bi þe, quaþ þemperour: as bi a gultie man do
þu schalt passi bi iugement: for þu toke on so
In strong prisoun and swiþe durk: sone he let him caste
þat he ne seȝ fot ne honde: he let him bynde faste
So longe he laie in prisoun: in hunger and in pyne
215 þat his lymes clonge awei: his bodie gan al fordwyne
He hadde leouere his deþ þeran: his lymes so forclonge to noȝte
So hi dude alle tofore here deþ: þat oure louerde to deþe broȝte
¶ A dai as þe gailer: into prisoun com
Pilatus cride so dulfulliche: þat gret deol to him he nom
220 "Haue reuþe of me, sire, he seide: for þin owe gentrice
Wel þu wost knyȝt ic am: and while was heȝ Iustice
And nou ic her clynge awei: and no siȝt iseo wiþ eye
Let me enes per charite: iseo siȝt er ic deye"
þe gayler hadde reuþe of him: such man he hadde ibeo
225 And of prisoun ladde him out: þe wordle forto seo
¶ þo pilatus com to liȝte: as þe boc haþ itold
And iseȝ his bodie alforswarted: his hurte ful ful cold
"Allas he seide þis dai abide: þat ich euere com in liȝt ·
Sire Renald for þi curteisie: grante me ane bone
230 ȝif me an appel to ete: for ic hit maie do sone"
þe gayler him tok an appel: he seide hit was vnriȝt
Vnpared an appel take: an heȝ man oþer a kniȝt
Such wrecche as ic nou am: ic was while heȝ Iustise
Len me a knyf þis appel to parie: for þin owe gentrise
235 þo þe gayler him tok a knyfe: him silue he slouȝ anon
And smot him deope in þe bodie: and lai ded as a ston
þo þe teþinge com to þemperour: þat bodie he let take
And caste hit wiþoute þe toun: among olde walles forsake
þer ne wende noman þerforþ: aboute in none side
240 þat he nas lame oþer wod: oþer sum auentoure him gan bitide
þer was þundre and liȝtninge: and gret tempest þer aboute
þat hi were witles and adrad: þat hi ne þerste no whar at-route
So þat þemperour let take: þe wrecche licame atte laste
And bere hit to þe watere of tybre: and þerinne hit caste

245 Þo com þer a gret tempest: þat þer aboute wel wide
     Þat schipes adreynte þere menie on: þer aboute in eche side
   ¶ Al þe contray þer aboute hem dradde: and nom hem to rede
     And in-to a watere fur fram men: þis licame gonne lede
     Bituene hulles and wyldernisse: and þerinne hi him caste
250 Þe þundre smot þer anon: and þe liʒtinge wel faste
     Þat bodie flet vp and doun: icast her and þere
     Mid weder and tempest of water: þat ech man hadde fere
     Amidde þe water þer stod a roche: þo þe licame was þer neʒ
     Þe roche clef amidde atuo: as al þat folc iseʒ
255 And as an arcwe schet of a bwe: þat bodie schet þerinne
     Þe roche schet to-gadere anon: þo þat bodie was wiþ-inne
     And þe wrecche bodie þer lyþ: ʒut to þis day
     Moche wo ʒut þer is þer aboute: as me iseo maie
     Þus pilatus endede his lyf: as he wel wel worþe was
260 God schulde ech cristenene man: fram so dulful cas. Amen.

        hic finiuntur gesta. Maledictorum. Inde et Pilati.

        ────────

              [End of the MS. Harl. 2277.]

        ──────────────

              XXV. A SONG OF MERCI.
     (Duplicate of the Vernon MS., Brit. Mus. Additional MS. 22,283, fol. 128, back,
                        col. 2.)

        Bi west. vnder a wilde* wode syde.
     2 In a launde. þer i. was lent.
        Wlanke deor. on grounde gan glide.
     4 And lyouns raunpyng. vppon bente.
        Beores. woluus. with mouþes wide.
     6 Þe smale bestes¹. þei al to-rent.
        Þer haukes vnto þare² pray þei hyde.
     8 Of whuche. to on. i. toke goode³ tent.

     * The Bodleian copy generally has *y* where the Brit. Mus. one has *i*,
     —as in wylde and glyde, line 3,—and ʒt for the Br. Mus. ht; also a
     final *e* after the *t* of rent, tent, hent, ment, l. 6, 7, 9, 11. It has also more
     capitals for the nouns; and more metrical points, which are printed here.
        ¹ Beestes.   ² heore.   ³ tok god.

A merlyon. a brid hedde[1] hent.

10 And in hir[2] foot. heo gan hit bringe.

Hit couþe not speke. but þus hit ment.

12 How merci passeþ alle þinge.

Merci was in þat. bryddes[3] Muvnde.

14 But þerof kneuӡ. þe hauk non.

For in hire foot. he[a] gan hit bynde.

16 And heolde hit stille. as eni ston.

Heo dud after. þe cours of kynde.

18 And fleiӡ in-to a treo anon.

þorw kynde. þe brid gan Merci fynde.

20 For on þe morwe. heo let hit gon.

Ful stille .i. stod. my self al on.

22 To herken. how þat bryd gan synge

A-wey wol wende. boþe murthe and moon.

24 And Merci passeþ. strengþe and riht.

Mony a wyse. seo we may.

26 God ordeynet[4] Merci. most of miht.

To beo a-boue. his werkes ay.

28 Whou deore Ihesu. schal beo[5] diht.

To demen vs. at domes day.

30 Vr sunne wol beo. so muche in siht.

We schul not wite. what we schul say.

32 Ful fresliche[6]. riht wol vs affray.

And blame vs for. vr mislyuyng.

34 þen dar non persone[7]. for vs to pray.

But Merci. passeþ alle þinge[8].

¶ Riht wolde sle vs. for vr sunne[9].

Miht wol don. execucion.

38 And rihtwis god. þenne[10] wol bigynne.

Forto[11] reherse vs. þis resoun.

40 I made þe Mon. ӡif þat þou mynne.

Of feture. liche. myn owne fasoun.

42 And after crepte. in-to þi kynne.

And for þe suffred passioun.

---

[1] had.   [2] hire.   [3] Briddes.   [a] heo.   [4] ordeyned.   [5] be.   [6] fersliche.
[7] p'se.   [8] þing.   [9] synne.   [10] Rihtwyse god. þen.   [11] Forte.

44 Of þornes kene. þeu was þe croun.
     Ful scharpe. vppon. myn hed standyng.
46 Myn herte [12] blood. ran from me doun.
     And i. forʒaf þe. alle þinge [1].
48 Myn herte [12] blood. for þe gan blede.
     To buye þe. from þe fendes blake [2].
50 And i. forʒaf þe. þi mysdede.
     What hast þou suffred. for my sake.
52 Me hungred. þou woldest not me fede.
     Ne neuer my furst. ne woldestou slake.
54 Whon .i. of herborwe. hedde gret nede.
     þou woldest not. to þin hous me take.
56 þou seʒe me .a. monge todes blake.
     Ful longe. in harde prisoun lyng.
58 Let seo what vnswere. constou make.
     Where were [3] þou kynde. in eny þing.
60 And hou .i. whenched [4]. al þi care.
     Lyft vp þin eʒe [5]. and þou maiʒt se.
62 My woundes wete. blodi al bare.
     As i. was rauht [6]. on roode tre.
64 þou seʒe me. for defaute forfare.
     In sekenes. and in pouerte.
66 ʒrt [7] of þi good. woldestou not spare.
     Ne ones come. to visite me.
68 Al eorþly þinge [1]. i. ʒaf to þe.
     Boþe beest and fysche [8]. and foul fleoyng.
70 And tolde þe. hou þat charite.
     And Merci. passeþ alle þing.
¶ Hou myhtou. eny Merci haue.
     þat neuer desiredest. non to do.
74 þou seʒe me naked. and cloþes craue. *
     Barehed. and Barefot. gan I. go.
76 On me þou vochedest no þing saue.

.

[12] B. M. hert.   [1] þing.   [2] B. M. feondes bolde.   [3] Wher weore.   [4] quenched.
[5] eiʒe.   [6] rauʒt.   [7] ʒit.   [8] fisch.
   * The next four lines are from the Bodleian copy, and are not in the
Brit. Mus. one.

But beede me wende. þi wones fro.
78 þou seʒe me ded. aboue to graue.
¶ On bere. seuen dayes and mo.
80 For luytel dette. i. ouʒte þe þo.
þou forbed. my buryinge [1].
82 þi Pater noster. seide not so.
For Merci passeþ. alle þinge.
¶ þeose are þe werkes of Merci. seuene.
Of whuche. crist wol vs areyne.
86 þat alle schul stoney. wiþ þat steuene.
þat euer tresoun. mihte ateyne.
88 For here [2] but yf [3] we make vs euene.
þer may no miht. ne ʒiftes ʒeyne.
90 þen [4] to þe kyng of heuene.
þe bok seiþ. þat we schul seyne.
92 Wher hastou lord. in prisoun leyne.
Whon were [5] þou. in eorþe dwellyng.
94 Whon seʒe we þe. in suche peyne.
Whon askedst þou. vs eny þing.
¶ Whon ʒe seʒe. oþer [6]. blynd. or lame.
þat for my loue. asked ʒou ouʒt.
98 Al þat ʒe duden. in my [7] name.
Hit was to me. boþe dede [8] & þouht.
100 But ʒe þat hated. cristendame.
And of my wraþpe. neuer ne rouht [9].
102 ʒour seruise schal. be [10] endeles schame.
Helle fuyr. þat slakes nouht [9].
104 And ʒe. þat with my blood .i. bouht [9].
þat loued me. in ʒoure lyuynge.
106 ʒe schul haue. þat ʒe haue souht [9].
Merci þat passeþ alle þinge.
¶ þis tyme schal tyde. hit is no nay.
And wel is hym. þat haþ þat grace.
110 For to plese. his god to pay.
And Merci secheþ [11]. while he haþ space.

[1] buriʒing. [2] heer. [3] ʒif. [4] þenne. [5] Whonne weore. [6] ouþer.
[7] myn. [8] deede. [9] ʒt for ht. [10] ben. [11] seche.

112 For beo vr moupe. crommed^a with¹ clay.
     Wormes blake. wol vs enbrace.
114 þenne is too late. Mon. in goode fay.
     To seche to amende. of þi trespace.
116 With¹ mekenes þou may. heuene purchase.
     Oþer meede. þar þe non bryng.
118 But knowe þi god. in vche a case.
     And loue hym best. of eny þing.
   ¶ To god a² mon. were holden meste.
     To loue. and his wrappe eschuwe.
122 Now is non. so vnkuynde a beeste.
     þat lasse doþ. þat weore hym duwe.
124 For beestes and foules. more and leeste.
     þe cours of kuynde³. alle þei suwe.
126 And whon⁴ we breken. godes heste.
     Aȝeynes kuynde. we ben vn-trewe.
128 For kuynde wolde. þat we hym knewe.
     And dradde hym moste^b. in vre doinge⁵.
130 Hit is no riht. þat he vs rewe.
     But Merci passeþ. alle þinge.
   ¶ Now harlotrie⁶. for murþe is holde.
     And vertues turnen⁷. in-to vice.
134 And symonye. haþ chirches solde.
     And lawe is waxen. couetise.
136 Vr feiþ is frele. to flecche and folde.
     For treuþe is put. to luytel prise.
138 Vr⁸ god. is glotonye. and golde.
     Dronkenes. lecherie⁶ and dyse.
140 Lo here⁹ vr lust. and vr⁸ likyng.
     ȝet ȝif we wole. repent¹⁰ and rise.
142 Merci passeþ. alle þinge.
   ¶ Vnlustily. vr lyf we lede.
144 Monhod and we. twynne in two.
     To heuene ne helle. take we non hede.
146 But on day come. a noþer go.

---

^a.?quommed.   ¹ wt.   ² and.   ³ kynde.   ⁴ whonne.   ^b most.
⁵ doing.   ⁶ y for ie.   ⁷ tornen.   ⁸ Vre.   ⁹ heer.   ¹⁰ repente.

Who is a Maister. now but meede.
148 And pruude. þat wakened al vr wo.
We stunt noþer[1]. for schame ne drede.
150 To teren vr god. from top to to.
For-swere his soule. his hert al-so[2].
152 And alle þe Membres[3]. þat we con[4] mynge.
Ful harde vengeaunce. wol falle o[5] þo.
154 But Merci passeþ alle þing[6].
¶ And corteis knihthod. and clergye.
156 þat wont were vices. to forsake.
Are now so roted[7]. in rybaudye.
158 þat oþer murthes. lust hem not make.
A wey is gentel. curtesye[8].
160 And lustines. his leue haþ take.
We loue so slouþe. and harlotrie.
162 We slepe. a[9] swolle swyn in lake.
þer wol no worschupe. with vs wake.
164 Til þat charyte. be made[10] a kyng.
And þenne schal. alle vre synnes[11] slake.
166 And Merci passeþ alle þing.
¶ I. Munge no more. of þis to ʒou.
168 Al þauʒ .i. kouþe. yf[12] þat .i. wolde.
For ʒe han herde[13]. whi and hou.
170 Bigon þis tale. þat .i. haue tolde.
And þis men knowen. wel i.-nouh.
172 For Merlions. feet ben colde.
Hit is heore[14] kuynde. on bank and bouh.
174 A. quik brid. to haue[15] and holde.
From foot to foot. to flytte[16] and folde.
176 To kepe hire. from clomesyng.
As i. an hauþorn. gan bi holde.
178 I. sauʒ my self. þe same þing.
Whon heo hedde holden. so al niht.
180 On morwe heo let hit gon a way.

---

[1] stunte neiþer. [2] herte also. [3] menbres. [4] cun. [5] on. [6] þinge.
[7] Rooted. [8] gentyl cortesye. [9] as. [10] beo mad. [11] þen schal. al
vr synne. [12] ʒif. [13] herd wel. [14] heor. [15] hauen. [16] flutte.

Wheþer genteri¹ tauȝt hire. so or nouht
182 J. con not telle ȝou. in goode² fay.
But god. as þu art ful of myȝt.
184 Þouȝ we plese þe. not to pay.
Graunt vs repentaunce. and respiȝt.
186 And schrift and hosel. or we day.
As þou art god. and Mon verray.
188 Þou beo vr help. at vr³ endyng.
Byfore⁴ þi face. þat we may⁴ say⁴.
190 Now Merci passeþ alle þing⁵.

> Explicit a songe of Merci.

XXVI. A SONGE OF DEO GRACIAS.·

(Duplicate of Vernon MS., Brit. Mus., fol. 129, col. 1.)

In a chirche. pere i. con knel.
2 Þis ender day. in on Morwenynge.
Me liked þe seruise. wondur wel.
4 For-þi þe lengore. con .i. lynge.
I seiȝ a clerk a boke forthe brynge.
6 Þat prikked was. in Mony a plas.
Fast he souht what be schulde synge.
8 And al was. Deo gracias.
Alle þe queristres in þat qwer.
10 On þat word. fast gon þei cri:
Þe noyse was goode. and .i. drouȝ neer.
12 And calde a prest ful priuely.
And seide syre. for ȝor curtesy.
14 Telle me ȝif ȝe haue spas.
What hit meneþ. and for whi.
16 ȝe singe. Deo gracias.
¶ In silke þat comely clerk. was clad.
18 And ouer a lettorne. leoned he.

---

¹ gentrie.   ² good.   ³ vre.   ⁴ ȝ for y.   ⁵ þinge.   · This and the
following Songs, I had not time to compare with the Bodleian copy.

And with his word. he made me glad.
20 And seide sone. i. schal telle þe.
Fadur and sone. in Trinite.
22 þe holygost ground of vr graas.
Also ofte siþe. þonke we.
24 As we sei. Deo gracias.
¶ To þonke and blesse hym we be bounde.
26 With alle þe murþes þat mon may mynne.
For al þe world in wo was wounde.
28 Til þat he crepte. in-to vr kynne.
A louesum buirde. he lihte with-Inne.
30 þe worþiest þat euer was.
And schedde hys blood for vr synne.
32 And þerfore. Deo gracias.
¶ þen seide þe prest. sone bi þi leue.
34 I. most scye forþ my seruise.
I. prey þe take hit. nouht in greue.
36 For þou hast herd al my deuyse.
Bi cause whi. hit is clerkes wise.
38 And holichirche. Muynde of hit maas.
Vn-to þe prince so muche of pride.
40 Forto synge. Deo gracias.
¶ Out of þat chirche. i. went my way.
42 And on þat word. was al my þouht.
And twenti tymes. i. con say.
44 God graunt þat i. forȝete hit nouht.
þouȝ .i. were out of bonechef brouht.
46 What help weore to me. to say allas.
In þe nome of god. what euer be wrouht.
48 I. schal seie. Deo gracias.
¶ In myschef and in bonchef boþe.
50 þat word is goode to say and synge.
And not to wayle and to be wroþe.
52 þauȝ al be nouht at vr likynge.
For langour schal not euer lynge.
54 And sumtyme plesaunce. wol ouerpas.
But ay in hope of amendynge.
56 I. schal say. Deo gracias.

A-Mende þat þu hast done amis.
58 And do wel þenne and haue no drede.
Wheþer so þou beo. in bale or blis.
60 Þi goode suffraunce. schal gete þe mede.
ȝif þou þi lyf in likyng lede.
62 Loke þou be kinde in vche a cans.
þonke þi god ȝif þou wel spede.
64 With þis word. Deo gracias.
¶ ȝif god haþ ȝiue þe vertues mo.
66 þen he haþ oþer two or þre.
þenne i. rede þou rule þe so.
68 Þat Men may speke worschupe bi þe.
Be ferd of pruyde and bost þou fle.
70 Þi vertues let no fulþe defaas.
But kepe þe clene corteis and fre.
72 And þenk on. Deo gracias.
¶ ȝif þou be made an officer.
74 And art a Mon of Muche miht.
What cause þou demest. loke hit be cler.
76 And reue no Mon from hym his riht.
ȝif þou be strong and fers to fiht
78 For envye neuer mon þou chas
But drede þi god. boþe day and niht.
80 And þenke on. Deo gracias.
¶ ȝif we þis word in herte wol haue.
82 And ay in loue and leute leende.
Of crist bi couenaunt. we mowe craue.
84 Þat ioye þat schal neuer haue ende.
Out of þis world. when we schul wende.
86 In-to his paleys forto paas.
And sitte A-Monge his seyntes hende.
88 And þere synge. Deo gracias.

       Explicit a songe of Deo gracias.

     [A songe of '·I· take my leue' follows.]

XXVII. DEUS CARITAS.

(Duplicate of Vernon MS., Brit. Mus., fol. 129, col. 1.)

Deus caritas est.

2 A deore god omnipotent:
Lord þou madest. boþe foul and best

4 On eorþe to Mon. þou here hit sent.
I. warne ȝow alle boþe more and leste.

6 Charite .i. rede þat ȝe hent.
For hit is cristes heste.

8 Þat schal come to þe iugement
¶ For whon he comeþ. at domes day

10 Þat al þis world. hit schal wel se.
Þe wikked he biddeþ to gon heore way.

12 In bittre penaunce for euere to be.
And to þe goode wol þat lord say

14 ȝe schul alle wende wiþ me.
In-to þe blysse for euer and ay.

16 Et qui manet in caritate.
¶ God þat made boþe heuene and helle.

18 Vr swete lord of Nazareth
Adam þat was. so fair of felle.

20 For his folyes. he suffred deth.
In god for soþe. he schal dwelle.

22 In charite ho so geth.
Hit is soþ. þat .i. ou telle.

24 Bi-holde᷈ and seo. In deo manet.
¶ Crist was toren vche a lym.

26 And on þe Roode. he was .i.-do.
Þe fende þat was. so derke and dym.

28 To þe crois he com þo.
Crist. al Charite is in hym.

30 Þere he ouercome vr fo.
Charite i. rede þat þou myn.

32 And þenne. Deus est in eo.
¶ Let Charite. nou a-wake.

34 And do hit. per neode is.

Heuene forsoþe. þenne maiȝt þou take.
36 And come to þat riche blis.
Nou crist for his Modur sake.
38 Let vs neuer þis place mys.
And schilde vs from. þe fcondes blake.
40 And sit deus in nobis.
¶ And charite .i. rede þat wc bygynne.
42 As bifore alle oþer games.
And schruyuc vs clene of vr synne.
44 For so dud petur Ion and Iames.
And perforc god. hem dwelled withinne.
46 For þei weore alle. withouten oþer blames.
Crist let vs heuenc wynne.
48 Et nos in ipso maneamus.
¶ God þat dwelleþ in gret solas.
50 In heuene þat riche regnyng.
And for vs þoled gret trespas.
52 Wondur muche at vre muntyng.
On þe Roode don he was.
54 In gret dispit icleped a kyng.
þenkeþ nouþe. on deus caritas.
56 And brynge vs alle to goode endyng.

Explicit Deus caritas.

XXVIII. ANOTHER SONGE OF DEO GRACIAS.
(Duplicate of Vernon MS. Brit. Mus. fol. 129, col. 1.)

Mi. word is Deo gracias.
2 In world wheþer me be wel or wo.
Hou schold. i. lauȝwe or sigge allas.
4 For leeue me wel. hit lastcþ o.
And þouȝ hit greue. hit wol ouer go.
6 As þouht chaungeþ. for suche is gras.
þerfore wheþer me be wel or wo.
8 I. sei not but Deo gratias.

¶ þouȝ .i. be riche of gold so red.
10 And liht to renne as is a ro.
. A noþur is boun to begge his bred.
12 With brestes blak and bleynes blo.
Whon .i. seo goode depart so.
14 To sum Mon god sent gret solas.
And sum Mon ay to lyue in wo.
16 þen sei .i. deo gracias.
¶ þou he be pore. and lyue in peyn.
18 A noþur Mon proudeþ. as doþ a poo.
Whon murthe is his and mournyng myn.
20 As may bifalle. to me and mo.
ȝif fortune wolde. be so my fo.
22 From me to turne. hire freoly faas.
Sippe god may sende. boþe weole and wo.
24 I. sei not. but deo gracias.
¶ A lord of worschupe ȝif .i. ware.
26 And were falle doun. in a wro.
Sekenesse sitteþ me. so sare.
28 And serwe wol neiȝ. myn hert slo.
þus am .i. bounden. from top to to.
30 And i. turment so. for my trespaas.
ȝit god may loose me. of þat wo.
32 And þenne .i. say. Deo gracias.
¶ Whon .i. hedde spendyng. here bifore.
34 þer wolde no felauschupe. founde me fro.
But herken and hiȝe. to myn horne.
36 For in myn hond þer stod non ho.
Nou appeereþ. non of þo.
38 So pouert apayred haþ my plas.
Ho may haue wele withoute wo.
40 þerfore .i. sey. Deo gracias.
¶ Almyhti corteis crouned kyng.
42 God graunt vs grace to rule vs so.
þat we may come to þi wonyng.
44 þere is weole. withouten wo.
Milde maide prey þi sone al so.
46 þat he forȝiue vs. vr trespas.

i

And aftur ward. in-to heuene go.
48 þere to synge. Deo gracias.

Explicit. A noþer songe of Deo gracias.

XXIX. A SONG—KNOWE þI SELF.

(Additional MS. 22,283; Brit. Mus. fol. 129, back, col. 1.)

In a Pistel þat Poul wrouht.
2 I. founde hit writen. and seide riht þis.
Vche cristen creature knowen hym self ouht.
4 His oune vessel. and soþe hit is.
Nere help of hym. þat vs deore bouht.
6 We were boren to luytel blis.
Whon alle þi goode dedus. beoþ þorw souȝt.
8 Seche and þou schalt. fynden a-mys.
Eueri mon schuld. knowen his.
10 And þat is luytel. as .i. trowe.
To teche vr self. crist vs wis.
12 For vche mon ouȝt hym self to knowe.
¶ Knowe þi self. what þou ware.
14 Whon þou were. of þi Moder born.
Ho was þi moder. þat þe bare.
16 And ho was þi fader. per biforn.
Knowe hou þei beoþ. forþe i-fare.
18 So schaltou. þeiȝ þou hedde sworn.
Knowe þou come hider. wiþ care.
20 þou nost neuer. ȝif þou bide til morn.
Hou lihtly. þou maiȝt be forlorn.
22 But þou þi synne schryue and schowe.
For lond or kip. catel or corn.
24 Vche Mon ouȝt hym self to knowe.
¶ Knowe þi lyf. hit may not last.
26 But as a blast. blouh out þi breth.
Tote and by a noþur mon tast.
28 Riht as a gleirtand glem. hit geth.

What is al. þat forþ is past.

30 Hit fareþ as fuir of heth.

þis worldes goode. a way wol hast.

32 For synnes seekenes. þi soule sleþ.

And þat is. a ful deolful deþ.

34 Go, saue þi soule and þou be slowe.

With þi Maistrie. medel þi meþ.

36 For vche mon ouȝt. hym self to knowe.

¶ ȝif þou þi self. knowe con.

38 Sitte doun. and take countures rounde.

Siþþe furst. þou monnes wit bigon.

40 Hou ofte synne. þe haþ ibounde.

And for vche a synne. lay þou doun on.

42 Til þou þi synnes. haue souȝt vp. and founde.

Counte. þi goode dedes eurichon.

44 A-bide þere a while. and stunt a stounde.

And ȝif þou fele þe syker and sounde.

46 þenke on þi god. as þe wel owe.

And ȝif þou art. in synne ibounde.

48 Amende þe. and þi self knowe.

Knowe what god. haþ for þe do.

50 Made þe aftur. his oune liknes.

Seiþe he come. from heuene also.

52 And diȝed for þe. in gret distres.

For þe he suffred. boþe pyne and wo.

54 Knowe þou hym. and alle his.

Whoso greueþ hym. is worþi to go.

56 To helle fuyr. but he hit redres.

And he beo demed. be rihtwisnes.

58 But his grace is. so wide isowe.

From his wraþe .i. rede vs bles.

60 For vche mon ouȝt. hym self to knowe.

¶ Knowe þi self. þat þou schalt dye.

62 But what tyme þou nost neuer ne whenne.

With an twynklyng of an eiȝe.

64 Eueriday þou hiȝest þe henne.

þi flesche foode. þe wormes wol fye.

66 Vche cristen mon. ouȝt þis to kenne.

Loke aboute. and wel aspye.
68 þis world doþ but bitraye menne.
And be war of þe fuir. þat euer schal brenne.
70 And þenk þou regnest here. but a þrowe.
Heuene blisse. þou schat haue þenne.
72 For vche mon ouȝt. hym self to knowe.
¶ Knowe þi flesche. þat wol rote.
74 For certes þou maiȝt not longe endure.
And nedes die. hennes þou mote.
76 þauȝ þou haue kyngdam and empyre.
And sone þou schalt. be forgote.
78 So schal souereyn, so schal syre.
Hoso leeueþ not þis .i. trowe he dote.
80 For eueri mok. most in-to myre.
Preye we to god. vr soules enspire.
82 Or we bene logged. in eorþe lowe.
Heuene to haue. to vr huire.
84 For vche mon ouȝt him self to knowe.
¶ Knowe þi kuynde Creatoure.
86 Knowe what he. for þe dide.
Knowe þis worldly. honoure.
88 Hou sone þat hit is forþ islyde.
Ende of ioye. is her doloure.
90 Strengþe stont vs in no stide.
But longyng. and beoing in laboure.
92 Vr bost vr brag. is sone ouerbide.
Arthur. and Ector. þat we dredde.
94 Dethe* haþ leide hem. wonderly lowe.   [* MS. Aethe]
Amende þe mon. euene forþ mydde.
96 For vchemon ouȝte. hym self to knowe.
¶ þi Concience schal þe saue and deme.
98 Wheþer þat þou. be ille or good.
Grope aboute and take good ȝeme.
100 þer maiȝt þou wite. but þou be wood.
þer schalt þou þe same seone.
102 Aske Merci. wiþ mylde mood.
Amende þe. þou wot what .i. mene.
104 Vche creature þat bereþ. bon and blood.

Prey we to god þat died on Roode.
106 Ar vr brethe beo. out i. blowe.
Þat cristes face. may bene vr foode.
108 For vche mon ouȝt. hym self to knowe.

Explicit. A song knowe þi self.

XXX. A SONG OF YESTERDAY.

(Additional MS. 22,283; Brit. Mus. fol. 129, back, col. 3.)

Whon men beoþ muriest. at heor mele.
2 With mete and drink. to maken hem glade.
With worschipe. and with worldliche wele.
4 Þei bene so sette. þei conne not sade.
Þei haue no deynte forto dele.
6 With þinges þat bene deuotly made.
Þei wene heore honoure and heore hele.
8 Schal euer last and neuer diffade.
But in heore hertes. i. wolde þei hade.
10 Whon þei gon ricchest men aray.
Hou sone þat god hem may degrade.
12 And sum tyme þenke on ȝusturday.
¶ Þis day as leef. we may be liht.
14 With alle þe murþes þat men may vise.
To Reuele with þise buyrdes briht.
16 Vche mon gayest on his gise.
At þe last. hit drawcþ to niht.
18 Þat slepe most make. his maistrise.
Whon þat he haþ kud his miht.
20 Þe morwe he buskeþ vp to rise.
Þenne alle drawcþ hem to fantasie.
22 Wher he is bicomen con no mon say.
And ȝif heo wuste. þei were ful wise.
24 For al is turned to ȝusterday.
¶ Whoso wolde þenke. vppon þis.
26 Miht fynde a goode enchesun whi.

To preue þis world. al wey i-wis.
28 Hit nis but fantum. and feiri.
þis eorþeli ioie þis worldly blis.
30 Is but a fykel fantasy.
For nou hit is. and nou hit nis.
32 þer may no mon þerinne affy.
Hit schaungeþ so oft and so sodeynly.
34 To day is here. to morwe a way.
A syker ground who wol him gy.
36 I. rede he þenke on ȝusterday.
¶ For þer nis non. so strong in stour.
38 Fro tyme þat he. ful waxen be.
From þat day forþ. eueriche an hour.
40 Of his strengþe he leost a quantite.
Ne no buyrde so briht in boure.
42 Of þritti wyntur. i. enseure þe.
þat heo ne schal fade as a flour.
44 Luyte. and luyte. leosen hir beute.
þe soþe ȝe may. ȝor self ise.
46 Beo ȝor eldres. in goode fay.
Whon ȝe bene grettest in ȝour degre.
48 I. rede ȝe þenke on ȝusturday.
¶ Nis non so fresch. on fote to fare.
50 Ne non so feir. on folde to fynde.
þat þei ne schal on bere. be brouȝt ful bare.
52 þis wrecched world nis but a wynde.
Ne non so styf. to stunt ne stare.
54 Ne non so bold. Beores to bynde.
þat he naþ warnynges to be ware.
56 For god is so corteis and so kynde.
Biholde þe lame. þe bedrede. þe blynde.
58 þat bit ȝou be war. whil þat ȝe may.
þei make a Mirour. to ȝor mynde.
60 To seo þe schap. of ȝusterday.
¶ þe lyf þat eny mon schal lede.
62 Beþ certeyn dayes atte last.
þen most vr terme. schort nede.
64 Be o day comen. a noþur is past.

Here-of and we wolde. take good hede.
66 And in vr hertes acountes cast.
Day bi day. withoute drede.
68 To-ward vr ende. we drawe ful fast.
þenne schal vr bodies in corþe be þrast.
70 Vr Careyns chaunged. vndur clay.
Here of we ouȝte be sore agast.
72 And we wolde þenke on ȝusterday.
¶ Salomon seide in his poysi.
74 He holdeþ wel bettre. with an hounde.
þat is likyng. and Ioly.
76 And of sekenesse. hol and sounde.
þen be a leon. þouȝ he ly.
78 Cold. and ded. vppon þe grounde.
Wher of serueþ. his victori.
80 þat was so styf. in vche a stounde.
þe most fool. i. herde respounde.
82 Is wysore. whil he lyue may.
þen he þat hedde. a þousond pounde.
84 And was buried. ȝusterday.
¶ Socrates seiþ. a word ful wys.
86 Hit were wel bettre forto se.
A mon þat nou parteþ. and dis.
88 þen a fest. of Rialte.
þe fest wol make. his flesche to ris.
90 And drawe his herte. to vanite.
þe body þat on þe bere lis.
92 Scheweþ þe same þat we schal be.
þat ferful fit. may no mon fle.
94 Ne with no whiles. wynne hit a way.
þerfore among al Iolyte.
96 Sumtyme þenke on ȝusterday.
¶ But ȝit me meruayles. ouer al.
98 þat god let monymon croke and elde.
Whon miht and strengþe is from hem fal.
100 þat þei may not. hem self awelde.
And now þise beggers most principal.
102 þat good ne profit. may non ȝelde.

To þi purpos vnswere. i. schal.
104 Whi god sent suche men. boote and belde.
Crist þat made boþe flour and felde.
106 Let suche men lyue. forsoþe to say.
Whon a ȝonge mon. on hem bihelde.
108 Scholde seo þe schap. of ȝusterday.
¶ A noþur skil. þer is for whi.
110 þat god let suche men lyue so longe.
For þei beoþ triacle. and remedi.
112 For synful men. þat han don wronge.
In hem. þe seuen dedes of Merci.
114 A Mon may. fulfille amonge.
And also þis proude men may þerbi.
116 A feir Mirour vndurfonge.
For þer nis non. so stif ne stronge.
118 Ne no lady. stout ne gay.
Biholde what ouer hor hed con honge.
120 And sumtyme þenke on ȝusterday.
¶ I. haue wust. sin. i. couþe meen.
122 þat children haþ. bi candel liht.
Heore schadewe on þe walle isen.
124 And ronne þer aftur. al þe niht.
Bisi aboute. þei han ben.
126 To cacchen hit with al heore miht.
And whon þei cacchen hit. best wold wen.
128 Sannest hit schet out. of heore siht.
þe schadewe cacchen. þei ne myht.
130 For no lynes. þat þei couþe lay.
þis schadewe. i. may likne a riht.
132 To þis world. and ȝusterday.
¶ In-to þis world. whon we beþ brouȝt.
134 We schul be tempted. to couetyse.
And al þi wit. schal be þorw souȝt.
136 To more good. þen þou may suffise.
Whon þou þenkest best. in þi þouht.
138 On richesse. forte regne and rise.
Al þi trauayle. turneþ to nouȝt.
140 For sodeynly on deþ þou dyese.

þi lyf þou hast ilad with lyȝes.
142 So þis world. gon þe bitray.
Þerfore. i. rede þou þis dispise.
144 And sumtyme þenke on ȝusterday.
¶ Mon, ȝif þi neiȝebor þe manas.
146 Oþur to culle. oþur to bete.
I. knowe me syker in þe cas.
148 Þat þou wold drede. þi neiȝebores þrete.
And neuer a day þi dore to pas.
150 Withoute syker. defense and grete.
And ben purueyed. in vche a plas.
152 Of sykernes. and helpe to gete.
Þin enemy woltou. not forȝete.
154 But ay be aferd. of his affray.
Ensaumple here of. i. wol ȝou trete.
156 To make ȝou þenke. on ȝusterday.
¶ Wel þou wost. withouten fayle.
158 Þat deþ haþ manast þe to die.
But whon þat he wol þe assayle.
160 Þat wost þou not. ne neuer may spye.
ȝif þou wost don bi my connsayle.
162 Wiþ syker defence. be ay redie.
For siker defence. in þis batayle.
164 Is clene lyf parfit and trye.
Put þi trust. in godus Mercie.
166 Hit is þe best. at al assay.
And euer among. þou þe ennuye.   [? enmiye]
168 In-to þis world. and ȝusterday.
¶ Sum men seiþ þat deþ is a þef.
170 And al vnwarned. wol on hym stele.
And. i. say nay. and make a pref.
172 Þat deþ is studefast trewe and lele.
And warneþ vche mon. of his gref.
174 Þat he wol o day. with hym dele.
Þe lyf þat is. to ȝou so leof.
176 He wol ȝou reue. and eke ȝor hele.
Þis poyntes. may no mon hym repele.
178 He comeþ so baldely. to pike his pray.

Whon men beoþ murgest. at heor mele.
180 I. rede ȝe þenke on ȝusterday.

     Explicit. A song. of ȝusterday.

XXXI. WHY I CAN'T BE A NUN.
(Bibl. Cotton, Vesp. D.IX, fol. 179.)

. . . .
And whan they had resceyvede her charge,
2 They spared nether mud ne myer,
But roden over Inglonde brode and large,
4 To seke owte nunryes in euery schyre:
Her hertys were alwey on her hyre,
6 And that scheude they wel in her workyng,
For they were as ferfent as ony fyre
8 To excecute her lordys byddyng.
And schortly to sey, no'man abode
10 That on thys erand schulde be sent.
In-to dyuers schyres dyuers men rode,
12 And one of hem be-gan in kent.
They token her leue and forthe they went;
14 And to eche of hem was ȝeven grete hyre,
And there fore they were so feruent
16 To seke owte nunryes in euery schyre.
But the townes names I ouyr pas,
18 For and I schulde telle alle in fere,
Hyt were a long tale for to here.
20 But on a boke I dare well swere,
In gode feythe and on womanhode,
22 None was forȝete, fer ne nere,
Thorowȝ ynglond long and brode.
24   [B]ut when they were com home aȝene
That roden owte message to bere,
26 Than my fader was fulle fayne
And callede hem to hym alle in fere

28 And seyde, "how sped ȝe there ȝe were,
⸱ How faren the nunnes that ȝe cam tylle?"
30 "Welle, syr," quod they, "and made vs gode chere,
And yowre desyre they wolle fulfylle."
32 "I thanke hem seres Iwys," quod he,
"Now am I glade, so god me spede:"
34 And than my fader loked on me,
"Dameselle," quod he, "now take gode hede,
36 For yowre entent god do yow mede,
ȝe seyde ȝe wolde be a nune
38 But ȝe may not fulfylle in dede
The purpose that ȝe haue be-gun."
40 "Fader, quod I, and sore I wept,
Wolle ȝe me here wythe wordys few;
42 I trow my wylle schalle be accept
Before owre souereyne lorde ihesu,
44 And to him I am, and wolle be, trew
Wythe alle my wylle and obcervaunce,
46 And I wolle not chonge hym for no new,
For I loue hym wythe owten variaunce;
48 And trewly me repenteth fulle sore
That my wylle my not be had."
50 Than my fader lowȝ and seyde no more,
But went his way and was fulle glade;
52 But than morned I, and was ryȝt sad,
And in my hert I was fulle wo:
54 'Alas', I thowȝt, 'my chawnce ys bad,
I trow that fortune be my fo.'
56 Than hyt befell in a mornyng of may,
In the same ȝcre as I seyde be-fore,
58 My pencyfnes wolde not a-way
But euer waxed more and more,
60 I walked a-lone and wepte sore
Wythe syhyngys and mornyng chere,
62 I seyde but lytylle and thowȝt the more,
For what I thowȝt no man myȝt here,
64 And in a gardyne I sportyd me
Euery day at dyuers howres,

66 To beholde and for to see
    The swete effecte of aprelle flowres,
68 The fayre herbys and gentyl flowrys
    And birde syngyng on euery spray,
70 But my longyng and my dolowrys
    For alle thys sport wolde not away.
72 The byrdys sate on the bowes grene
    And syngyng fulle meryly & made gode chere
74 Her federys were fulle fayre and schene
    And alle they maden mery in her manere.
76 Than went I in-to a fayre herbere,
    And set me on my kneys allone,
78 To god I made my prayowre,
    And on thys wyse I made my mone—
80 "Lorde god that alle vertu hast
    And haddyst wythe-owten begynnyng,
82 Kepe me that I may lyue chaste
    For the corupcion of synnyng;
84 For thowȝ my fadyr and alle my kyn
    For-sake me thus in necessite,
86 ȝyt I hope suche grace to wyn
    That owre lord ihesu wolle resceyue me.
88 Souereyne lord omnipotent,
    Now be my comfort, swete Ihesu.
90 Before the alle thyng ys present,
    Alle that evyr was, and alle þat ys,
92 Alle that schalle be aftyr thys,
    Thow knowest alle thyng bothe most and lest.
94 Now ihesu kyng of hevyn blys,
    Wysse me thy seruant what ys best,
96 For now I am alle desolate,
    And of gode cownesayle destitute.
98 Lord to my mornyng be mediate,
    For thow are oonly my refute,
100 To the for comfort I make my sute
    To haue that ioy that lastythe ay,
102 For her loue that bare that frute,
    Swete ihesu, miserere mei!

104 I can no more, but trust in the
 In whom ys alle wysdom an wyt;
106 And thow wost what ys best for me,
 For alle thyng in thy syȝt ys pyt.
108 Loo here I thyne hand-mayde syt
 Dyspysede and in poynte to spylle;
110 My cawse to the, lorde, I commytte;   ✎
 Now do to me aftyr thy wylle."
112 And at that worde for-feynte I fylle
 Among the herbes fresche and fyne;
114 Vn-to a benche of camomylle
 My wofulle hede I dyd inclyne,
116 And so I lay in fulle grete pyne,
 And cowde not cese but alwey wepe,
118 And sore I syȝhed many a tyme
 And prayed my lorde he wolde me kepe.
120   And at the last a sclepe was Ibrowȝt
 And alle a-lone in this gardyne.
122 And than com a fayre lady, as me thowȝt,
 And called me by name 'kateryne',
124 And seyde "a-wake, dowȝtyr myne,
 And to my talkyng take entent;
126 To bryng thyne hert owte of pyne,
 And to comfort the, now haue I ment.
128 Kateryne", sche sayde, "loke vp and haue"
 And than I behelde welle her fygure,—
130 I pray to god in hevyn her saue,—
 For hyt was the most godely creature
132 That euer I saw, I yow ensuer,
 As I wolle telle yow or I go,
134 For I behelde welle her feture,
 Her bewte, and her clothyng also,
136 And me thowȝt I was as wakyng tho;
 And I behelde that lady so
138 That I forgate alle my mornyng,
 For hyt was to me a wondyr thyng
140 That lady to beholden and see,

    Sche was so fayre wythe-owten lesyng
142 Bothe of clothyng and of bewte,
    Thys that was so godely arrayed.
144 Sche comfortythe me in dyuers wyse,
    And spake to me in dyuers wyse,
146 And bad me anone I schulde aryse.
    And me thow3t I rose and knelyd thryes,
148 And seyde to her wythe grete reuerence,
    "What ys yowr name, dame empryse?"
150 Sche seyde "my name ys experience;
    And, dow3ter, my techyng may not fayle;
152 For what so I teche, hyt ys fulle trew,
    And now at thys tyme for thyne avayle
154 I am com hedyr on the to rew;
    And wythe the help of cryste ihesu
156 I hope hyt schalle be for the best,
    For suche thynges as I schalle the sche,
158 I tro hyt schalle set thyne hert in rest."
       "Thanke yow, lady," quod I than,
160   "And there-of hertely I yow pray;
    And I, as lowly as I can,
162 Wolle do yow servyse ny3t and day;
    And what 3e byd me do or say
164 To yow I promyt obedyence,
    And bryng me owte of thys carefulle way,
166 My gode dere lady experience."
    Than me thow3t sche toke me by the honde
168 As I knelyd vp-on my kne
    And vp a-none sche bad me ryse,
170 And on thys wyse seyde to me,
    "Kateryne, thys day schalt thow see
172 And howse of wommen reguler,
    And diligent loke that thow be,
174 And note ry3t welle what þow seest there."
    Than me thou3t sche led me forthe a pace
176 Thorow3 a medow fayre and grene,
    And sone sche brow3t me to a place,
178 In erthe ys none so fayre I wene,

Of ryalle byldyng so I mene,
180 Hyt schyned wythe-owte so fayre and clere,
But syn had made hyt fulle vnclene
182 Wythe-in, as ʒe schalle aftyr here.
"What place ys thys þat stondythe hyre",
184 Quod I to hyre þat dyd me lyde.
"Kateryne, sche sayd, we wyl go nere,
186 And what you scyst, take good hede."
Than at the ʒates in we ʒede,
188 Boldly as thowʒ we had be at home,
And I thowʒt, 'now cryst vs spede'.
190 Than to the cloyster sone we com,
For hyt was a howse of nunes in trewthe,
192 Of dyuers orderys bothe old and yong,
But not welle gouernede, and þat was rowthe,
194 Aftyr the rewle of sad levyng.
For where that selfe-wylle ys reygnyng,
196 The whyche causethe dyscord and debate,
And resun hathe none enteryng,
198 That howse may not be fortunate.
For arystotelle, who so redythe
200 In the fyrst boke of hys moralite,
Playnely sayethe that euery man nedethe
202 To be ware of the vnresonabylite
That comethe of the sensualite,
204 And not hys bestely condiciones sewe,
But let resun haue the soueraynte,
206 And so he schalle purches vertu.'
But what in that place I saw
208 That to religion schulde not long,
Perauenture ʒe wolde desyre to know,
210 And who was dwellyng hem a-mong.
Sum what schalle I telle yow wyth tong,
212 And sum what cownseyle kepe I schalle,
And so I was tawʒt whan I was yong,
214 To here and se, and sey not alle.
But there was a lady, that hyʒ dame pride;
216 In grete reputacion they her toke

And pore dame mekenes sate be syde,
218 To her vnnethys ony wolde loke,
But alle as who scythe I her forsoke,
220 And set not by her nether most ne lest;
Dame ypocryte loke vp-on a boke
222 And bete her selfe vp on the brest.
On euery syde than lokede vp I,
224 And fast I cast myne ye a-bowte;
Yf I cowde se be-holde or a-spy,
226 I wolde haue sene dame devowte.
And sche was but wythe few of that row¡t;
228 For dame sclowthe and dame veyne glory
By vyolens had put her owte;
230 And than in my hert I was fulle sory.
But dame envy was there dwellyng
232 The whyche can sethe stryfe in euery state.
And a nother lady was there wonnyng
234 That hy¡t dame loue vn-ordynate,
In that place bothe erly and late
236 Dame lust, dame wantowne, and dame nyce,
They ware so there enhabyted, I wate,
238 That few token hede to goddys servyse.
Dame chastyte, I dare welle say,
240 In that couent had lytylle chere,
But oft in poynte to go her way,
242 Sche was so lytelle beloved there;
But sum her loved in hert fulle dere,
244 And there weren that dyd not so,
And sum set no thyng by her,
246 But ¡afe her gode leue for to go.
And at that place I saw muche more,
248 But alle I thenk not to dyscrye,
But I wolle sey as I seyde be-fore.
250 And yt ys a poynte of curtesy;
For whoso chateryt lyke a py
252 And tellethe alle that he herethe and seethe,
He schalle be put owte of company,
254 And scho the gose, thus wysdum vs lerethe.

And in that place fulle besyly
256 I walked whyle I myʒt enduer,
And saw how dame enevy
258 In euery corner had grete cure;
Sche bare the keyes of many a dore.
260 And than experience to me came,
And seyde, kateryne, I the ensuer,
262 Thys lady ys but seldom fro home.
Than dame pacience and dame charyte
264 In that nunry fulle sore I sowʒt;
I wolde fayne haue wyst where they had be,
266 For in that couent were they nowʒt;
But an owte chamber for hem was wrowʒt,
268 And there they dweldyn wyth-owtyn stryfe,
And many gode women to them sowʒt
270 And were fulle wyfulle of her lyfe,
Also a-nother lady there was
272 That hyʒt dame dysobedyent
And sche set nowʒt by her priores.
274 And than me thowʒt alle was schent,
For sugettys schulde evyr be dylygent
276 Bothe in worde, in wylle, and dede,
To plese her souereynes wyth gode entent,
278 And hem obey, ellys god forbede.
And of alle the defawtes that I cowde se
280 Thorowʒ schewyng of experience,
Hyt was one of the most that grevyd me,
282 The wantyng of obedyence.
For hyt schulde be chese in consciens,
284 Alle relygius rule wytnesseth the same,
And when I saw her in no reverence,
286 I myʒt no lenger abyde for schame,
For they setten not by obedyence.
288 And than for wo myne hert gan blede,
Ne they haddeu her in no reuerence,
290 But few or none to her toke hede.
And than I sped me thens a grete spede,
292 That couent was so fulle of syn;

k

And than experience dyd me lede
294 Owte at the ꝫates there we com In.
　　And when we were both wyth-owte,
296 Vp on the gras we setten vs downe,
　　And then we he-helde the place abowte,
298 And there we talkeden as vs lest.
　　And than I prayed experience for to haue wyst
300 Why sche schewed me thys nunery,
　　Sche seyde "now we bene here in rest,
302 I thenk for to tellen the why.
　　Thy fyrst desyre and thyne entent
304 Was to bene a nune professede,
　　And for thy fader wolde not consent,
306 Thyne hert wyth mornyng was sore oppressede,
　　And thow wyst not what to do was best;
308 And I seyde, I wolde cese thy grevawnce,
　　And now for the most part in euery cost
310 I haue schewed the nunnes gouernawnce.
　　For as thow seest wyth-in yonder walle
312 Suche bene the nunnes in euery warde,
　　As for the most part, I say not alle,
314 God forbede, for than hyt were harde,
　　For sum bene devowte, holy, and towarde,
316 And holden the ryꝫt way to blysse;
　　And sum bene feble, lewde, and frowarde,
318 Now god amend that ys amys!
　　And now kateryne, I haue alle do
320 For thy comfort that longeth to me,
　　And now let vs aryse and go
322 Vn-to the herber there I com tó the."
　　Than in thys herber sche let be me.
324 I thanked her wyth grete reuerence,
　　I pray to god I-blessyd be sche,
326 Thys fayre lady experience.
　　And whan sche was gone, I wakede anone.
328 And I thowꝫ how I may gouerned be,
　　For nun wold I neuere be none,
330 For suche defawtes that I haue see.

But ȝyf they myȝt amendyd be,
332 And forsake her syn both day and nyȝt,
God ȝyf me grace that day to se,
334 And ellys hyt wolle not be a ryȝt.
But here perauenture sum man wolde say,
336 And to hys conceyte so hyt schulde seme,
That I forsoke sone a perfyte way
33S For a fantesy or for a dreme.
For dreme was hyt none, ne fantasye,
340 Hyt was vn-to me a gratius mene,

[A piece of the MS. containing the whole of the first 4 lines, and part
of the next four, is torn off here.]

That . . . .
342 Holy wryt w . . . .
Pleynely go rede hyt wh . . .
344 And hyt ys wretyn in Genesye,
In the fowre and thyrty Chapytylle,
346 How dyna, for sche bode not stylle
But went owte to see thynges in veyne,
34S Sche was defowled a-ȝenst her wylle,
And there-fore thowsandys of peple were sclayn.
350 Yowre barbe, your wymppylle and your vayle,
Yowre mantelle and yowre devowte clothyng,
352 Maketh men wyth-owten fayle
To wene ȝe be holy in levyng.
354 And so hyt ys an holy thyng
To bene in habyte reguler;
356 Than, as by owtewarde aray in semyng,
Beth so wyth-in my ladyes dere.
358 A fayre garlond of yve grene
Whyche hangeth at a taverne dore,
360 Hyt ys a false token as I wene,
But yf there be wyne gode and sewer;
362 Ryȝt so but ȝe your vyces for-bere,
And let alle lewde custom be broken,
364 So god me spede, I yow ensewer
Ellys yowre habyte ys no trew token
366 . . . . hyng

. . . .
368 . . . .
. . . . . yng . . . nde gode levyng,
370 . . yf they be wyth-in the contrary,
In holy schrypture wyth-owte lesyng
372 They bene called the chyldryn of false ypocrasy.
Now, ladyes, taketh gode hede to thys exhortacion
374 That I haue taw3t yow in thys lore,
And beholde the gode conuersacion
376 Of gode women here be-fore,
Fulle holy vyrgynes many a store,
378 The whyche levedyn here relygyiusly,
And now in ioy and blysse therefore
380 They haue possession enlesly,—
Seynte clare and seynte edyth also,
382 Seynte scolastica and seynte Brigytte,
Seynte Radegunde, and many mo
384 That weren[1] professed in nunnes habyte.
They fulle besy were wyth alle her wytte
386 To be ware of syn, and fle there froo,
And now for evyr they bene qwyte
388 From alle maner sorow and woo,—
Seynte audre, seynte freswyth, & seynte Emerlde (?)
390 Seynte wythbuge & seynte Myldrede,
Seynte sexburge & seynte Ermenylde,—
392 Of alle these holy women we rede.

[? Incomplete.]

XXXII. OLD AGE.

(Harl. 913, p. 54 back; printed Rel. Ant. II., p. 210.)

1. Elde makiþ me geld. an[2] growen al grai.
when eld me wol feld. nykkest[3] þer no nai.
eld nul meld. no murþes of mai
when eld me wold aweld. mi wele is a wai

---

[1] MS. wereren.   [2] The ands are written a'.   [3] MS. blotched.

eld wold keld. an cling so the clai.

wiþ eld I mot held. an hien to mi dai.

2. When eld blowid he is blode. his ble is sone abatid.

al we wilniþ to ben old. wy is eld ihatid.

moch me anueþ. þat mi dribil druiþ. and mi wrot wet.

eld me awarpeþ. þat mi schuldern scharpiþ. and ʒouþe me haþ let.

3. Ihc ne mai no more ⎫
grope vnder gore ⎬ þoʒ mi wil wold ʒete:

y-ʒoket ic am of ʒore ⎫
wiþ last an luþer lore ⎬ an sunne me haþ bi-set.

4. iset ic am wiþ sunne ⎫
þat i ne mai noʒt munne ⎬ non murþis wiþ muþe:

eld me haþ amarrid ⎫
ic wene he he bi-charred ⎬ þat trusteþ to ʒuþe.

5. Al þus eld me for-dede ⎫
þus he toggiþ vte mi ded ⎬ an drawiþ ham on rewe.

Y ne mai more of loue done ⎫
mi pilkoc pisseþ on mi schone ⎬ vch schenlon[1] me bischrew.

6. Mine hed is hore & al for-fare ⎫
i-hewid as a grei mare ⎬ Mi bodi wexit lewe[2]

when i bi-hold on mi schennen ⎫
m'in dimmiþ al for-dwynnen ⎬ Mi frendis waxiþ fewe.

7. Now i pirtle i pofte. i poute. ⎫
i snurpe i snobbe i sneipe on snovte. ⎬ þroʒ kund i comble an kelde

i lench i len on lyme i lasse ⎫
i poke i pomple i palle i passe ⎬ as galliþ gome i-geld.

8. i riuele i roxle i rake i rouwe ⎫
i clyng i cluche i croke i couwe ⎬ þus he wol me a-weld:

i grunt i grone i grenne i gruche ⎫
i nese i nappe i nifle i nuche ⎬ an al þis wilneþ eld.

9. i stunt i stomere i stomble as sledde. ⎫
i blind i bleri i bert in bedde. ⎬ Such sond is me sent:

i spitte i spatle in speche i sporne ⎫
i werne i lutle þerfor i murne ⎬ þus is mi wel iwent.

10. i spend an marrit is mi main ⎫
an wold wil ʒuþe a-ʒayn ⎬ as falc i falow an felde:

---

[1] puer.   [2] debile.

i was heordmon nov am holle ⎫
al folk of me beþ wel folle   ⎬ such willing is after elde.

11. eld me haþ so hard ihent ⎫
seo wouw spakliy[1] he me spent ⎬ arerid ig of rote:
vch toþ fram oþer is trent. ⎭

þe tunge wlaseþ wend þerwiþ ⎫
lostles lowteþ in uch a liþ ⎬ he fint me vnder fote. Amen.
i mot be þat eld beþ   ⎭

XXXIII. EARTH.
(Harl. 913, p. 62; Rel. Ant. II, p. 216.)

1. Whan erþ haþ erþ iwonne wiþ wow ⎫
þan erþ mai of erþ nim hir inow ⎬
erþ vp erþ falliþ fol frow[2]   ⎬
erþ toward erþ delful him drow. ⎭

Of erþ þou were makid. and mon þou art ilich: ⎫
in on erþ awaked þe pore and þe riche   ⎬

2. Terram per inuri ⎫   ⎧cum terra lucr⎫
   tunc de terra copi⎬am ⎨terra sorci   ⎬atur

   terra super are ⎫   ⎧subito frustr⎫
   se traxit ad arid⎬am ⎨terraque trist⎬atur

   De terra plasmaris⎫   ⎧simile virr   ⎫
   vna terra pauper ⎬es ⎨ac dites sunt pr⎬oni

3. Erþ geþ on erþ. wrikkend in weden. ⎫
   erþ toward erþ. wormes to feden   ⎬
   erþ beriþ to erþ. al is lif deden ⎬
   when erþ is in erþe. heo muntid[3] þi meden. ⎭

   When erþ is in erþe. þe rof is on þe chynne. ⎫
   þan schullen an hundred wormes. wroten on þe skin. ⎭

4. Vesta pergit uesti⎫   ⎧super vestem v[4]⎫
   artatur et uermi ⎬bus ⎨vesta pastum d ⎬are

---

[1] The Rel. Ant. reads 'spakky', but the true word is evidently 'spakly'
= quickly or certainly. H. C.

[2] Glossed 'festine'.   [3] metitur.   [4] vare, to deck it out with var,
fur. Bond.

ac cum gestis omni⎫
cnm uesta sit scrobi⎭ bus
    ⎧ad uestam migr ⎫
    ⎩quis rult suspir⎭ are

Cum sit uesta ponit⎫
tunc in cute candid ⎭ a
    ⎧doma tangit m ⎫
    ⎩verrunt[1] uermes c⎭ entum

5. Erþ askiþ erþ. and erþ hir answerid ⎫
   whi erþ hatid erþ. and erþ erþ verrid ⎪
   erþ haþ erþ. and erþ erþ teriþ   ⎬   . .
   erþ geeþ on erþ. and erþ erþ berriþ. ⎭

   Of erþ þow were bi-gun. on erþ þou schalt end ⎫
   al þat þou in erþ wonne. to erþ schal hit wend ⎭

6. Humus humum repet ⎫
   humum quare neglig ⎪ it
   humus humum porrig ⎪
   super humum perag ⎭
       ⎧et responsum d ⎫
       ⎪et humo fru   ⎪ atur
       ⎨sic et oper   ⎬
       ⎩humo que port ⎭

   humo sic incip ⎫ eris
   quod humo quesi ⎭
       ⎧ac humo me ⎫ abis
       ⎩humo totum d⎭

7. Erþ get hit on erþ. maistrie and miȝte: ⎫
   al we beþ erþ. to erþ we beþ idiȝte.   ⎪
   erþ askeþ carayne. of king and of kniȝt.⎬
   whan erþ is in erþ. so lowȝ he be liȝt. ⎭

   Whan þi riȝt and þi wowȝ. wendiþ þe bi-for: ⎫
   be þou þre niȝt in a þrouȝ. þi frendschip is ilor. ⎭

8. Terra vincit braui ⎫
   totus cetus homin ⎪ vm
   ops cadauer milit ⎪
   cum detur in tumul ⎭
       ⎧terra collucr ⎫
       ⎪de terra portr ⎪ atur.
       ⎨que regis scrut⎬
       ⎩mox terra vor ⎭

   Cum ius et iustici⎫ vm
   pauci per trinocti ⎭
       ⎧coram te migr ⎫ abunt.
       ⎩mortem deplor ⎭

9. Erþ is a palfrei. to king and to quene ⎫
   erþ is ar lang wei. þouw we lutil wenc ⎪
   þat weriþ grouer and groy. and schrud so schene ⎬
   whan erþ makiþ is liuerei. he grauiþ vs in grene. ⎭

   Whan erþ haþ erþ wiþ streinþ þus geten. ⎫
   alast he haþ is leinþ. miseislich i-meten. ⎭

10. Dic uestam[2] dextrar⎫ ium
    iter longum mar   ⎭
       ⎧regique regi   ⎫ ne
       ⎩quod est sine fi ⎭

---

[1] Glossed 'trahunt'. [2] est tam.

indumentum uar ⎱
omne dat corrod ⎰ ium.   dans cedit scuti ⎱
                   nos tradit rui ⎰ ne

Cum per fortitudi ⎱
capit longitudi ⎰ nem   tenet hanc lucra ⎱
                    misere meta ⎰ tam

11. Erþ gette on erþ. gersom and gold ⎫
    erþ is þi moder. in erþ is þi mold |
    erþ uppon erþ. be þi soule hold |
    er erþe go to erþe. bild þi long bold ⎭
    Erþ bild castles. and erþe bilt toures. ⎱
    whan erþ is on erþe. blak beþ þe boures. ⎰

12. Humus querit plurim ⎫
    humus est mater tu |
    anime sis famul   } a   super humum bo ⎫
    domum dei perpetr ⎭   in quam sumas dor |
                                   super humum pro } na.
                                   mundo cum coro ⎭
    Ops turres edific ⎱
    quin* fatum capi ⎰ at   ac castra de pe ⎱
                          penora sunt te ⎰ tra.   * or quando.

13. þenk man in lond. on þi last ende ⎫
    whar-of þou com. and whoder schaltou wend. |
    make þe wel at on. wiþ him þat is so hend. |
    and dred þe of þe dome. lest sin þe schend. ⎭
    For he is king of blis. and mon of moche mede ⎱
    þat deliþ þe dai fram niȝt. and leuiþ lif and dede. ⎰

14. De fine nouissim ⎫
    huc quo veneris uic |
    miti prudentissim   } o   mauors medite ⎫
    hesites iudic   ⎭   dic quo gradie |
                                   concordare de } ris
                                   ne noxa dampne ⎭
    Quia rex est glori ⎱
    mutat noctem de di ⎰ e   dans mensura rest ⎱
                          vitam mortem prest ⎰ at.   Amen.

XXXIV. "OF MEN LIF þAT WONIþ IN LOND'.
A Satire on the Monks and People of Kildare.
(Harl. MS. 913, p. 7.)[1]

1. Hail seint michel wiþ þe lange sper
    fair beþ þi winges vp þi scholder

[1] Printed Rel. Ant. II, p. 174. Mr. Wright says, 'see an account of the MS. in Mr. Crofton Croker's Popular Songs of Ireland, pp. 282-7.'

þou hast a rede kirtil a-non to þi fote
þou ert best angle þat euer god makid
þis uers is ful wel iwroȝt
hit is of wel furre y-broȝt

2. Hail seint cristofre wiþ þi lang stake
  þou ber ur louerd ihesu crist ouer þe brod lake
  mani grete kunger swimmeþ abute þi fete
  hou mani hering to peni at west chep in London
  þis uers is of holi writte
  hit com of noble witte

3. Seint mari bastard þe maudlein-is sone
  to be wel iclopid wel was þi wone
  þou berist a box on þi hond ipeintid al of gold
  woned þou wer to be hend. ȝiue us sum of þi spicis
  þis uers is imakid wel
  of consonans and wowel

4. Hail seint dominik with þi lang staffe
  hit is at þe ouir end crokid as·a gaffe
  þou berist a bok on þi bak. ic wen hit is a bible
  þoȝ þou be a gode clerk. be þou noȝt to heiȝ.
  Trie rime la god hit wote
  soch an opir an erþe i note

5. Hail seint franceis wiþ þi mani foulis
  kites and crowis. reuenes and owles
  fure and .xx.ti wild ges and a poucok
  mani bold begger siwiþ þi route
  þis uers is ful wel isette
  swiþe furre hit was i-vette

6. Hail be ȝe freris wiþ þe white copis
  ȝe habbiþ a hus at drochda[1] war men makiþ ropis
  euir ȝe beþ roilend þe londis al a-boute
  of þe watir daissers ȝe robbiþ þe churchis
  maister he was swiþe gode
  þat þis sentence vnderstode

7. Hail be ȝe gilmins wiþ ȝur blake gunes
  ȝe leuith ȝe wildirnis and fillip þe tiuns

---

[1] Drogheda.

Menur wiþ-oute. and prechur wiþ-inne
ʒur abite is of gadering þat is mochiʒ schame
sleilich is þis uers iseid
hit wer harme adun ileiid

8. Hail ʒe holi monkes wiþ ʒur corrin
late and rape ifillid of ale and wine
depe cun ʒe bouse þat is al ʒure care
wiþ seint benet-is scurge lome ʒe disciplineþ
takeþ hed al to me
þat þis is sleche ʒe mow wel se

9. Hail be ʒe nonnes of seint mari house
goddes bourmaidnes and his owen spouse
ofte mistrediþ ʒe ʒur schone. ʒur fete beþ ful tendre
daþeit þe sotter þat tawiþ ʒure leþir
swiþe wel ʒe vnder-stode
þat makid þis ditee so gode

10. Hail be ʒe prestis wiþ ʒur brode bokes
þoʒ ʒur crune be ischaue. fair beþ ʒur crokes
ʒow and oþer lewidmen deleþ bot a honue
whan ʒe deliþ holibrede. ʒiue me botte a litil
Sikirlich he was a clerk
þat wrochete þis craftilich werke

11. Hail be ʒe marchans wiþ ʒur gret packes
of draperie auoir-depeise and ʒur wol sackes
gold siluer stones riche markes and ek pundes
litil ʒiue ʒe þer-of to þe wrech pouer
sleiʒ he was and ful of witte
þat þis lore put in writte

12. Hail be ʒe tailurs wiþ ʒure scharpe sheres
to mak wronge hodes ʒe kittiþ lome gores
a-ʒens midwinter hote beþ ʒur neldes
þoʒ ʒur semes semiþ fair. hi lestiþ litil while
þe clerk þat þis baston wrowʒte
wel he woke and slepe riʒte nowʒte

13. Hail be ʒe sutlers wiþ ʒour mani lestes
wiþ ʒour blote¹ hides of selcuþ bestis

---

¹ May be *r*, blotched.

and trobles and treisuses bochevanpe and alles
blak and loþlich beþ ȝur teþ hori was þat route
nis þis bastun wel ipiȝte
euch word him sitte ariȝte

14. Hail be ȝe skinners wiþ ȝure drenche kiue
who so smilliþ þer-to. wo is him aliue
whan þat hit þonneriþ. ȝe mote þer-in schite
daþeit ȝur curteisic. ȝe stinkeþ al þe strete
worþ hit wer þat he wer king
þat ditid þis trie þing

15. Hail be ȝe potters wiþ ȝur bole ax
fair beþ ȝur barmhatres, ȝolow beþ ȝur fax
ȝe stondiþ at þe schamil. brod ferlich bernes
fleiis ȝow folowiþe, ȝe swolowiþe y-now
þe best clark of al þis tun
craftfullich makid þis bastun

16. Hail be ȝe bakers wiþ ȝur louis smale
of white bred and of blake. ful mani and fale
ȝe pincheþ on þe riȝt white aȝen goddes law
to þe fair pillori ich rede ȝe tak hede
þis uers is i-wrowȝte so welle
þat no tung i-wis mai telle

17. Hail be ȝe brewesters wiþ ȝur galuns
potels and quarters ouer al þe tounes
ȝur thowrnes beriþ moch awai, schame hab þe gyle
beþ i-war of þe coking-stole, þe lak is dep and hori
sikerlich he was a clerk
þat so sleilich wroȝte þis werk

18. Hail be ȝe hokesters dun bi þe lake
wiþ candles and golokes and þe pottes blak
tripis and kine fete. and schepen heuedes
wiþ þe hori tromcheri hori is ȝure inne
he is sori of his lif
þat is fast to such a wif

19. Fi a debles kaites þat kemiþ þe wolle
al þe·schindes of þe tronn an heiȝ opon ȝur sculle
ȝe makid me sech a goshorne ouer al þe wowes
þer-for ich makid on of ȝou sit opon a hechil

he was noble clerk and gode
þat þis dep lore vnderstode
20. Makiþ glad mi frendis ʒe sittiþ to long stille
spekiþ now and gladieþ and drinkeþ al ʒur fille
ʒe habbeþ ihird of men lif þat woniþ in lond
drinkiþ dep and makiþ glade, ne hab ʒe non oþer nede
þis song is y-seid of me
euer i-blessid mote ʒe be.   *Explicit.*

XXXV. THE LAND OF COKAYGNE.
(Harl. MS. 913, fol. 3.)

(Printed in Hickes's Thesaurus part 1, p. 231; and (modernised) in Ellis's
Specimens, vol. 1. In the MS., only the first lines of the divisions ¶
of the poem begin with capital letters, and there are no commas.)

1 Fur in see bi west spayngne.
Is a lond ihote cokaygne.
þer nis lond under heuen-riche.
4 Of wel of godnis hit iliche.
þoʒ paradis be miri and briʒt.
Cokaygn is of fairir siʒt.
What is þer in paradis.
8 Bot grasse and flure and grene-ris.
þoʒ þer be ioi and grete dute.
þer nis mete bote frute.
þer n'is halle, bure, no benche.
12 Bot watir, man-is þursto quenche.
Beþ þer no man but two.
Hely and enok also.
Clinglich may hi go.
16 Whar þer woniþ men no mo.
¶   In cokaygne is met and drink.
Wiþ vte care. how and swink.
þe met is trie. þe drink is clere.
20 To none. russin, and sopper.

I sigge for soþ, boute were.
þer n'is lond on erthe is pere.
Vnder heuen n'is lond iwisse.
24 Of so mochil ioi and blisse.
¶ þer is mani swete siȝte.
Al is dai, n'is þer no niȝte.
þer n'is baret noþer strif.
28 N'is þer no deþ, ac euer lif.
þer n'is lac of met no cloþ.
þer n'is man no womman wroþ.
þer n'is serpent, wolf no fox.
32 Hors, no capil, kowe. no ox.
þer n'is schepe. no swine no gote.
No non horwȝ-la, god it wot.
Nother harate, nother stode.
36 þe lond is ful of oþer gode.
N'is þer flei. fle, no lowse.
In cloþ, in toune. bed, no house.
þer n'is dunnir, slete, no hawle.
40 No non vile worme no snawile.
No non storme, rein, no winde.
þer n'is man no womman blinde.
Ok al is game, Ioi, and gle.
44 Wel is him þat þer mai be.
¶ þer beþ riuers gret and fiue.
Of oile, melk, honi and wine.
Watir seruiþ þer to no þing.
48 Bot to siȝt and to waiissing.
þer is maner frute.
Al is solas and dedute.
¶ þer is a wel fair abbei.
52 Of white monkes and of grei.
þer beþ bowris and halles.
Al of pasteiis beþ þe walles.
Of fleis, of fissc, and rich met.
56 þe likfullist þat man mai et.
Fluren cakes beþ þe scingles alle.
Of cherche. cloister. boure. and halle.

Þe pinnes beþ fat podinges.
60 Rich met to princeȝ and kinges.
Man mai þer-of et inoȝ.
Al wiþ riȝt, and noȝt wiþ woȝ.
Al is commune to ȝung and old.
64 To stoute and sterne, mek and bold.
¶   Þer is a cloister fair and liȝt.
Brod and lang, of sembli siȝt.
Þe pilers of þat cloistre alle
68 Beþ i-turned of cristale.
Wiþ har-las and capitale.
Of grene Jaspe and rede corale.
In þe praer is a tre.
72 Swiþe likful for to se.
Þe rote is gingeuir and galingale.
Þe siouns beþ al sedwale.
Trie maces beþ þe flure.
76 Þe rind, canel of swet odur.
Þe frute gilofre of gode smakke.
Of cucubes þer n'is no lakke.
Þer beþ rosis of rede ble.
80 And lilie likful for to se.
Þai faloweþ neuer day no niȝt.
Þis aȝt be a swet[e] siȝt.
¶ Þer beþ .iiij. willis in þe abbei.
84 Of triacle and halwei.
Of baum and ek piement.
Euer ernend to riȝt rent.
Of þai stremis al þe molde.
88 Stonis preciuse and golde.
Þer is saphir and vniune.
Carbuncle and astiune.
Smaragde. lugre. and prassiune.
92 Beril. onix. topasiune.
Ametist and crisolite.
Calcedun and epetite.
¶   Þer beþ briddes mani and fale.
96 Þrostil, þruisse, and niȝtingale.

Chalandre and wodwale.
And oþer briddes wiþout tale.
Þat stinteþ neuer by har miȝt.
100 Miri to sing dai and niȝt.

[Here a few lines seem to be lost.]

¶ ȝite I do ȝow mo to witte.
Þe Gees irostid on þe spitte.
Fleeȝ to þat abbai, god hit wot.
104 And grediþ 'gees al hote, al hot.'
Hi bringeþ garlek gret plente.
Þe best idiȝt þat man mai se.
Þe leuerokes þat beþ cuþ.
108 Liȝtiþ adun to man-is muþ.
Idiȝt in stu ful swiþe wel.
Pudrid wiþ gilofre and canel.
N'is no spech of no drink.
112 Ak take inoȝ wiþ-vte swink.

¶ Whan þe monkes geeþ to masse.
All þe fenestres þat beþ of glasse.
Turneþ in to cristal briȝt.
116 To ȝiue monkes more liȝt.
When þe masses beþ iseiid.
And þe bokes up ileiid.
Þe cristal turniþ in to glasse.
120 In state þat hit raþer wasse.

¶   Þe ȝung monkes euch dai.
Aftir met goþ to plai.
N'is þer hauk no fule so swifte.
124 Bettir fleing bi þe lifte.
Þan þe monkes heiȝ of mode.
Wiþ har sleuis and har hode.

¶ Whan þe abbot seeþ ham flee.
128 Þat he holt for moch glee.
Ak naþeles al þar amang.
He biddiþ ham liȝt to eue-sang.
Þe monkes liȝtiþ noȝt adun.
132 Ac furre fleeþ in o randun.

¶ Whan þe abbot him iseeþ.
Þat is monkis fram him fleeþ.

He takeþ maidin of þo route.
136 And turniþ vp her white toute.
And bètiþ þe taburs wiþ is hond.
To make is monkes liȝt to lond.
¶ Whan is monkes þat iseeþ.
140 To þe maid dun hi fleeþ.
And geþ þe wench al abute.
And þakkeþ al hir white toute.
And siþ aftir her swinke.
144 Wendith meklich hom to drinke.
And geth to har collacione.
A wel fair processione.
¶   Anoþer abbei is þerbi.
148 For soth a gret fair nunnerie.
Up a riuer of swet milke.
Whar is plente grete of silk .
Whan þe somer-is dai is hote.
152 þe ȝung nunnes takith a bote.
And doth ham forth in that riuer.
Bothe with oris and with stere.
When hi beth fur from the abbei.
156 Hi makith ham nakid for to plei.
And lepith dune in-to the brimme.
And doth ham sleilich for to swimme.
þe ȝung monkes [1] þat hi sceth.
160 Hi doth ham up, and forþ hi fleeþ.
And commiþ to þe nunnes anon.
And euch monke him taketh on.
And snellich berith forth har prei.
164 To the mochil grei abbei.
And techith the nunnes an oreisun.
With iambleue vp and dun.
¶ þe monke þat wol be stalun gode.
168 And kan set a-riȝt is hode.
He schal hab wiþute danger.
.xii. wiues euche ȝere.

_____
[1] MS. monkeþ.

Al þroȝ riȝt and noȝt þroȝ grace.
172 For to do him silf solace.
And þilk monk þat clepiþ best.
And doþ his likam al to rest.
Of him is hoppe, god hit wote.
176 To be sone uadir abbot.
¶   Whose wl com þat lond to.
Ful grete penance he mot do.
Seue ȝere in swine-is dritte.
180 He mot wade, wol ȝe i-witte.
Al anon up to þe chynne.
So he schal þe lond[e] winne.
¶   Lordinges gode and hend.
184 Mot ȝe neuer of world wend.
For ȝe stond to ȝure cheance.
And fulfille that penance.
Þat ȝe mote þat lond ise.
188 And neuer more turne a-ȝe.
Prey we god so mote hit be.
Amen, per seinte charite.   *finit.*

XXXVI. FIVE EVIL THINGS.

Bissop lorles.
Kyng redeles.
ȝung man rechles.
Old man witles.
Womman ssamles.
I swer bi heuen kyng.
Þos beþ fiue liþer þing.

NOTE to Poem II, p. 7, *XV Signa Ante Iudicium.*

The Rev. J. Small of the University Library, Edinburgh, has kindly
furnished me (through our member, Mr. Muir) with another English, and
a Latin, version of these Signs before the Judgment. They form pages
25-28 of a small volume that Mr. Small has now in the press, *English
Metrical Homilies, from MSS. of the Fourteenth Century.*

. . . .

> And bides us lok til grouand tres;
> For quen men leues on thaim sees,
> Men wat that ful ner es somer comand,
> And ribt sua mai we understand
> Quen we se thir takenis cume,
> That nerhand es the dai of dom.
> > Bot for Crist spekes of takeninge
> > That tithand of this dom sal bringe,
> Forthi es god that I you telle
> Sum thing of thir takeninges snelle:
> Sain Jerom telles that fiften
> Ferli takeninges sal be sen
> Bifor the day of dom, and sal
> Ilkan of thaim on ser[1] dai fal.

(1) The first dai sal al the se
Boln and ris and heyer be
Than ani fel of al the land,
And als a felle up sal it stand,
The heyt thar-of sal passe the felles
Bi sexti fot, als Jerom telles,

(2) And als mikel the tother day
Sal it sattel and wit away,
And be lauer than it nou esse,
For water sal it haf wel lesse.

(3) The thride dai, mersuine and qualle
And other gret fisces alle
Sal yel, and mak sa reuful ber
That soru sal it be to her.

---

[1] *seir,* several.

(4) The ferthe day freis water and se
Sal bren als fir and glouand be.

(5) The fift day sal greses and tres
Suet blodi deu that grisli bes.

(6) The sexte day sal doun falle
Werdes werks bathe tours and halle.

(7) The seuend day sal stanes gret
Togider smit and bremly bete.

(8) And al the erthe the achtande day
Sal stir and quae and al folc slay.

(9) The neynd day the fels alle
Be mad al cuin wit erthe salle.

(10) The tend day sal folc up crep,
Als wod men of pittes dep.

(11) The elleft day sal banes rise
And stand on graues thar men nou lies.

(12) The tuelft day sal sternes falle.

(13) The thretend day sal quek men dey alle,
Wit other ded men to rise,
And com wit thaim to gret asise.

(14) The faurtend day at a schift
Sal bathe brin bathe erthe and lift.

(15) The fifetende day thai bathe
Sal be mad newe and fair ful rathe,
And al ded men sal rise,
And cum bifor Crist our iustise.

Unde Versus de ejusdem Signis.

Signis ter quinis se prodet ad ultima finis
Mundani motus Domino soli modo notus.

(1) In signo primo surget mare stans quasi murus
Erigat, in proprios post pauca sinus rediturus,
Atque quater denis cubitis transcendere montes
Cernetur, paucique fluent in flumina fontes.

(2) Oculet in signo sic se maris unda secundo,
Ut vix aspectum capiat. Diuersa profundo

12

(3) Monstra super fluctus post hec ubi nata patebunt,
Rugitusque sui celos horrore mouebunt.

(4) Quarto cum fluuiis ardebunt equoris unde,
Fontibus ut[1] latices effundant non erit unde.

(5) Rorem sanguineum quinto deducet ab [herbis]
Horror et arboribus lacrimis perfusus acerbis.

(6) Hinc turres et tecta cadent, que[2] diruet edes
Sexta dies, omnis que solo ruet ardua sedes;

(7) Augebit lapidum conflictus in orbe timorem,
Terribilemque dabit collisio seua fragorem.

(8) Concuciet terram post hec motus generalis,
Omnia conturbans, horrendus, et exitialis.

(9) Omnibus equatis in plano terra jacebit,
Strata superficies nichil asperitatis habebit.

(10) Hinc velud amentes exibunt ante latentes
In latebris homines et fari nulla valentes.

(11) Sicca super tumbis post hec surgencia stabunt.

(12) Casus stellarum signans discrimine finem
Nesciet ulterius clarum deducere finem.

(13) Corpore uiuentes simul absque mora morientur,
Ut pariter clangente tuba cuncti repetentur.

(14) Optimus inde status celum terramque nouabit,
Luce sub eterna, quem nulla dies uariabit;

(15) Conuocet ut cunctos cum buccina protinus urgens
Iudicis ante pedes ueniet plebs tota resurgens.

NOTE to Poem VII, p. 21-2, and to Dr. Guest's Letter in the Preface, p. v.

The following is the passage from *the History of English Rhythms* (vol. 1, pp. 136-7) referred to by its author.

"INVERSE RHIME

is that which exists between the last accented syllable of the first section, and the first accented syllable of the second. It appears to have flourished most in the fifteenth and sixteenth centuries. I do not remember any instance of it in the Anglo-Saxon, but it is probably of native growth.

[1] et.   [2] quia.

A kindred dialect, the Icelandic, had, at an early period, a species of
rhime closely resembling the present—the second verse always beginning
with the last accented syllable of the first. It is singular that the French
had, in the sixteenth century, a rhime like the Icelandic, called by them
la rime entrelassée. The present rhime differed from both, as it was
contained in one verse ... We will begin with the verse of four accents.

> These steps | both *reach* | : and *teach* | thee shall |
> To come | by *thrift* | : to *shift* | withal | . *Tusser*.
> The pi | per *loud* | : and *loud* | er blew | ,
> The dan | cers *quick* | : and *quick* | er flew | . *Burns*."

M. Eugene Oswald has kindly supplied me with the following specimen
of the French rhyme similar to that of the text, though about 250 years
later.

"Clément Marot. 1542.

Chanson III.

> Dieu gard ma Maistresse, et Re*gente*,
> *Gente* [1] de corps, et de façon,
> *Son* cueur tien [2] le mien en sa *tente*
> *Tant* et plus d'ung ardant [3] frisson.
> *S'on* m'oyt [4] poulser sur ma chan*son*
> Son de uoix [5], au Harpes doul*cettes*,
> *C'est E*spoir, qui sans marris*son*
> *Songer* me faict en amour*ettes*.

[1] gentille.   [2] tient.   [3] ardent.
[4] Old Pres. of *ouïr*, whence *oyer* and *oyez*. Old Infinitive *oyr* :—"le
Roy envoia guerre celi cordelier pour le *oyr* parler." *Joinville*.
[5] Of course, *voix*.—*Variante*, of later edition, son de *Lucz* = *luth*.

The second and third stanzas do not keep up this law of rhyme, but
have other curious artifices of form.—I do not think the form a common
one.—E. O."

INDEX.

LIST OF WORDS &c.

not in Coleridge's *Glossarial Index*, 1250-1300, A.D.

———

a, *prep.*, in, a two, p. 14, st. 77.

a, *prep.*, at or with, p. 145, l. 291.

a, *interj.*, ah, p. 1, st. 2b.

afonge, *v.a.*, take, p. 41.

ajt, *v.n.*, ought, p. 8, st. 5.

alive, *adj.*, p. 63, l. 142.

all, *pron.*, p 146, l. 319.

alone, *adv.*, only, p. 3, st. 17.

although, *conj.*, p. 123, l. 168.

amove, *v.n.*, p. 11, l. 148.

anap, *v.n.*, take with sleep, bedrowse, p. 78, l. 278.

anoveward, *prep.*, upon, p. 56, l. 341.

aoure, *v.a.*, honour, worship, Fr. *aourer*, L. *adorare*, p. 90, l. 32.

apan, *prep.*, upon, p. 5, st. 36.

arraign, *v.a.*, p. 121, l. 85.

array, *v.n.*, p. 133, l. 10.

arsmetrike, *sb.*, geometry &c., p. 77, l. 222.

art, *sb.*, the liberal Arts, p. 77, l. 220.

as, *conj.* or *rel.pron.*, that, which, p. 77, l. 223; in which, p. 57, l. 362.

ash, *sb.*, ash-tree, p. 52, l. 171.

aslay, *v.a.*, *pret.* aslouj, p. 53, l. 193; p. 58, l. 26.

atom, *adv.*, at home, p. 62, l. 89.

attain, *v.a.*, p. 121, l. 87.

avail, *sb.*, help, comfort, p. 142, l. 153.

await, *v.a.*, watch, p. 53, l. 238.

awield, *v.a.*, rule, manage, p. 149, st. 8; p. 135, l. 100.

awinne, *v.a*, win, get, p. 73, l. 107.

awolde, *v a.*, move, wield, p. 80, l. 336.

barb, *sb.*, a nun's face-veil or muffler, p. 147, l. 350.

barehead, *adj.*, p. 120, l. 75.

beastly, *adj.*, p. 143, l. 204.

because, p. 125, l. 37.

become (to), *v.a.*, turn (into), p. 51, l. 129.

become, *v.n.*, go to, p. 53, l. 238.

bedrid, *sb.*, the bedridden, p. 134, l. 57.

begin (of), *v.n.*, spring (from), p. 151, st. 5.

beguile, *v.n.*, p. 59, l. 39.

behold after, *v.n.*, look after, p. 52, l. 160.

bench, *sb.*, bank? p. 141, l. 114.

bent, *sb.*, a grassy plain, p. 118, l. 4.

bert, *v.n.*, break wind, p. 145, st. 9.

bespeak, *v.a*, plan, plot, p. 51, l. 144.

bespit, *v.n.*, spit on, p. 20.

best, for the, p. 142, l. 156.

bet, *adv.*, *cp.*, better, p. 50, l. 107.

betake, *v.a.*, p. 71, l. 31.

bethink, *v.a.*, think of, purpose, plot, p. 50, l. 110.

betide, *v.a.*, p. 51, l. 142.

betray, *v.n.*, p. 59, l. 39.

bid (beden), *v.a.*, pray (prayers), p. 61, l. 71.

bigete, *sb.*, gain, p. 57, l. 358.

bimean, *v.n.*, regret, p 82, l. 347.

bipeach, *v.a.*, deceive, p. 18, st. 10.

biset in, *v.a*, place, bestow on, p. 38, l. 148.

bitter, *adj.*, severe, harsh, p 4, st. 33.

bitter, *adv.*, bitterly, p. 5, st. 37.

blain, *sb.*, A.S. *blægen*, a pustule, p. 129, l. 12.

bleed, *v.n.*, p. 10, st. 101.

blind, *v.a.*, make blind, p. 3.

blossom, *sb.*, p 51, l. 120.

bob, *v.a.*, beat, p. 14, l. 59.

body, *sb.*, corpse, p. 14, l. 74.

boldlier, *adv.*, cp , p. 45, l. 69.

bonechef, *sb.*, prosperity, p. 125, l. 49, (mischief, *sb.*, adversity, *ib.*).

book, *sb.*, Bible, p. 138, l. 20.

boten, *v.n.*, become cured, p. 47, l. 151. A.S. *bétan*.

both, *conj.*, p. 4, st. 31.

bouten, *prep.*, without, p. 39, l. 184.

brag, *sb.*, A.S. *brægan*, to spread, pretend, p. 132, l. 92.

bring forth, *v.a.*, bring up (a child), p. 51, l. 135.

building, *sb.*, p. 143, l. 1.

bur, *sb.*, lady, maiden, girl, p. 50, l. 85.

busk, *v.n.*, make ready, p. 133, l. 20.

but (bote), *conj.*, except, p. 5, st. 37; p. 60, l. 24.

buttock, *sb.*, p. 75, l. 163.

buxom, *v.n.*, bow, obey, p. 82, l. 367.

by, *prep*, through, p. 159, l. 124.

bye, *v.a*, *pret.* byde, bow, p. 75, l. 167.

bymene, *v.a.?* p. 61, l. 51; p. 57, l. 357.

calewe, *sb.*, bald-pate, p. 37, l. 89, A.S. *calo*, bald.

camomile, *sb.*, p. 141, l. 114.

can or cunne thonk, give thanks, p. 21.

cast, *v.a.?* add up, p. 77, l. 223.

castle, *sb.*, p. 152, st. 11.

catel, *sb.*, riches, goods, p. 6, st. 45.

cease, *v.a.*, cause to cease, stop, p. 146, l 308

chapitle, *sb.*, chapter (of Genesis), p. 147, l. 344.

chaser, *sb.*, hunter, a horse, p. 10, st. 109, O.Fr. *chasseres*.

chaste, *adj.*, pure (generally), p. 140, l. 82.

chatter, *v.n.*, p. 144, l. 251.

cherubin, *sb. pl.*, p. 11, st. 149.

chief, *sb*, metropolis, p. 49, l. 50.

chorister—queristere—, *sb.*, p. 124, l. 9.

chough, *sb.*, the bird, A.S. *ceo*, p. 76, l. 185.

circle, *sb.*, p. 77, l. 232.

cleanly, *adv.*, right out, p. 61, l. 65.

clemde, *pret.* of climb, p. 51, l. 123.

clive, *sb.*, acclivity, p. 33, l. 175.

clomesyng, *part.*, stiffening from cold, A.S. *clom*, band, clasp.

clothing, *sb.*, p. 142, l. 142.

comble, *v.n.?* p. 149, st. 7.

come within, *v.a.*, overcome, p. 58, l. 42.

conceit, *sb.*, conception, fancy, p. 147, l. 336.

conde, *sb.?* slit, wound, p. 20.

condition, *sb.*, p. 143, l. 204.

continually, *adv.*, p. 77, l. 220.

conversation, *sb*, life, p. 148, l. 375.

core, *v.a.?* p. 14, l. 45.

cost, *sb.*, side, part, p. 146, l. 309.

counsel, *sb*, keep counsel, p. 143, l. 212.

counter, *sb.*, thing for counting with, p. 131, l. 38.

country, *adj.* (c. man), p. 55, l. 291.

course, *sb.*, succession, p. 77, l. 222; p. 122, l. 125.

crop, *v.a.*, breed, produce, p. 2, st. 10.

crop, *sb.*, top (of a tree), p. 10, st. 97.

cure, *sb.*, charge, p. 145, l. 258.

dasher, *sb.*, p. 153, st. 6.

deadly (sin), *adj*, p. 59, l. 54.

deal, *v.a.*, separate, p. 152, st. 13.

death, *adj.* (death throes), p. 64, l. 101.

debate, *sb.*, p. 143, l. 196.

deep, *sb.*, deep water, p. 62, l. 84.

deface, *v.a.*, p. 126, l. 70.

defence,*sb.*,forbiddance,prohibition, p. 16, l. 15.

deil or del, *sb.*, sorrow, p.15, l.83.

delivre, *adj.*, free, p. 78, l. 290; O.Fr. *delivre*, libre, affranchi, Roq.

desire, *sb.*, p. 146, l. 303.

destitute, *adj.*, p. 140, l. 97.

deverse or diverse, *v.n.*, p.11,st.129.

devoutly, *adv.*, p. 133, l. 6.

diffade, *v.n.*, fade away, p. 133, l. 8.

diligent, *adj.*, p. 145, l. 275.

discipline, *sb.* (of flogging), p. 74, l. 114.

disobedient, *adj.* as *sb.*, p.145, l.272.

dispute (in divinity), *v.n.*, p. 77, l. 255.

disturb *of* for *in* or *from*, p. 82, l. 338.

diverse, *adj.*, different, p. 54, l. 261.

divinity, *sb.*, the study divinity, p. 77, l. 238.

do, *v.a.*, put, row, p. 160, l. 152; get (up), rise, p. 160, l. 159.

do, *phr.*, have done! p. 97, l. 279.

doat, *v.n.*, p. 132, l. 79.

doing, *sb.*, p. 122, l. 129.

dolour, *sb.*, p. 132, l. 89.

dotus, *adj.*, fearful, O.Fr. *dotus*.

draw, *v.a.*, pull (one's hair), p. 97, l. 266.

draw, *v.a.*, play (a lay on a harp), p. 39, l. 170.

dread, *v.a.*, p. 8, st. 13.

drunkenness, *sb.*, p 122, l. 130.

due, *adj.*, p. 122, l. 123.

dunnir, *sb.*, thunder, p. 157, l. 39.

durne, *adj.*, dark, p. 52, l. 157.

durneliche, *adv.*, secretly, p. 55, l. 283, A.S. *dyrnan*, to hide.

dute, *sb.*, treasure, prize, p.13, l.24.

each, *adj.*, every, p. 50, l. 86.

east, *adj.*, p. 48, l. 18.

Eastland, *sb.*, Norfolk, Suffolk, Ely, and Cambridge, p. 49, l. 63.

effect, *sb.*, p. 140, l. 67.

eie, *sb.*, awe, p. 22, st. 10.

eirmonger, *sb.*, egg-monger, p. 45, l. 69.

either, *adj.*, both, p. 57, l. 355.

election, *sb.*, p. 81, l. 326.

embrace, *v.a.*, p. 122, l. 113.

empire, *sb.*, p. 132, l. 76.

endlessly, *adv.*, p. 148, l. 380.

endure, *v.n.*, p. 145, l. 256.

english, *sb.*, p. 54, l. 260.

enhabit, *v.n.*, p. 144, l. 237.

ensure, *v.a.*, assure, p. 145, l. 261; p. 147.

epistle—pistel—, *sb.*, p. 130, l. 1.

er, *adv.*, before, formerly, p. 50, l. 90.

erne, *v.n.*, run, p. 9, st. 49.

erore, *adj.*, *cp.*, former, p.55, l.290.

eschew, *v.a.*, p. 122, l. 121.

even, *adv.*, as far as, p. 52, l. 190.

execution, *sb.*, beheading, p. 119, l. 37.

exhortation, *sb.*, p. 148, l. 373.

experience, *sb.*, p. 142, l. 150.

falc, *sb.*, a plant, p. 149, st. 10.

fantasy, *sb.*, p. 134, l. 30.

fashion, fasoun, *sb.*, making, shape, p. 119, l. 41.

fast *to* for *on*, p. 71, l. 24.

fawe, *adv.*, p. 63, l. 154.

fearful, *adj.*, p. 135, l. 93.

fervent, *adj.*, eager, p. 138, l. 7.

fese, *v.n.*, drive, A.S. *fesian*, drive away, p. 12, st. 169.

fiercely—fresliche—, *adv.*, p. 119, l. 32.

fignre, *sb.*, geometrical f., p. 77, l. 223.

file, *adj.*, foul (base of filth), p. 1, st. 3.

fill, *sb.* (eat one's fill), p. 81, l. 391.

fiz, *sb.*, son, p. 12, st. 179.

flecche, *v.n.*, bend, give way, p. 62, l. 116.

fleme, ? *sb.*, outlaw, A.S. *flyma*, one who flees; a runaway, p. 37, l. 101.

flit, *v.a.*, change, shift, p. 123, l. 175.

fold, *sb.*, time, p. 24, st. 27.

folly, *sb.*, a sinful act, p. 57, l. 3.

forbear, *v.n.*, refrain from, p. 147, l. 362.

forcroked, *adj.*, bent up, p. 80, l. 341.

foreign—furrene—, *adj.*? p. 90, l. 20.

form, *sb.*, treaty (by deed or articles), p. 56, l. 311, 314.

forolthed, *pp.*, befouled, p. 75, l. 175.

for-roti, *v.n.*, rot completely away, p. 17.

forte, *conj.*, until, p. 52, l. 168.

forth, *prep.*, up, p. 51, l. 135.

forth-mydde, *adv.*, forthwith, p. 132, l. 95.

fortranailled, *pp.*, thoroughly tired with travel, p. 56, l. 313.

frail, *adj.*, p. 122, l. 136.

fresh—uerisse—, *adj.* (of water), p. 11, st. 125.

frow, *adv.*, glossed *festine*, p. 150.

froward, *adj.*, p. 146, l. 317.

furst, *sb.*, thirst, p. 120, l. 53.

fye, *v.a.*, ? eat, p. 131, l. 65.

garden, *sb.*, p. 141, l. 121.

gentise, *sb.*, birth, bearing, p. 69, l. 136.

ghastly, *adj.*, p. 63, l. 147.

giddyhood, *sb.*, folly, A.S. *gydig*, giddy, p. 90, l. 13.

ʒime, *v.n.*, keep, hoard, A.S. *giman*, take care of, p. 3, st. 18.

glad *with*, pleased with, p. 69, l. 121.

gleirtand, *adj.*, glittering, p. 130, l. 28.

glisminge, *adv.*, gleamingly, p. 21.

glory, vain, *sb.*, p. 144, l. 228.

go, *p.p.* igo, p. 99, l. 23.

go to, *v.n.*, go at them, fall on, begin, p. 4, st. 31.

God forbid! p. 146, l. 314.

goose, *prov.* "shoe the goose", p. 144, l. 254. Rabelais' *ferroyt les cigalles* (Garg. liv. 1, chap. xi) is translated 'he shoed the geese' in 'Sir T. Urquart and Mr. Motteux's translation' (1818. Reprint of Ozell's edition of 1737, vol. 1, p. 167). Cotgrave has *Ferrer les cigales*. 'To spend the time in trifling, to undertake a foolish businesse; to lose time altogether ... *Ferrer les oyes*. as, *Ferrer les cigales*.' cp. 'It is as much pity to see a woman weepe, as it is to see a goose goe barefooted.' Withal's Dict. ed. 1634, p. 579, in Nares.

grace, *sb.*, spirit, power, p. 1, st. 1.

grave, *v.a.*, engrave, cut, p. 73, l. 91.

gridiron, *sb.*, p. 65, l. 202, 204.

harbour, *sb.* (in a garden), p. 140, l. 76.

harlotry, *sb.*, p. 122, l. 132.

harm, *sb.*, evil, p. 13, st. 19.

harp, *v.a.*, play on the harp, p. 39, l. 179.

hawthorn, *adj.*, p. 52, l. 187; *sb.*, p. 123, l. 177.

heath, *sb.*, p. 131, l. 30.

heavy, *v.n.*, grow heavy, p. 62, l. 96.

herdman, *sb.*, p. 150.

hereforth, *adv.*, p. 62, l. 94.

hexist, *adj*, *sp.*, highest, p. 60, l. 8, 10.

highly, *adv.*, p. 55, l. 276.

hive, *sb.*, p. 16, l. 31.

hold, *v.a.*, consider, p. 2, st. 13; give or have (feasts), p. 3, st. 23.

hore, *sb.*, ? sin or filth, p. 71, l. 8; sin, p. 13, st. 17.

horrid, *adj.*, p. 18, st. 10.

horsehair, *sb.*, p. 75, l. 158.

hostess — osteste —, *sb*, p. 73.

hypocrisy, p. 148, l. 372.

icche, *v.n.*, budge, stir, p. 104, l. 106.

idojt, *pp.* of dow, to prosper, p. 64. l. 182.

ifere, *adv.*, together, p. 11, st. 117.

illespyl, *sb.*, hedgehog, A.S. *il*, *igil*, a hedgehog, *pylce*, a garment of skin with the hair.

in, *prep.*, on, p. 99, l. 42.

inspire, *v.a.*, p. 132, l. 81.

iredi, *adj.*, ready, p. 58, l. 27.

is, *adj*, his, p. 2, st. 12.

is, *adj.*, his, for its, p. 9, st. 61.

-is, *gen. term.*, p. 2, st. 13; p. 8, st. 5, &c.

isee, *v.a.*, see, p. 2, st. 14.

ivy, *sb*, A.S. *ifig*, p. 147, l. 358.

iþej, ? *pp.* of þe, do, p. 35, l. 28.

keld, *v.n.*, make cold, p. 149, l. 1; become cold, p. 149, st. 7.

kene, *v.n.*, p. 65, l. 212.

kill, *v.a.*, p. 62, l. 102.

kind, *adj.*, merciful, p. 132, l. 85.

kingdom, *sb.*, reign, p. 50, l. 79.

kinriche, *sb.*, holder of a kingdom or domain, A.S. *eynrice*, kingdom.

kith, *sb.*, p. 130, l. 23.

kithe, *v.n.*, make known, show, p. 15, l. 100.

langour, *sb.*, mourning, O.Fr. *laigner*, se plaindre, murmurer, p. 125, l. 53.

lap, *v.a.*, wrap, p. 5, st. 39.

larder, *sb.*, p. 54, l. 236.

lasse, *v.n.* ? p. 149, st. 8.

latin, *sb.*, p. 1, st. 2a.

leave, *v.n.*, p. 15, st. 5.

lectern, *sb.*, p. 124, l. 18.

leman, *sb.* (of Christ), p. 21, st. 15.

lest, *v. imp.*, it pleased, p. 146, l. 298.

lewe, *adj.*, glossed *debile*, p. 149, st. 6.

lifeday, *sb.*, life, p. 50, l. 93.

like, *Proverb*, 'ech þing loueþ his iliche', p. 109, l. 66.

liking, *adj.*, pleasant; but ? read *livyng*, p. 135, l. 75.

line, *sb.* (a red line), p. 89, l. 98.

lisnisse, *sb.*, loosing, remission, p. 61, l. 75.

liþerhede, *sb.*, wickedness, p. 50, l. 88.

little, *adv.*, p. 144, l. 132.

lolich, *adv.*, loathsomely, p. 2, st. 7.

long, *phr.*, ever the longer the more, p. 35, l. 33.

long, *v.n.*, belong, p. 143, l. 208.

losed, ? *pp.*, praised, p. 77, l. 245.

lostles, *adj.*, ? listless, p. 150, st. 11.

loud — lude —, *adv.*, p. 4, st. 31.

lowly, *adv.*, p. 142, l. 161.

lustiness, *sb.*, valour, p. 123, l. 160.

lusting, *sb.*, (good) desire, p. 18, st. 8.

lute, *sb.*, (base of little), p. 56, l. 327.

lutles, *gen.* of lutel, little, p. 81, l. 396.

lyne, *r.n.*, lie (down), p. 41.

main, *sb.*, chance, p. 149, st. 10.

maner, *sb.*, ? manor, or *manoir*, mansion, manor- or dwelling-house, p. 53, l. 200.

manslaȝt, *sb.*, murderer, p. 16, l. 35.

match — found his match, p. 59, l. 48.

mean, *sb.*, p. 148, l. 340.

meatless, *adj.*, without food, p. 53, l. 240.

medel, *r.a.*, mix, p. 131, l. 35.

mediate, *adj.*, propitious, p. 140, l. 98.

members, *sb. pl.*, genital organs, p. 58, l. 25.

merlyon, *sb.*, a kind of hawk, a merlin, p. 119, l. 9, &c.

merry, *adv.*, p. 159, l. 100.

mete, *adj.*, bad, p. 29, st. 116. ? A.S. *mǽte*, moderate, little. Piers Plowman's Crede, l. 85: 'tweye myteynes as *meter*', worn out, worthless.

-mighty *of* for *over*, p. 99, l. 47.

mischief, *sb.*, adversity, p. 125, l. 49.

mislere, *v.a.*, misinform, deceive, p. 57, l. 6.

misliving, *sb.*, p. 119, l. 33.

mok, *sb.?*, p. 132, l. 80.

mone, *sb.*, complaint, p. 58, l. 11.

mont, *sb.*, mountain, p. 10, st. 85.

morality, *sb.*, p. 143, l. 200.

mould, *sb.*, form, shape, p. 152, st. 11.

mow (corn), *v.a.*, p. 23, st. 11.

much, *adj.*, big (man), p. 63, l. 147.

munge, *v.a.*, mention, p. 123, l. 167.

munne, *r.a.*, mind, care for, p. 149, st. 4.

muntyng, *sb.*, p. 128, l. 52.

must, *pret.*, could, p. 54, l. 249.

near — nere —, *adr., cp.*, p. 143, l. 185.

necessity, *sb.*, time of need, p. 140, l. 85.

needs, *adr.*, of necessity, p. 13, st. 39.

nigh, *prep.*, p. 58, l. 21.

nime, *r.n.*, take by a vision, entrance, p. 39, l. 174.

no, *conj.*, nor, p. 2, st. 11.

north, *adj.*, p. 48, l. 17.

nourish, *v.n.*, be brought up, p. 35, l. 26.

nurse — norice —, *sb.*, p. 51, l. 135.

observance, *sb.*, p. 139, l. 45.

odour, *sb.*, p. 158.

officer, *sb.*, p. 126, l. 73.

ofgast, *adj.*, afraid, agast, p. 53, l. 212.

ofsake, *v.a.*, deny, p. 61, l. 60.

omnipotent, *adj.*, p. 140, l. 88.

onde, *sb.*, envy, p. 20, l. 52.

one, *phr.*, make at one, p. 152, st. 13.

out, *adj.*, outside, p. 145, l. 267.

outrage, *sb.*, evil deed, p. 50, l. 95.

outward, *adj.*, p. 147, l. 356.

overbid, *r.a.*, p. 132, l. 92.

overtrow, *v.a.*, know well, p. 55, l. 292.

palm (of the hand), *sb.*, p. 77, l. 232.

pameri, *sb.*, palm branch or staff, p. 76, l. 208, 209.

patience, *sb.*, p. 145, l. 263.

pensiveness, *sb.*, p. 139, l. 58.

perche, *sb.*, staff, rod, p. 61, l. 80.

phantasy, *sb.*, p. 134, l. 30.

pike, *sb.*, prickle, spine, p. 88, l. 47.

pilte, *r.n.*, ? pelt, p. 16, l. 12.

—, put, crucify, p. 14, l. 56; put, set, p. 13, l. 29.

pistel, *sb.*, epistle, p. 130, l. 1.

plainly, *adv.*, p. 143, l. 201.

play, *v.n.*, amuse, p 51, l. 150.

plays, *sb. pl.*, games, p. 67, l. 68.

plesaunce, *sb.*, mirth, p. 125, l. 54.

poesy, *sb.*, p. 135, l. 73.

pofte, *v.n*, puff, p. 149, st. 7.

pose, *sb.*, ? cold, running at the nose, p. 37, l. 92.

poverty, *sb.*, p. 5, st. 41.

powder, *sb.*, ? chalk powder, p. 77, l. 223.

preach, *v.a.*, preach to, teach, p. 68, l. 90.

present, *adj.*, p. 140, l. 90.

prioress, *sb.*, p. 75, l. 150.

procuracy, *sb.*, p. 79, l. 320.

professed, *p p.*, vowed, p. 146, l. 304; p. 148, l. 383.

profound, *adj.*, wise, learned, p. 77, l. 221.

promit, *v.a.*, promise, p. 142, l. 164.

proud, *v.n.*, become proud, show off, p. 129, l. 18.

psalter, *sb.* (sautere), p. 57, l. 356.

pudri, *v.a.*, stuff, fill, p. 2, st. 7; p. 159, l. 110.

quantity, *sb.*, p. 134, l. 40.

quench, *v.a.*, p. 74, l. 111.

quittor, *sb.*, p. 75.

rather, *adv.*, formerly, earlier, p. 159, l. 120.

redress, *v.a.*, p. 131, l. 56.

regular, *adj.*, under religious rule, p. 142, l. 172.

reigning, ? *sb.*, kingdom, p. 128, l. 50.

religiously, *adv.*, p. 148, l. 378.

remedy, *sb.*, p. 136, l. 111.

reputation, *sb.*, repute, p. 143, l. 216.

respond, *v.n.*, p. 135, l. 81.

revel, *v.n.*, p. 133, l. 15.

rifedly — riuedlich —, *adv.*, p. 15, l. 103.

rovcisoun, *sb.*, p. 80, l. 348, Fr. *Rouraisons*, *voraisons*: Rogations, temps de prières; do *rogare*. Roquefort.

royalty — rialte —, p. 135, l. 89.

rudde, *v.a.*, redden with blood, p. 75, l. 172.

rue, *v.a.*, repent, p. 5, st. 37.

run *of*, for run (or stream) *with*, p. 4, st. 29.

sad, *adj.*, serious, religious, p. 143, l. 194.

sautere, *sb.*, psalter, p. 57, l. 356.

say, *phr.*, say at one mouth, p. 15, l. 85.

sced, *sb.*, shed ?, p. 33, st. 183.

sceft, *sb.*, creature, p. 24, st. 42.

schindful, *adj.*, disgraceful, p. 57, l. 366.

schindisse, *sb.*, disgrace, infamy, p. 57, l. 365, A.S. *scendnys*.

scholar, *sb.*, p. 77, l. 256.

sed, *sb.*, satiety, A.S. *sæd*, satisfied, sated.

seeming, *sb.*, appearance, p. 147, l. 356.

self, *adj.*, himself, p. 97, l. 290.

selfwill, *sb.*, p. 143, l. 195.

sembli, *adj.*, semely, p. 158, l. 65.

sensuality, *sb.*, p. 143, l. 203.

seraphin, *sb. pl.*, p. 11, st. 149.

serve *to*, *v.n.*, be of use for, p. 157, l. 47.

set, *v.n.*, fight, p. 56, l. 310.

set by, *v.a.*, value, care for, p. 144, l. 220; p. 145, l. 287.

sharp, *v.n.*, become sharp, p. 149, st. 2.

shingle — scingle —, *sb.*, tile, p. 157, l. 57.

shire, *sb.*, men of a shire, p. 56, l. 309.

showing, *sb.*, p. 145, l. 280.

sign, *v.a.*, make a sign (of the cross) on, p. 72, l. 66.

simony, *sb.*, p. 75, l. 145; p. 122, l. 134.

sit down *at*, for *to*, p. 39, l. 172.

smite, *v.a.*, cut, p. 51, l. 127.

soler, *sb.*, upper chamber, p. 56, l. 340.

some, for 'some part', p. 48, l. 31.

sooth, *sb.*, truth, true thing, p. 99, l. 39.

sore, *adv.*, sorely, p. 5, st. 37; p.4, st. 28.

sovereign, *adj.*, p. 140, l. 88.

spene, *v.a*, (base of) spend, p. 6, st. 47.

spill, *v.a.*, lose, waste (time), p. 52, l. 163.

stead, *sb.*, help, p. 132, l. 90.

stepmother, *sb.*, p. 45, l. 88.

stinie, *v.a.*, ? look at, p. 20, st. 5.

stoney, *v.n.*, be astonished, p. 121, l. 86.

stour, *sb.*, p. 134, l. 37.

string, *sb.*, p. 75, l. 156.

subject (of a superior), *sb.*, p. 145, l. 275.

sueven, *sb.*, dream, p. 51, l. 147; p. 52, l. 192.

summer, *adj.*, p. 54, l. 236.

sure, *adj.*, safe, sound (wine), p. 147, l. 361.

sunel, *sb.*, (soul,) seasoning, p. 23, st. 23.

sweetheart, *sb.*, p. 51, l. 142.

swell, *v.n.*, *p.part.* swolle, p. 123, l. 162.

swevening, *sb.*, dream, vision, p. 50, l. 116.

swilc, *conj.*, such as, like, p. 24, st. 40.

swondrie, *v.n.*, doze, p. 77, l. 257.

talking, *sb.*, p. 141, l. 125.

targe, *v.a.*, tarry, p. 52, l. 179.

tent, *sb.*, attention, heed, p. 118, l. 8.

that there, *pron.*, that, p. 89, l. 82.

the ? *v.a.*, *pp.*, iþeჳ, do, p. 35, l. 28.

there, *comp. pron.*, where, in the places where, p. 139, l. 28; p. 146, l. 294.

theredown, *adv.*, p. 53, l. 206.

thick, *adv*, p. 51, l. 121.

thorn, *sb.*, thorn-tree, p. 54, l. 267.

threatening, *sb.*, p. 54, l. 248.

throuჳ, *sb.*, coffin, A.S. þruh, p. 70, l. 168.

tit, tyt, happens to, p. 65, l. 219; p. 44, l. 58.

to-geanes, *prep.*, against, p. 33, l. 175.

torment, *v.a.*, p. 75, l. 170.

toward (and froward), *adj.*, good, p. 146, l. 315.

travail, *v.n.*, work, p. 52, l. 163.

tray, *v.a.*, betray, p. 13, st. 41.

tree, *sb.*, wood, p 63, l. 122.

tresche, *sb.* (*Danse, bal, assemblée*; *jeux de baladins*), p. 67, l. 67.

trespass, *sb.*, outrage, p. 128, l. 51.

trust—triste—, *sb.*, p. 17, st. 5.

tug out, *v.a.*, p. 149, st. 5.

ulthe, *sb.*, age, A.S. *yldo*, age, p. 90, l. 6.

underget, *v. a.*, undertake, p. 55, l. 291; get at, find out, p. 66.

undergo, *v. a.*, undertake, p. 55, l. 280.

university, *sb.*, p. 78.

unlike, *adv.*, unequally, p. 20, l. 55.

unlustily, *adv.*, in an unmanly way, p. 122, l. 143.

unordinate, *adj.*, p. 144, l. 234.

unreasonability, *sb.*, p. 143, l. 202.

unwinne, *sb.*, distress, A.S. *wyn*, joy, p. 21.

unypyned, *adj.*, unpunished, p. 75, l. 173.

vanity, *sb.*, empty show, p. 2, st. 13.

veil, *sb.*, p. 147.

vessel, *sb.*, p. 130, l. 4.
victory, *sb.*, p. 135, l. 79.
virst, *sb.*, ? drink, satisfaction of thirst, p. 7, st. 57.
virtue, *sb.*, miracle, p. 63, l. 127.
vise, *r.n.*, devise, p. 133, l. 14.

wanting, *sb.*, p. 145, l. 282.
ward, *v. n.*, ward, take care of, p 51, l. 151.
ward, *sb.*, place, p. 146, l. 312.
warning, *sb.*, p. 134, l. 55.
weave, *r.n.*, *pp.* iwone, p. 75, l. 156.
wencle, *sb.*, girl, A.S. *wencle*, maid, p 48.
were, *sb.*, care, p. 7, st. 59.
west, *adj.*, p. 49, l. 62.
what, *comp.pron.*, that which, p 141, l. 106.
whatlokest, *adv.*, *cp.*, soonest, p. 56, l. 315.
while, *conj.*, p. 2, st. 15.
while, *adv*, formerly, p. 49, l. 73.

why, *sb* , the reason why, p. 146, l. 302.
winter, *sb.*, year, p. 14, st. 53.
wiste, *pret.*, iwist, *pp.*, watched, p. 41, l. 38, 40.
within, *prep.*, p. 128, l. 45.
witness, *v. a.*, p. 145, l. 284.
witty, *adj.*, possessing wits, having a mind, p. 53, l. 219.
wlank, *adj* , A. S. *wlanc*, lofty, proud, p. 118.
word, *phr.*, the last word binds the tale, p. 6, st. 52.
worthi, *v. a*, honour, p. 16, l. 18.
wraxli, *v.n.*, wrestle, p. 45, l. 70 (in Coleridge's Gloss. as *wrayli*).
wrekke of, *v. a.*, revenge on, p. 4, st. 30.
wunienge, *sb.*, dwelling, p. 33, l. 179.

yet, *conj.*, p. 122, l. 141.
yield, *v a.*, pay back, p. 58, l. 44.

www.ingramcontent.com/pod-product-compliance
Lightning Source LLC
Chambersburg PA
CBHW020611030726
47497CB00007B/2189